W9-AVN-323

by Stephen R. Davis

WILEY

John Wiley & Sons, Inc.

Beginning Programming with C++ For Dummies®

Published by
John Wiley & Sons, Inc.
111 River Street
Hoboken, NJ 07030-5774

www.wiley.com

Copyright © 2010 by John Wiley & Sons, Inc., Hoboken, New Jersey

Published by John Wiley & Sons, Inc., Hoboken, New Jersey

Published simultaneously in Canada

Library of Congress Control Number: 2010930969

ISBN 978-0-470-61797-7 (pbk); ISBN 978-0-470-90948-5 (ebk); ISBN 978-0-470-90949-2 (ebk); ISBN 978-0-470-90950-8 (ebk)

Manufactured in the United States of America

10 9 8 7 6 5 4

WILEY

Publisher's Acknowledgments

We're proud of this book; please send us your comments at http://dummies.custhelp.com. For other comments, please contact our Customer Care Department within the U.S. at 877-762-2974, outside the U.S. at 317-572-3993, or fax 317-572-4002.

Some of the people who helped bring this book to market include the following:

Acquisitions, Editorial, and Vertical Websites

Project Editor: Nicole Sholly

Senior Acquisitions Editor: Katie Feltman

Copy Editor: Melba Hopper

Technical Editor: Danny Kalev

Editorial Manager: Kevin Kirschner

Vertical Websites Project Manager: Laura Moss-Hollister

Vertical Websites Assistant Project Manager: Jenny Swisher

Vertical Websites Associate Producer: Shawn Patrick

Editorial Assistant: Leslie Saxman

Sr. Editorial Assistant: Cherie Case

Cartoons: Rich Tennant (www.the5thwave.com)

Composition Services

Project Coordinator: Patrick Redmond

Layout and Graphics: Ashley Chamberlain, Nikki Gately

Proofreaders: Rebecca Denoncour, Christine Sabooni

Indexer: Valerie Haynes Perry

Publishing and Editorial for Technology Dummies

 Richard Swadley, Vice President and Executive Group Publisher

 Andy Cummings, Vice President and Publisher

 Mary Bednarek, Executive Acquisitions Director

 Mary C. Corder, Editorial Director

Publishing for Consumer Dummies

 Kathleen Nebenhaus, Vice President and Executive Publisher

Composition Services

 Debbie Stailey, Director of Composition Services

Dedication

To Janet for helping me be the best Dummy that I can be.

Author's Acknowledgments

I find it very strange that only a single name appears on the cover of any book, but especially a book like this. In reality, many people contribute to the creation of a *For Dummies* book. From the beginning, acquisitions editor Katie Feltman and my agent, Claudette Moore, were involved in guiding and molding the book's content. A number of editors work behind the scene to make a book like this possible. However, I would like to call out for special mention my project editor, Nicole Sholly. Also, the Technical Editor, Danny Kalev, saved me from embarrassment on several occasions.

Finally, a summary of the animal activity around my house. For those of you who have not read any of my other books, I should warn you that this has become a regular feature of my *For Dummies* books.

My two dogs, Scooter and Trude, have been gone for almost 8 years now. We moved to the "big city" about five years ago which meant giving away our dogs Chester and Sadie (both of which are doing quite well with other families). We tried to keep the two Great Danes, Monty and Bonnie, but they were just too much for the back yard. We were forced to give them away as well. No sooner did I give away the two Danes than my son showed up with his two smallish Catahoola-mix mutts from the pound, Lolli and Bodie. I kept these two for several years until my son was settled enough in his own house to take them off my hands (any day now).

If you are having problems getting started, I maintain a FAQ of common problems at www.stephendavis.com. You can e-mail me questions from there if you don't see your problem. I can't write your program (you don't know how often I get asked to do people's homework assignments), but I try to answer most questions.

Publisher's Acknowledgments

We're proud of this book; please send us your comments at http://dummies.custhelp.com. For other comments, please contact our Customer Care Department within the U.S. at 877-762-2974, outside the U.S. at 317-572-3993, or fax 317-572-4002.

Some of the people who helped bring this book to market include the following:

Acquisitions, Editorial, and Media Development

Project Editor: Nicole Sholly

Senior Acquisitions Editor: Katie Feltman

Copy Editor: Melba Hopper

Technical Editor: Danny Kalev

Editorial Manager: Kevin Kirschner

Media Development Project Manager: Laura Moss-Hollister

Media Development Assistant Project Manager: Jenny Swisher

Media Development Associate Producer: Shawn Patrick

Editorial Assistant: Leslie Saxman

Sr. Editorial Assistant: Cherie Case

Cartoons: Rich Tennant (www.the5thwave.com)

Composition Services

Project Coordinator: Patrick Redmond

Layout and Graphics: Ashley Chamberlain, Nikki Gately

Proofreaders: Rebecca Denoncour, Christine Sabooni

Indexer: Valerie Haynes Perry

Publishing and Editorial for Technology Dummies

    Richard Swadley, Vice President and Executive Group Publisher

    Andy Cummings, Vice President and Publisher

    Mary Bednarek, Executive Acquisitions Director

    Mary C. Corder, Editorial Director

Publishing for Consumer Dummies

    Diane Graves Steele, Vice President and Publisher

Composition Services

    Debbie Stailey, Director of Composition Services

Contents at a Glance

Table of Contents

Introduction

Welcome to *Beginning Programming with C++ For Dummies.* This book is intended for the reader who wants to learn to program.

Somehow over the years, programming has become associated with mathematics and logic calculus and other complicated things. I never quite understood that. Programming is a skill like writing advertising or drawing or photography. It does require the ability to think a problem through, but I've known some really good programmers who had zero math skills. Some people are naturally good at it and pick it up quickly, others not so good and not so quick. Nevertheless, anyone with enough patience and "stick-to-itiveness" can learn to program a computer. Even me.

About Beginning Programming with C++ For Dummies

Learning to program necessarily means learning a programming language. This book is based upon the C++ programming language. A Windows version of the suggested compiler is included on the CD-ROM accompanying this book. Macintosh and Linux versions are available for download at www. codeblocks.org. (Don't worry: I include step-by-step instructions for how to install the package and build your first program in the book.)

The goal of this book is to teach you the basics of programming in C++, not to inundate you with every detail of the C++ programming language. At the end of this book, you will be able to write a reasonably sophisticated program in C++. You will also be in a position to quickly grasp a number of other similar languages, such as Java and C#.NET.

In this book, you will discover what a program is, how it works, plus how to do the following:

- ✔ Install the CodeBlocks C++ compiler and use it to build a program
- ✔ Create and evaluate expressions
- ✔ Direct the flow of control through your program

- Create data structures that better model the real world
- Define and use C++ pointers
- Manipulate character strings to generate the output the way you want to see it
- Write to and read from files

Foolish Assumptions

I try to make very few assumptions in this book about the reader, but I do assume the following:

- **You have a computer.** Most readers will have computers that run Windows; however, the programs in this book run equally well on Windows, Macintosh, Linux, and Unix. In fact, since C++ is a standardized language, these programs should run on any computer that has a C++ compiler.

- **You know the basics of how to use your computer.** For example, I assume that you know how to run a program, copy a file, create a folder, and so on.

- **You know how to navigate through menus.** I include lots of instructions like "Click on File and then Open." If you can follow that instruction, then you're good to go.

- **You are new to programming.** I don't assume that you know anything about programming. Heck, I don't even assume that you know what programming is.

Conventions Used in This Book

To help you navigate this book as efficiently as possible, I use a few conventions:

- C++ terms are in monofont typeface, `like this`.
- New terms are emphasized with *italics* (and defined).
- Numbered steps that you need to follow and characters you need to type are set in **bold**.

What You Don't Have to Read

I encourage you to read one part of the book; then put the book away and play for a while before moving to the next part. The book is organized so that by the end of each part, you have mastered enough new material to go out and write programs.

I'd like to add the following advice:

- ✔ If you already know what programming is but nothing about C++, you can skip Chapter 1.

- ✔ I recommend that you use the CodeBlocks compiler that comes with the book, even if you want to use a different C++ compiler after you finish the book. However, if you insist and don't want to use CodeBlocks, you can skip Chapter 2.

- ✔ Skim through Chapter 3 if you've already done a little computer programming.

- ✔ Start concentrating at Chapter 4, even if you have experience with other languages such as BASIC.

- ✔ You can stop reading after Chapter 20 if you're starting to feel saturated. Chapter 21 opens up the new topic of object-oriented programming — you don't want to take that on until you feel really comfortable with what you've learned so far.

- ✔ You can skip any of the TechnicalStuff icons.

How This Book Is Organized

Beginning Programming with C++ For Dummies is split into seven parts. You don't have to read it sequentially, and you don't even have to read all the sections in any particular chapter. You can use the Table of Contents and the Index to find the information you need and quickly get your answer. In this section, I briefly describe what you'll find in each part.

Part 1: Let's Get Started

This part describes what programs are and how they work. Using a fictitious tire-changing computer, I take you through several algorithms for removing a tire from a car to give you a feel for how programs work. You'll also get CodeBlocks up and running on your computer before leaving this part.

Part II: Writing a Program: Decisions, Decisions

This part introduces you to the basics of programming with C++. You will find out how to declare integer variables and how to write simple expressions. You'll even discover how to make decisions within a program, but you won't be much of an expert by the time you finish this part.

Part III: Becoming a Functional Programmer

Here you learn how to direct the flow of control within your programs. You'll find out how to loop, how to break your code into modules (and why), and how to build these separate modules back into a single program. At the end of this part, you'll be able to write real programs that actually solve problems.

Part IV: Data Structures

This part expands your knowledge of data types. Earlier sections of the book are limited to integers; in this part, you work with characters, decimals, and arrays; and you even get to define your own types. Finally, this is the part where you master the most dreaded topic, the C++ pointer.

Part V: Object-Oriented Programming

This is where you expand your knowledge into object-oriented techniques, the stuff that differentiates C++ from its predecessors, most notably C. (Don't worry if you don't know what object-oriented programming is — you aren't supposed to yet.) You'll want to be comfortable with the material in Parts I through IV before jumping into this part, but you'll be a much stronger programmer by the time you finish it.

Part VI: Advanced Strokes

This is a collection of topics that are important but that didn't fit in the earlier parts. For example, here's where I discuss how to create, read to, and write from files.

Part VII: The Part of Tens

This part includes lists of what to do (and what not to do) when programming to avoid creating bugs needlessly. In addition, this part includes some advice about what topics to study next, should you decide to expand your knowledge of C++.

The CD-ROM Appendix

This part describes what's on the enclosed CD-ROM and how to install it.

Icons Used in This Book

What's a *Dummies* book without icons pointing you in the direction of really great information that's sure to help you along your way? In this section, I briefly describe each icon I use in this book.

The Tip icon points out helpful information that is likely to make your job easier.

This icon marks a generally interesting and useful fact — something that you might want to remember for later use. I also use this icon to remind you of some fact that you may have skipped over in an earlier chapter.

The Warning icon highlights lurking danger. With this icon, I'm telling you to pay attention and proceed with caution.

When you see this icon, you know that there's techie stuff nearby. If you're not feeling very techie, you can skip this info.

This icon denotes the programs that are included on this book's CD-ROM.

Where to Go from Here

You can find a set of errata and Frequently Asked Questions for this and all my books at www.stephendavis.com. You will also find a link to my e-mail address there. Feel free to send me your questions and comments (that's how I learn). It's through reader input that these books can improve.

Now you've stalled long enough, it's time to turn to Chapter 1 and start discovering how to program!

Part I
Let's Get Started

"We're outsourcing everything but our core competency. Once we find out what that is, we'll begin the outsourcing process."

In this part . . .

You will learn what it means to program a computer. You will also get your first taste of programming — I take you through the steps to enter, build, and execute your first program. It will all be a bit mysterious in this part, but things will clear up soon, I promise.

Chapter 1

What Is a Program?

*I*n this chapter, you will learn what a program is and what it means to write a program. You'll practice on a Human Computer. You'll then see some program snippets written for a real computer. Finally, you'll see your first code snippet written in C++.

Up until now all of the programs running on your computer were written by someone else. Very soon now, that won't be true anymore. You will be joining the ranks of the few, the proud: the programmers.

How Does My Son Differ from a Computer?

A computer is an amazingly fast but incredibly stupid machine. A computer can do anything you tell it (within reason), but it does *exactly* what it's told — nothing more and nothing less.

In this respect, a computer is almost the exact opposite of a human: humans respond intuitively. When I was learning a second language, I learned that it wasn't enough to understand what was being said — it's just as important and considerably more difficult to understand what was left unsaid. This is information that the speaker shares with the listener through common experience or education — things that don't need to be said.

For example, I say things to my son like, "Wash the dishes" (for all the good it does me). This seems like clear enough instructions, but the vast majority of the information contained in that sentence is implied and unspoken.

Let's assume that my son knows what dishes are and that dirty dishes are normally in the sink. But what about knives and forks? After all, I only said dishes, I didn't say anything about eating utensils, and don't even get me started on glassware. And did I mean wash them manually, or is it okay to load them up into the dishwasher to be washed, rinsed, and dried automatically?

But the fact is, "Wash the dishes" is sufficient instruction for my son. He can decompose that sentence and combine it with information that we both share, including an extensive working knowledge of dirty dishes, to come up with a meaningful understanding of what I want him to do — whether he does it or not is a different story. I would guess that he can perform all the mental gymnastics necessary to understand that sentence in about the same amount of time that it takes me to say it — about 1 to 2 seconds.

A computer can't make heads or tails out of something as vague as "wash the dishes." You have to tell the computer exactly what to do with each different type of dish, how to wash a fork, versus a spoon, versus a cup. When does the program stop washing a dish (that is, how does it know when a dish is clean)? When does it stop washing (that is, how does it know when it's finished)?

My son has gobs of memory — it isn't clear exactly how much memory a normal human has, but it's boat loads. Unfortunately, human memory is fuzzy. For example, witnesses to crimes are notoriously bad at recalling details even a short time after the event. Two witnesses to the same event often disagree radically on what transpired.

Computers also have gobs of memory, and that's very good. Once stored, a computer can retrieve a fact as often as you like without change. As expensive as memory was back in the early 1980s, the original IBM PC had only 16K (that's 16 thousand bytes). This could be expanded to a whopping 64K. Compare this with the 1GB to 3GB of main storage available in most computers today (1GB is *one billion bytes*).

As expensive as memory was, however, the IBM PC included extra memory chips and decoding hardware to detect a memory failure. If a memory chip went bad, this circuitry was sure to find it and report it before the program went haywire. This so-called Parity Memory was no longer offered after only a few years, and as far as I know, it is unavailable today except in specific applications where extreme reliability is required — because the memory boards almost never fail.

On the other hand, humans are very good at certain types of processing that computers do poorly, if at all. For example, humans are very good at pulling the meaning out of a sentence garbled by large amounts of background noise. By contrast, digital cell phones have the infuriating habit of just going silent whenever the noise level gets above a built-in threshold.

Programming a "Human Computer"

Before I dive into showing you how to write programs for computer consumption, I start by showing you a program to guide human behavior so that you can better see what you're up against. Writing a program to guide a human is much easier than writing programs for computer hardware because we have a lot of familiarity with and understanding of humans and how they work (I assume). We also share a common human language to start with. But to make things fair, assume that the human computer has been instructed to be particularly literal — so the program will have to be very specific. Our guinea pig computer intends to take each instruction quite literally.

The problem I have chosen is to instruct our human computer in the changing of a flat tire.

The algorithm

The instructions for changing a flat tire are straightforward and go something like the following:

1. Raise the car.

2. Remove the lug nuts that affix the faulty tire to the car.

3. Remove the tire.

4. Mount the new tire.

5. Install the lug nuts.

6. Lower the car.

(I know that technically the lug nuts hold the wheel onto the car and not the tire, but that distinction isn't important here. I use the terms "wheel" and "tire" synonymously in this discussion.)

As detailed as these instructions might seem to be, this is not a program. This is called an *algorithm*. An algorithm is a description of the steps to be performed, usually at a high level of abstraction. An algorithm is detailed but general. I could use this algorithm to repair any of the flat tires that I have experienced or ever will experience. But an algorithm does not contain sufficient detail for even our intentionally obtuse human computer to perform the task.

The Tire Changing Language

Before we can write a program, we need a language that we can all agree on. For the remainder of this book, that language will be C++, but I use the newly invented TCL (Tire Changing Language) for this example. I have specifically adapted TCL to the problem of changing tires.

TCL includes a few nouns common in the tire-changing world:

- ✔ car
- ✔ tire
- ✔ nut
- ✔ jack
- ✔ toolbox
- ✔ spare tire
- ✔ wrench

TCL also includes the following verbs:

- ✔ grab
- ✔ move
- ✔ release
- ✔ turn

Finally, the TCL-executing processor will need the ability to count and to make simple decisions.

This is all that the tire-changing robot understands. Any other command that's not part of Tire Changing Language generates a blank stare of incomprehension from the human tire-changing processor.

The program

Now it's time to convert the algorithm, written in everyday English, into a program written in Tire Changing Language. Take the phrase, "Remove the lug nuts." Actually, quite a bit is left unstated in that sentence. The word "remove" is not in the processor's vocabulary. In addition, no mention is made of the wrench at all.

The following steps implement the phrase "Remove a lug nut" using only the verbs and nouns contained in Tire Changing Language:

1. Grab wrench.

2. Move wrench to lug nut.

3. Turn wrench counterclockwise five times.

4. Move wrench to toolbox.

5. Release wrench.

I didn't explain the syntax of Tire Changing Language. For example, the fact that every command starts with a single verb or that the verb "grab" requires a single noun as its object and that "turn" requires a noun, a direction, and a count of the number of turns to make. Even so, the program snippet should be easy enough to read (remember that this is not a book about Tire Changing Language).

You can skate by on Tire Changing Language, but you will have to learn the grammar of each C++ command.

The program begins at Step 1 and continues through each step in turn until reaching Step 5. In programming terminology, we say that the program flows from Step 1 through Step 5. Of course, the program's not going anywhere — the processor is doing all the work, but the term "program flow" is a common convention.

Even a cursory examination of this program reveals a problem: What if there is no lug nut? I suppose it's harmless to spin the wrench around a bolt with no nut on it, but doing so wastes time and isn't my idea of a good solution. The Tire Changing Language needs a branching capability that allows the program to take one path or another depending upon external conditions. We need an IF statement like the following:

1. Grab wrench.

2. If lug nut is present

3. {

4. Move wrench to lug nut.

5. Turn wrench counterclockwise five times.

6. }

7. Move wrench to toolbox.

8. Release wrench.

The program starts with Step 1 just as before and grabs a wrench. In the second step, however, before the program waves the wrench uselessly around an empty bolt, it checks to see if a lug nut is present. If so, flow continues on with Steps 3, 4, and 5 as before. If not, however, program flow skips these unnecessary steps and goes straight on to Step 7 to return the wrench to the toolbox.

In computerese, you say that the program executes the logical expression "is lug nut present?" This expression returns either a true (yes, the lug nut is present) or a false (no, there is no lug nut there).

What I call steps, a programming language would normally call a *statement*. An *expression* is a type of statement that returns a value, such as 1 + 2 is an expression. A *logical expression* is an expression that returns a true or false value, such as "is the author of this book handsome?" is `true`.

The braces in Tire Changing Language are necessary to tell the program which steps are to be skipped if the condition is not true. Steps 4 and 5 are executed only if the condition is true.

I realize that there's no need to grab a wrench if there's no lug to remove, but work with me here.

This improved program still has a problem: How do you know that 5 turns of the wrench will be sufficient to remove the lug nut? It most certainly will not be for most of the tires with which I am familiar. You could increase the number of turns to something that seems likely to be more than enough, say 25 turns. If the lug nut comes loose after the twentieth turn, for example, the wrench will turn an extra 5 times. This is a harmless but wasteful solution.

A better approach is to add some type of "loop and test" statement to the Tire Changing Language:

1. Grab wrench.

2. If lug nut is present

3. {

4.   Move wrench to lug nut.

5.   While (lug nut attached to car)

6.   {

7.   Turn wrench counterclockwise one turn.

8.   }

9. }

10. Move wrench to toolbox.

11. Release wrench.

Here the program flows from Step 1 through Step 4 just as before. In Step 5, however, the processor must make a decision: Is the lug nut attached? On the first pass, we will assume that the answer is yes so that the processor will execute Step 7 and turn the wrench counterclockwise one turn. At this point, the program returns to Step 5 and repeats the test. If the lug nut is still attached, the processor repeats Step 7 before returning to Step 5 again. Eventually, the lug nut will come loose and the condition in Step 5 will return a false. At this point, control within the program will pass on to Step 9, and the program will continue as before.

This solution is superior to its predecessor: It makes no assumptions about the number of turns required to remove a lug nut. It is not wasteful by requiring the processor to turn a lug nut that is no longer attached, nor does it fail because the lug nut is only half removed.

As nice as this solution is, however, it still has a problem: It removes only a single lug nut. Most medium-sized cars have five nuts on each wheel. We could repeat Steps 2 through 9 five times, once for each lug nut. However, this doesn't work very well either. Most compact cars have only four lug nuts, and large pickups have up to eight.

The following program expands our grammar to include the ability to loop across lug nuts. This program works irrespective of the number of lug nuts on the wheel:

1. Grab wrench.

2. For each lug bolt on wheel

3. {

4.   If lug nut is present

5.   {

6.   Move wrench to lug nut.

7.   While (lug nut attached to car)

8.   {

9.   Turn wrench counterclockwise one turn.

10.   }

11.   }

12. }

13. Move wrench to toolbox.

14. Release wrench.

This program begins just as before with the grabbing of a wrench from the toolbox. Beginning with Step 2, however, the program loops through Step 12 for each lug nut bolt on the wheel.

Notice how Steps 7 through 10 are still repeated for each wheel. This is known as a *nested* loop. Steps 7 through 10 are called the inner loop, while Steps 2 through 12 are the outer loop.

The complete program consists of the addition of similar implementations of each of the steps in the algorithm.

Computer processors

Removing the wheel from a car seems like such a simple task, and yet it takes 11 instructions in a language designed specifically for tire changing just to get the lug nuts off. Once completed, this program is likely to include over 60 or 70 steps with numerous loops. Even more if you add in logic to check for error conditions like stripped or missing lug nuts.

Think of how many instructions have to be executed just to do something as mundane as move a window about on the display screen (remember that a typical screen may have 1280 x 1024 or a little over a million pixels or more displayed). Fortunately, though stupid, a computer processor is very fast. For example, the processor that's in your PC can likely execute several billion instructions per second. The instructions in your generic processor don't do very much — it takes several instructions just to move one pixel — but when you can rip through a billion or so at a time, scrolling a mere million pixels becomes child's play.

The computer will not do anything that it hasn't already been programmed for. The creation of a Tire Changing Language was not enough to replace my flat tire — someone had to write the program instructions to map out step by step what the computer will do. And writing a real-world program designed to handle all of the special conditions that can arise is not an easy task. Writing an industrial-strength program is probably the most challenging enterprise you can undertake.

So the question becomes: "Why bother?" Because once the computer is properly programmed, it can perform the required function repeatedly, tirelessly, and usually at a greater rate than is possible under human control.

Computer Languages

The Tire Changing Language isn't a real computer language, of course. Real computers don't have machine instructions like "grab" or "turn." Worse yet, computers "think" using a series of ones and zeros. Each internal command is nothing more than a sequence of binary numbers. Real computers have instructions like 01011101, which might add 1 to a number contained in a special purpose register. As difficult as programming in TCL might be, programming by writing long strings of numbers is even harder.

The native language of the computer is known as *machine language* and is usually represented as a sequence of numbers written either in binary (base 2) or hexadecimal (base 16). The following represents the first 64 bytes from the Conversion program in Chapter 3.

```
<main+0>:  01010101 10001001 11100101 10000011 11100100 11110000 10000011 11101100
<main+8>:  00100000 11101000 00011010 01000000 00000000 00000000 11000111 01000100
<main+16>: 00100100 00000100 00100100 01110000 01000111 00000000 11000111 00000100
<main+24>: 00100100 10000000 01011111 01000111 00000000 11101000 10100110 10001100
<main+32>: 00000110 00000000 10001101 01000100 00100100 00010100 10001001 01000100
```

Fortunately, no one writes programs in machine language anymore. Very early on, someone figured out that it is much easier for a human to understand ADD 1,REG1 as "add 1 to the value contained in register 1," rather than 01011101. In the "post-machine language era," the programmer wrote her programs in this so-called *assembly language* and then submitted it to a program called an *assembler* that converted each of these instructions into their machine-language equivalent.

The programs that people write are known as *source code* because they are the source of all evil. The ones and zeros that the computer actually executes are called *object code* because they are the object of so much frustration.

The following represents the first few assembler instructions from the `Conversion` program when compiled to run on an Intel processor executing Windows. This is the same information previously shown in binary form.

```
<main>:        push    %ebp
<main+1>:      mov     %esp,%ebp
<main+3>:      and     $0xfffffff0,%esp
<main+6>:      sub     $0x20,%esp
<main+9>:      call    0x40530c <__main>
<main+14>:     movl    $0x477024,0x4(%esp)
<main+22>:     movl    $0x475f80,(%esp)
<main+29>:     call    0x469fac <operator<<>
<main+34>:     lea     0x14(%esp),%eax
<main+38>:     mov     %eax,0x4(%esp)
```

This is still not very intelligible, but it's clearly a lot better than just a bunch of ones and zeros. Don't worry — you won't have to write any assembly language code in this book either.

The computer does not actually ever execute the assembly language instructions. It executes the machine instructions that result from converting the assembly instructions.

High level languages

Assembly language might be easier to remember, but there's still a lot of distance between an algorithm like the tire-changing algorithm and a sequence of MOVEs and ADDs. In the 1950s, people started devising progressively more expressive languages that could be automatically converted into machine language by a program called a *compiler*. These were called *high level languages* because they were written at a higher level of abstraction than assembly language.

One of the first of these languages was COBOL (Common Business Oriented Language). The idea behind COBOL was to allow the programmer to write commands that were as much like English sentences as possible. Suddenly programmers were writing sentences like the following to convert temperature from Celsius to Fahrenheit (believe it or not, this is exactly what the machine and assembly language snippets shown earlier do):

```
INPUT CELSIUS_TEMP
SET FAHRENHEIT_TEMP TO CELSIUS_TEMP * 9/5 + 32
WRITE FAHRENHEIT_TEMP
```

The first line of this program reads a number from the keyboard or a file and stores it into the variable CELSIUS_TEMP. The next line multiplies this number by ⅘ and adds 32 to the result to calculate the equivalent temperature in Fahrenheit. The program stores this result into a variable called FAHRENHEIT_TEMP. The last line of the program writes this converted value to the display.

People continued to create different programming languages, each with its own strengths and weaknesses. Some languages, like COBOL, were very wordy but easy to read. Other languages were designed for very specific areas like database languages or the languages used to create interactive Web pages. These languages include powerful constructs designed for one specific problem area.

The C++ language

C++ (pronounced "C plus plus," by the way) is a symbolically oriented high level language. C++ started out life as simply C in the 1970s at Bell Labs. A couple of guys were working on a new idea for an operating system known as Unix (the predecessor to Linux and Mac OS and still used across industry and academia today). The original C language created at Bell Labs was modified slightly and adopted as a worldwide ISO standard in early 1980. C++ was created as an extension to the basic C language mostly by adding the features that I discuss in Parts V and VI of this book.When I say that C++ is symbolic, I mean that it isn't very wordy, preferring to use symbols rather than long words like in COBOL. However, C++ is easy to read once you are accustomed to what all the symbols mean. The same Celsius to Fahrenheit conversion code shown in COBOL earlier appears as follows in C++:

```
cin >> celsiusTemp;
fahrenheitTemp = celsiusTemp * 9 / 5 + 32;
cout << fahrenheitTemp;
```

The first line reads a value into the variable celsiusTemp. The subsequent calculation converts this Celsius temperature to Fahrenheit like before, and the third line outputs the result.

C++ has several other advantages compared with other high level languages. For one, C++ is universal. There is a C++ compiler for almost every computer in existence.

In addition, C++ is efficient. The more things a high level language tries to do automatically to make your programming job easier, the less efficient the machine code generated tends to be. That doesn't make much of a difference for a small program like most of those in this book, but it can make a big difference when manipulating large amounts of data, like moving pixels around on the screen, or when you want blazing real-time performance. It's not an accident that Unix and Windows are written in C++ and the Macintosh O/S is written in a language very similar to C++.

Chapter 2

Installing Code::Blocks

In This Chapter

▶ Reviewing the compilation process

▶ Installing the Code::Blocks development environment

▶ Testing your installation with a default program

▶ Reviewing the common installation errors

*I*n this chapter, you will review what it takes to create executable programs from C++ source code that you can run on the Windows, Linux, or Macintosh computer. You will then install the Code::Blocks integrated development environment used in the remainder of the book, and you will build a default test program to check out your installation. If all is working, by the time you reach the end of this chapter, you will be ready to start writing and building C++ programs of your own — with a little help, of course!

Reviewing the Compilation Process

You need two programs to create your own C++ programs. First, you need a text editor that you can use to enter your C++ instructions. Any editor capable of generating straight ASCII text letters will work. I have written programs using the Notepad editor that comes with Windows. However, an editor that knows something about the syntax of C++ is preferable since it can save you a lot of typing and sometimes highlight mistakes that you might be making as you type, in much the same way that a spelling checker highlights misspelled words in a word processor.

The second program you will need is a compiler that converts your C++ source statements into machine language that the computer can understand and interpret. This process of converting from source C++ statements to object machine code is called *building*. Graphically, the process looks something like that shown in Figure 2-1.

The process of building a program actually has two steps: The C++ compiler first converts your C++ source code statements into a machine executable format in a step known as *compiling*. It then combines the machine instructions from your program with instructions from a set of libraries that come standard with C++ in a second step known as *linking* to create a complete executable program.

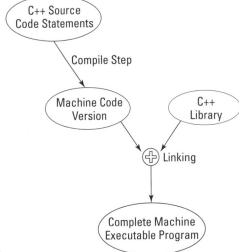

Figure 2-1:
The C++ program development process.

Most C++ compilers these days come in what is known as an Integrated Development Environment or IDE. These IDEs include the editor, the compiler, and several other useful development programs together in a common package. Not only does this save you from the need to purchase these programs separately, but combining them into a single package produces several productivity benefits. First, the editor can invoke the compiler quickly without the need for you to switch back and forth manually. In addition, the editors in most IDEs provide quick and efficient means for finding and fixing coding errors.

Some IDEs include visual programming tools that allow the programmer to draw common windows such as dialog boxes on the display — the IDE generates the C++ code necessary to display these boxes automatically.

As nice as that sounds, the automatically generated code only displays the windows. A programmer still has to generate the real code that gets executed whenever the operator selects buttons within those windows.

Invariably, these visual IDEs are tightly coupled into one or the other operating system. For example, the popular Visual Studio is strongly tied into the

.NET environment in Windows. It is not possible to use Visual Studio without learning the .NET environment and something about Windows along with C++ (or one of the other .NET languages). In addition, the resulting programs only run in a .NET environment.

In this book, you will use a public domain C++ IDE known as Code::Blocks. Versions of Code::Blocks exist for Windows, Linux, and MacOS — a version for Windows is included on the CD-ROM accompanying this book. Versions of Code::Blocks for Macintosh and Linux are available for free download at www. codeblocks.org.

You will use Code::Blocks to generate the programs in this book. These programs are known as _Console Applications_ since they take input from and display text back to a console window. While this isn't as sexy as windowed development, staying with Console Applications will allow you to focus on C++ and not be distracted by the requirements of a windowed environment. In addition, using Console Applications will allow the programs in the book to run the same on all environments that are supported by Code::Blocks.

Installing Code::Blocks

Beginning Programming with C++ For Dummies includes a version of Code::Blocks for Windows on the CD-ROM. This section provides detailed installation instructions for this version. The steps necessary to download and install versions of Code::Blocks from www.codeblocks.org will be similar.

1. **Insert the enclosed CD-ROM into your computer.**

   That's straightforward enough.

2. **Read the End User License Agreement (EULA) and select Accept.**

3. **Select the Software tab and then select Code::Blocks to install the Code::Blocks environment.**

   On some versions of Windows, you may see a message appear that "An unidentified program wants access to your computer." Of course, that unidentified program is the Code::Blocks Setup program.

4. **Select Allow.**

   Setup now unpacks the files it needs to start and run the Code::Blocks Setup Wizard. This may take about a minute. Once it finishes, the startup window shown in Figure 2-2 appears.

5. **Close any other programs that you may be executing and select Next.**

   The Setup Wizard displays the generic End User License Agreement (EULA). There's nothing much here to get excited about.

Figure 2-2:
The
Code::Blocks
Setup
Wizard
guides you
through the
installation
process.

6. **Select I Agree.**

   The Setup Wizard then displays a list of the components that you may
   choose to install. The defaults are okay, but you may want to also check
   the Desktop Shortcut option as shown in Figure 2-3. Doing this provides
   an icon on the desktop that you can use to start Code::Blocks without
   going through the Program Files menu.

Figure 2-3:
Checking
Desktop
Shortcut
creates an
icon that
you can
use to start
Code::Blocks
more
quickly.

7. **Select Next.**

   The next window asks you to choose the install location. This window
   also tells you how much hard disk space Code::Blocks requires (about
   150MB, depending upon the options you've selected) and how much
   space is available on your hard drive. If you don't have enough free disk
   space, you'll have to delete some of those YouTube videos you've cap-
   tured to make room before you continue.

8. **The default install location is fine, so once you have enough disk space, select Install.**

   At this point, the Code::Blocks Setup Wizard really goes to work. It extracts umpteen dozen files that it installs in a myriad of subdirectories too complicated for mere mortals. This process may take several minutes.

9. **When the installation is complete, a dialog box appears asking you whether you want to run Code::Blocks now. Select No.**

   If all has gone well so far, the Installation Complete window shown in Figure 2-4 appears.

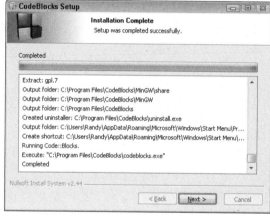

Figure 2-4:
The Installation Complete window signals that Code::Blocks has been successfully installed.

10. **Click Next.**

    Finally, the Completing the Code::Blocks Setup Wizard window appears. This final step creates the icons necessary to start the application.

11. **Click Finish.**

You've done it! You've installed Code::Blocks. All that remains now is to test whether it works, and then you'll be ready to start programming.

Testing the Code::Blocks Installation

In this section, you will build a default program that comes with Code::Blocks. This program does nothing more than display "Hello, world!" on the display, but building and running this program successfully will verify that you've installed Code::Blocks properly.

1. **Start Code::Blocks by double-clicking on the Code::Blocks icon created on the Desktop or selecting Programs⇨Code::Blocks⇨Code::Blocks.**

   This should open a window like the one shown in Figure 2-5.

   Across the top of the window are the usual menu options starting with File, Edit, View, and so on. The window at the upper right, the one that says "Start here," is where the source code will go when you get that far. The window at the lower right is where Code::Blocks displays messages to the user. Compiler error messages appear in this space. The window on the left labeled Management is where Code::Blocks keeps track of the files that make up the programs. It should be empty now since you have yet to create a program. The first thing you will need to do is create a project.

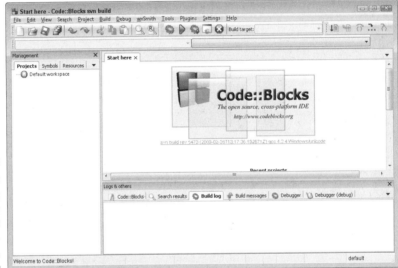

Figure 2-5:
The opening
screen of the
Code::Blocks
environ-
ment.

What's a project?

You want Code::Blocks to create only Console Applications, but it can create a lot of different types of programs. For Windows programmers, Code::Blocks can create Dynamic Link Libraries (also known simply as DLLs). It can create Windows applications. It can create both static and dynamically linked libraries for Linux and MacOS.

In addition, Code::Blocks allows the programmer to set different options on the ways each of these targets is built. I will show you how to adjust a few of these settings in later chapters. And finally, Code::Blocks remembers how you have your windows configured for each project. When you return to the project, Code::Blocks restores the windows to their last configuration to save you time.

Code::Blocks stores the information it needs about the type of program that you are building, the optional settings, and the window layout in two project files. The settings are stored in a file with the same name as the program but carrying the extension .cbp. The window configuration is stored in a file with the same name but with the extension .layout.

Creating the project

1. **Select File⇨New⇨Projects to open the window shown in Figure 2-6.**

   This is a list of all of the types of applications that Code::Blocks knows how to build.

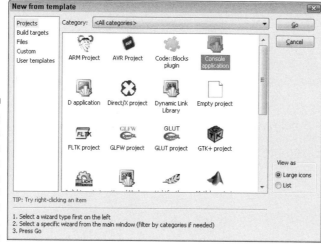

Figure 2-6: Select the Console Application from the many types of targets offered.

Fortunately, you will be concentrating on just one, the Console Application.

2. **Select Console Application and select Go.**

   Code::Blocks responds with the display shown in Figure 2-7. Here Code::Blocks is offering you the option to create either a C or a C++ program.

3. **Select C++ and click Next.**

   Code::Blocks opens a dialog box where you will enter the name and optional subfolder for your project. First, click on the little ... button to create a folder to hold your Projects, navigate to the root of your working disk (on a Windows machine, it'll be either C or D, most likely C). Select the Make New Folder button at the bottom left of the window. Name the new folder Beginning_Programming-CPP.

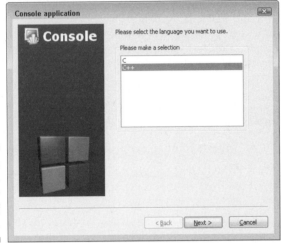

Figure 2-7:
Select C++
as your
language of
choice.

4. **Click OK when your display looks like the one shown in Figure 2-8.**

The folder that you create to hold your project must not contain any spaces in the name. In addition, none of the folders in the path should contain spaces. That automatically eliminates placing your projects on the Desktop since the path to the Desktop contains spaces. You should also avoid spaces in the name of the Project. You can use underscores to separate words instead. The Code::Blocks compiler gets confused with spaces in the filenames and generates obscure and largely meaningless errors.

Figure 2-8:
Create
the folder
`Begin`
`ning_`
`Program`
`ming–`
`CPP` into
which you
will collect
your C++
projects.

Now enter the name of the Project as **HelloWorld**. Notice that Code::Blocks automatically creates a subfolder of the same name to contain the files that make up the project.

5. **Click Next when your display looks like Figure 2-9.**

Figure 2-9:
Call your
first project
HelloWorld.

6. **When Code::Blocks asks how you want your subfolders set up, you can accept the default configuration, as shown in Figure 2-10. Select Finish.**

You can select the Back button to back up to a previous menu in the preceding steps if you screw something up. However, you may have to reenter any data you entered when you go forward again. Once you select Finish, you can no longer return and change your selections. If you screw up and want to redo the project, you will first need to remove the Project: Right-click on HelloWorld in the Management window and select Close Project. Now you can delete the folder `Beginning_Programming-CPP\HelloWorld` and start over again.

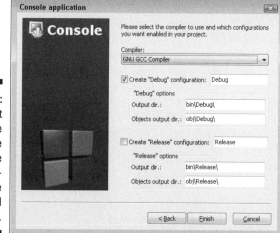

Figure 2-10:
Select
Finish on the
final page
to complete
the cre-
ation of the
HelloWorld
Project.

Testing your default project

Code::Blocks creates a Console Application project and even populates it with a working program when you select Finish on the Project Wizard. To see that program, click on the plus (+) sign next to Sources in the Management window on the left side of the display. The drop-down list reveals one file, `main.cpp`. Double-click on `main.cpp` to display the following simple program in the source code entry window on the right:

```cpp
#include <iostream>

using namespace std;

int main()
{
    cout << "Hello world!" << endl;
    return 0;
}
```

I'll skip over what some of this stuff means for now, but the crux of the program starts after the open brace following `main()`. This is where execution begins. The line

```cpp
cout << "Hello world!" << endl;
```

says output the line "Hello, world!" to the `cout`, which by default is the command line. The next line

```cpp
return 0;
```

causes control to return to the operating system, which effectively terminates the program.

1. **Select Build⇨Build to build the C++ source statements into an executable machine language program.**

   (You can press Ctrl+F9 or click the Build icon if you prefer.) Immediately, you should see the Build Log tab appear in the lower-right screen followed by a series of lengthy commands, as shown in Figure 2-11. This is Code::Blocks telling the C++ compiler how to build the test program using the settings stored in the project file. The details aren't important. What is important, however, is that the final two lines of the Build Log window should be

   ```
   Process terminated with status 0 (0 minutes, 1 seconds)
   0 errors, 0 warnings
   ```

The terminated status of 0 means that the build process worked properly. The "0 errors, 0 warnings" means that the program compiled without errors or warnings. (The build time of 1 second is not important.)

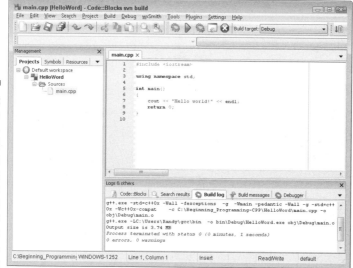

Figure 2-11: Building the default program should result in a working program with no errors and no warnings.

If you don't get a status of 0 with 0 errors and 0 warnings, then something is wrong with your installation or with the project. The most common sources of error are

- You already had a gcc compiler installed on your computer before you installed Code::Blocks. Code::Blocks uses a special version of the GNU gcc compiler, but it will use any other gcc compiler that you may already have installed on your computer. Your safest bet is to uninstall Code::Blocks, uninstall your other gcc compiler, and reinstall Code::Blocks from scratch.

- You built your project in a directory that contains a space in the name; for example, you built your project on the Desktop. Be sure to build your project in the folder `Beginning_Programming-CPP` in the root of your user disk (most likely C on a Windows machine).

- You built a project directly from the enclosed CD-ROM that came with the book. (This doesn't apply to the steps here, but it is a common source of error anyway. You can't build your program on a read-only storage medium like a CD-ROM. You will have to copy the files from the CD-ROM to the hard drive first.)

2. Select Build⇨Run (Ctrl+F10) to execute the program.

Immediately a window should pop open with the message "Hello, world!" followed by the return code of zero and the message "Press any key to continue," as shown in Figure 2-12.

3. Press Enter.

The window will disappear and control returns to the Code::Blocks text editor.

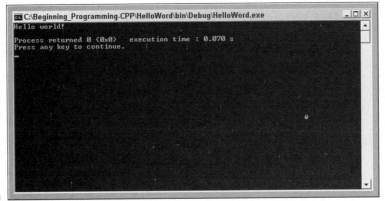

Figure 2-12:
The default program displays "Hello, world!" and waits for you to press a key.

If you were able to see the "Hello, world!" message by executing the program, then congratulations! You've installed your development environment and built and executed your first C++ program successfully. If you did not, then delete the `Beginning_Programming_CPP` folder, uninstall Code::Blocks, and try again, carefully comparing your display to the figures shown in this chapter. If you are still having problems, refer to www.stephendavis.com for pointers as to what might be wrong, as well as a link to my e-mail where you can send me questions and comments. I cannot do your programming homework for you, but I can answer questions to get you started.

Chapter 3

Writing Your First Program

*T*his chapter will guide you through the creation of your first program in C++. You will be using the Code::Blocks C++ environment. It will all be a bit "cookbookish" since this is your first time. I explain all of the parts that make up this program in subsequent chapters beginning with Part II, but for now you'll be asked to accept a few things on faith. Soon all will be revealed, and everything you do in this chapter will make perfect sense.

Creating a New Project

As always, you must create a new project to house your program. Follow the abbreviated steps here (or you can use the detailed steps from Chapter 2):

1. **With Code::Blocks open, select File⇨New⇨Project.**

2. **Select Console Applications and select Go (or double-click on the Console Applications icon).**

3. **Select C++ as your language of choice and select Next.**

4. **Enter** Conversion **as the Project Title.**

   If you followed the steps in Chapter 2, the "Folder to create project in" should already be set to Beginning_Programming-CPP. If not, it's not too late to click the ... button and create the folder in the root of your working disk. (This is described in detail in Chapter 2.) The Code::Blocks Wizard fills in the name of the Project and the name of the resulting program for you.

When you're done, your window should look like that shown in Figure 3-1.

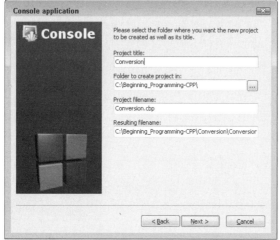

5. **Select Next.**

   The next window allows you to change the target folders. The defaults are fine.

6. **Select Finish.**

Code::Blocks creates a new Project and adds it to the earlier `HelloWorld` project. (See the "Organizing projects" sidebar for an explanation of why this happens.) The resulting display should look like Figure 3-2.

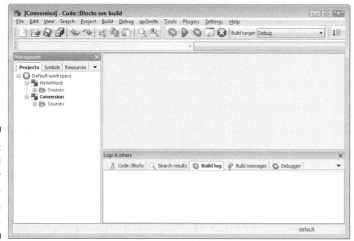

Organizing projects

You may be curious as to why Code::Blocks added the new Conversion project to the existing HelloWorld project rather than replacing it. A large effort involving multiple developers may be broken up into a number of different programs that are all designed to work together. To support this, Code::Blocks allows you to have any number of different projects loaded at once.

The collection of all projects is called a *workspace*. Since you didn't specify a workspace when you started Code::Blocks, the projects you've created so far have been going into the *default workspace*. Only one project in the workspace can be active at a time. This is the project that appears in bold (refer to Figure 3-2 again, and you'll notice that `Conversion` is bolded while `HelloWorld` is not). Any Code::Blocks commands you perform are directed at the active project. By default, the last project you created is the active project,

but you can change the active project by right-clicking on it in the Management window and selecting Activate Project (the first option in the list).

If you were to take a peek in the `Beginning_Programming-CPP` folder right now, you would notice two subfolders: `HelloWorld` and `Conversion`. Both of these subfolders include a project file with the extension .cbp that contains the compiler settings, a layout file with the extension layout that describes the way you want your windows set up when working on this project, and the file `main.cpp` that contains the C++ program created by the application wizard. `HelloWorld` contains a further subfolder named `Debug`.

C++ programs can have any name that you like, but it should end in .cpp. You will see how to create multiple C++ source files with different names in Chapter 12.

Entering Your Program

It is now time to enter your first program using the following steps:

1. **Make sure that Conversion is bolded in the Management window (refer to Figure 3-2).**

   This indicates that it's the active project. If it is not, right-click on Conversion and select Activate Project from the drop-down menu.

2. **Close any source file windows that may be open by selecting File⇨ Close all files.**

   Alternatively, you can close just the source files you want by clicking on the small X next to the name of the file in the editor tab. You don't want to inadvertently edit the wrong source file.

3. **Open the Sources folder by clicking on the small plus sign next to Sources underneath Conversion in the Management window.**

   The drop-down menu should reveal the single file `main.cpp`.

Filename extensions

Windows has a bad habit of hiding the filename extensions when displaying filenames. For some applications this may be a good idea, but this is almost never a good idea for a programmer. With extensions hidden, Windows may display three or four files with the same name `HelloWorld`. This confusing state of affairs is easily cleared up when you display file extensions and realize that they are all different.

You should disable the Windows Hide Extensions feature. Exactly how you do this depends upon what version of Windows you are using:

✔ Windows 2000: Select Start⇨Settings⇨ Control Panel⇨Folder Options.

✔ Windows XP with Default View: Select Start⇨Control Panel⇨Performance and Maintenance⇨File Types.

✔ Windows XP with Classic view: Select Start⇨Control Panel⇨Folder options.

✔ Windows Vista with Default view: Select Start⇨Control Panel⇨Appearance and Personalization⇨Show hidden files and folders.

✔ Windows Vista with Classic view: Select Start⇨Settings⇨Control Panel⇨Folder options.

Now navigate to the View tab of the Folder Options dialog box that appears. Scroll down until you find "Hide extensions for known file types." Make sure that this box is unchecked. Select OK to close the dialog box.

4. **Double-click `main.cpp` to open the file in the editor.**

5. **Edit the contents of `main.cpp` by entering the following program exactly as it appears here.**

   The result is shown in Figure 3-3.

   This is definitely the hard part, so take your time and be patient:

```
//
// Conversion - Program to convert temperature from
//              Celsius degrees into Fahrenheit:
//              Fahrenheit = Celsius * (212 - 32)/100 + 32
//
#include <cstdio>
#include <cstdlib>
#include <iostream>
using namespace std;

int main(int nNumberofArgs, char* pszArgs[])
{
  // enter the temperature in Celsius
  int celsius;
  cout << "Enter the temperature in Celsius:";
  cin >> celsius;

  // convert Celsius into Fahrenheit values
  int fahrenheit;
```

```
    fahrenheit = celsius * 9/5 + 32;

    // output the results (followed by a NewLine)
    cout << "Fahrenheit value is:";
    cout << fahrenheit << endl;

    // wait until user is ready before terminating program
    // to allow the user to see the program results
    system("PAUSE");
    return 0;
}
```

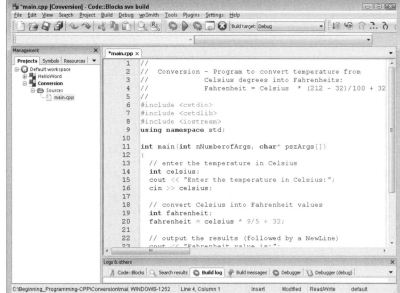

Figure 3-3:
The edited
`main.`
`cpp` file
of the
Conversion
program.

What do I mean by "exactly as you see here"? C++ is very picky about syntax. It frowns on missing semicolons or misspelled words. It doesn't care about extra spaces as long as they don't appear in the middle of a word. For example `int fahren heit;` is not the same as `int fahrenheit;` but `int    fahrenheit;` is okay. C++ treats tabs, spaces, and newlines all the same, referring to them all as simply whitespace.

Maybe it was just me, but it took me a long time to get used to the fact that C++ differentiates between uppercase and lowercase. Thus, `int Fahrenheit;` is not the same thing as `int fahrenheit;`. One final hint: C++ ignores anything that appears after a `//`, so you don't have to worry about getting that stuff right.

6. **Save the file by selecting File⇨Save all files.**

Building the Program

Now comes the most nerve-racking part of the entire software development process: building your program. It's during this step that C++ reviews your handiwork to see if it can make any sense out of what you've written.

Programmers are eternal optimists. Somewhere, deep in our hearts, we truly believe that every time we hit the Build button, everything is going to work, but it almost never does. Invariably, a missing semicolon or a misspelled word will disappoint C++ and bring a hail of error messages, like so much criticism from our elementary school teachers, crashing down around our ears.

Actually building the program takes just one step: You select Build⇨Build or press Ctrl+F9 or click the little Build icon.

Finding What Could Go Wrong

No offense, but the Build step almost certainly did not come off without error. A Gold Star program is one that works the first time you build and execute it. You will almost never write a Gold Star program in your entire programming career.

Fortunately, the Code::Blocks editor is so well integrated with the compiler that it can automatically direct you very close to your errors. Most times, it can place the cursor in the exact row that contains the error. To prove the point, let me take you through a couple of example errors.

These are just two of the myriad ways to screw up in C++. I can't possibly show you all of them. Learning how to interpret what the compiler is trying to tell you with its error and warning messages is an important part of learning the language. It can come only from many months of practice and gaining experience with the language. Hopefully, these two examples will get you jump-started.

Misspelled commands

Misspelled commands are the easiest errors to identify and correct. To demonstrate the point, I added an extra t to line 14 in the preceding code so that it now reads

```
intt celsius;
```

Unlike int, the word intt has no meaning to C++. Building the resulting program generated the display shown in Figure 3-4.

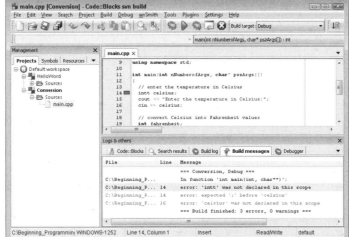

Figure 3-4:
The error
messages
resulting
from mis-
spelling
int.

Notice first the small, red block on Line 14 indicating that there is a problem somewhere on this line. You can read all about it down in the Build Messages tab in the lower-right window. Here you can see the following messages:

```
    In function 'int main(int, char**)':
14 error: 'intt' was not declared in this scope
14 error: expected ';' before 'celsius'
16 error: 'celsius' was not declared in this scope
```

The first line indicates the name of the function containing the error. I don't present functions until Chapter 12, but it's easy to believe that all of the code in this program is in a function called main. The next line is the key. This says essentially that C++ didn't understand what intt is on line 14 of the program. The error message is a bit cryptic, but suffice it to say you'll get this same error message almost every time you misspell something. The remaining error messages are just by-products of the original error.

One C++ error can generate a cascade of error messages. It is possible to identify and fix multiple errors in a single build attempt, but it takes experience to figure out which errors stem from which others. For now, focus on the first error message. Fix it and rebuild the program.

Why is C++ so picky?

You will quickly come to appreciate that C++ is about as picky as a judge at a spelling bee. Everything has to be just so, or the compiler won't accept it. Interestingly enough, it doesn't have to be that way: Some languages choose to try to make sense out of whatever you give it. The most extreme version of this was a language promulgated by IBM for its mainframes in the 1970s known as PL/1 (this stood for "Programming Language 1"). One version of this compiler would try to make sense out of whatever you threw at it. We nerds used to get immense fun during late nights at the computer center by torturing the compiler with a program consisting of nothing but the word "IF" or "WHILE." Through some tortured logic, PL/1 would construct an entire program out of this one command.

The other camp in programming languages, the camp to which C++ belongs, holds the opposite view: These languages compel the programmer to state exactly what she intends. Everything must be spelled out. Each declaration is checked against each and every usage to make sure that everything matches. No missing semicolon or incorrectly declared label goes unpunished.

It turns out that the tough love approach adopted by C++ is actually more efficient. The problem with the PL/1 "free love" approach is that it was almost always wrong in its understanding of what I intended. PL/1 ended up creating a program that compiled but did something other than what I intended when it executed. C++ generates a compiler error if something doesn't check out to force me to express my intentions clearly and unambiguously.

It turns out that it's a lot easier to find and fix the compile time errors generated by C++ than the so-called runtime errors created by a compiler that assumes it understands what I want but gets it wrong.

Missing semicolon

Another common error is to leave off a semicolon. The message that this error generates can be a little confusing. To demonstrate, I removed the semicolon from the declaration on line 14 so that it reads

```
int celsius
cout << "Enter the temperature in Celsius:";
```

The error reported by C++ for this offense points not to line 14 but to the following line 15:

```
15 error: expected initialization before 'cout'
16 error: 'celsius' was not declared in this scope
```

This is easier to understand when you consider that C++ considers newlines as just a different form of space. Without the semicolon, C++ runs the two lines together. There is no separate line 14 anymore. C++ can interpret the first part, but it doesn't understand the run-on sentence that starts with cout.

Missing semicolons often generate error messages that bear little resemblance to the actual error message, and they are almost always on the next line after the actual error. If you suspect a missing semicolon, start on the line with the reported error and scan backwards.

Using the Enclosed CD-ROM

If you just can't get the program entered correctly, you can always copy the program from the enclosed CD-ROM. (If you have questions regarding using the CD-ROM, see the Appendix; it details what you'll find on the CD-ROM, as well as troubleshooting tips, should you need them.)

You should really try to enter the program by hand first before you give up and resort to the CD-ROM. It's only through working through your mistakes that you develop a feel for how the language works.

You have several ways to use the enclosed CD-ROM. The most straightforward is to copy and paste the contents of the file on the CD into your own as follows:

1. **Insert the enclosed CD-ROM into your computer.**

2. **Select File⇨Open from within Code::Blocks. Navigate to the `X:\`
   `Beginning_Programming-CPP\Conversion` where *X* is the letter of
   your CD-ROM drive.**

3. **Select the file `main.cpp`.**

   Code::Blocks will open the file (in ReadOnly mode) in a new tab in the editor window.

4. **Select Edit⇨Select All or press Ctrl+A.**

   This will select the entire contents of the source file.

5. **Select Edit⇨Copy or press Ctrl+C.**

   This will copy the entire file to the clipboard.

6. **Select the main tab corresponding to your program.**

7. **Select Edit⇨Select All or press Ctrl+A again.**

8. **Select Edit⇨Paste or press Ctrl+V.**

   This will overwrite the entire contents of the `main.cpp` that you've been working on with the contents of the corresponding file on the CD-ROM.

9. **Close the tab containing the CD-ROM version of the file by clicking on
   the small X next to the filename.**

Running the Program

You can execute the program once you get a clean compile (that is, 0 errors and 0 warnings) by following these steps:

1. **Select Build⇨Run or press Ctrl+F10.**

   This will execute the program without the debugger. (Don't worry if you don't know what a *debugger* is; I teach you how to use it in Chapter 20.)

   The program opens an 80 column by 25 row window and prompts you to enter a temperature in degrees Celsius.

2. **Enter a known temperature like 100 degrees. Press Enter.**

   The program immediately responds with the equivalent temperature in Fahrenheit of 212:

   ```
   Enter the temperature in Celsius:100
   Fahrenheit value is:212
   Press any key to continue . . .
   ```

3. **Press Enter twice to exit the program and return to the editor.**

How the Program Works

Even though this is your first program, I didn't want to leave this chapter without giving you some idea of how this program works.

The template

The first part of the program I call the "Beginning Programming Template." This will be the same magic incantation used for all programs in this book. It goes like this:

```
//
//   ProgramName - short explanation of what the
//                 program does
//
#include <cstdio>
#include <cstdlib>
#include <iostream>
using namespace std;

int main(int nNumberofArgs, char* pszArgs[])
```

```
{
  // program goes here

  // wait until user is ready before terminating program
  // to allow the user to see the program results
  system("PAUSE");
  return 0;
}
```

Comments

The first few lines in this template appear to be free-form text. Either this "code" was meant for human consumption or the computer is a lot smarter than anyone's ever given it credit for. These first four lines are known as *comments.* A comment is a line or portion of a line that is ignored by the C++ compiler. Comments enable the programmer to explain what she was doing or thinking while writing a particular segment of code.

A C++ comment begins with double forward slashes and ends with a newline. You can put any character you want in a comment, and comments can be as long as you like, though it is customary to limit them to 80 characters or so because that's what fits within a normal screen width.

Note: You may think it odd to have a command in C++, or any other programming language, that is specifically ignored by the compiler; yet, all programming languages have some form of comment. It is critical that the programmer be able to explain what was going through her mind when a piece of code was written. It may not be obvious to the next person who picks up the program and uses it or modifies it. In fact, it may not be obvious to the programmer herself after only a few days working on something else.

Include files

The next few lines are called *include statements* because they cause the contents of the named file to be included at that point in the program. Include files always start with the statement `#include` in column 1 followed by the name of the file to include. I'll explain further in Chapter 12. Just consider them magic for now.

main

Every program must have a `main()` somewhere in it. Program execution begins at the open brace immediately following `main()` and terminates at the return statement immediately prior to the closed brace. An explanation of the exact format of the declaration for `main()` will have to wait.

Notice that the standard template ends with the statement `system("PAUSE")` prior to the `return 0`. This command causes the program to wait for the user to enter a key before the program terminates.

The call to `system("PAUSE")` isn't necessary as long as you're running your programs from the Code::Blocks environment. Code::Blocks waits for the user to enter a key before closing the console application window anyway. However, not all environments are so understanding. Leave this off and very often C++ will close the application window before you have a chance to read the output from the program. I get lots of hate mail when that happens.

The Conversion program

The remainder of the `Conversion` program sans the template appears as follows:

```
// enter the temperature in Celsius
int celsius;
cout << "Enter the temperature in Celsius:";
cin >> celsius;

// convert Celsius into Fahrenheit values
int fahrenheit;
fahrenheit = celsius * 9/5 + 32;

// output the results (followed by a NewLine)
cout << "Fahrenheit value is:";
cout << fahrenheit << endl;
```

Skipping over the comment lines, which C++ ignores anyway, this program starts by declaring a variable called `celsius`. A variable is a place you can use to store a number or character.

The next line displays the prompt to the user to `"Enter the temperature in Celsius:"`. The object `cout` points to the console window by default.

The next line reads whatever number the operator enters and stores it into the variable `celsius` declared earlier.

The next two lines declare a second variable `fahrenheit`, which it then sets equal to the value of the variable `celsius * 9 / 5 + 32`, which is the conversion formula from Celsius to Fahrenheit temperature.

The final two lines output the string `"Fahrenheit value is:"` and the value calculated and stored into the variable `fahrenheit` immediately above.

Part II
Writing a Program: Decisions, Decisions

The 5th Wave   By Rich Tennant

Maintenance is chagrined to find out the squeak in Clark's disk drive is really a whistle in Clark's nose.

In this part . . .

Now that you're familiar with how to write and build a program, you can start learning about C++ itself. This part introduces you to the basic elements of C++: the variable declaration and the expression. You'll even find out how to make a decision in your program if you can stand it. Finally, you'll see some beginning techniques for finding errors in your programs.

Chapter 4

Integer Expressions

- -

In This Chapter

▶ Declaring variables

▶ Creating expressions

▶ Decomposing compound expressions

▶ Analyzing the assignment operator

▶ Incrementing variables with the unary operator

- -

*I*n this chapter, you will be studying integer declarations and expressions. Algebra class introduced you to the concepts of variables and expressions. The teacher would write something on the board like

```
x = 1
```

This defines a *variable* x and sets it equal to the value 1 until some subsequent statement changes it for some reason. The term x becomes a replacement for 1. The teacher would then write the following *expression*:

```
y = 2x
```

Because I know that x is 1, I now know that y is equal to 2. This was a real breakthrough in the seventh grade. All conventional computer languages follow this same pattern of creating and manipulating variables.

Declaring Variables

An integer *variable declaration* starts with the keyword int followed by the name of a variable and a semicolon, as in the following example:

```
int n1;         // declare a variable n1
```

All variables in C++ must be declared before they can be used. A variable declaration reserves a small amount of space in memory, just enough for a single integer, and assigns it a name. You can declare more than one variable in the same declaration, as in the following example, but it's not a good idea for reasons that will become clear as you work through subsequent chapters:

```
int n2, n3;    // declare two variables n2 and n3
```

A *keyword* is a word that has meaning to C++. You cannot name a variable the same as a keyword. Thus, you cannot create a variable with the name `int`. However, since keywords are case-sensitive, you could create a variable `Int` or `INT`. You will be introduced to further keywords throughout the chapters.

The fact that the keyword `int` is used instead of `integer` is just a reflection of the overall terseness of the C++ language. The creators of the language must have been poor typists and wanted to minimize the amount of typing they had to do.

Unlike in algebra class, the range of an integer in C++ is not unlimited. However, it is very large indeed. If you exceed the range of an int, you will get the wrong answer. I will discuss variable size and range in Chapter 14.

Variable names

You can name a variable anything you like with the following restrictions:

- ✔ The first letter of the variable must be a character in the sequence a through z, A through Z, or underscore ('_').
- ✔ Every letter after the first must be a character in the sequence a through z, A through Z, underscore ('_'), or the digits 0 through 9.
- ✔ A variable name can be of any length. All characters are significant.

The following are legal variable names:

```
int myVariable;
int MyVariable;
int myNumber2Variable;
int _myVariable;
int my_Variable;
```

The following are not legal variable names:

```
int myPercentage%;       // contains illegal character
int 2ndVariable;         // starts with a digit
int my Variable;         // contains a space
```

Variable names should be descriptive. Variable names like x are discouraged.

Assigning a value to a variable

Every variable has a value from the moment it's declared. However, until you assign it a value, a variable will just assume whatever garbage value happens to be in that memory location when it's allocated. That means that you don't know what the value is, and it's likely to change every time you run the program.

You can assign a variable a value using the equals sign as in the following example:

```
int n;          // declare a variable n
n = 1;          // set it to 1
```

This looks remarkably similar to the assignment statement in algebra class, but the effect is not quite the same. In C++, the assignment statement says "take the value on the right-hand side of the equals sign" (in this case 1) "and store it into the location on the left-hand side, overwriting whatever was there before" (in this case n).

You can see the difference in the following expression:

```
n = n + 1;      // increment the variable n
```

This statement would make absolutely no sense in algebra class. How could n be both equal to n and n + 1 at the same time? However, this statement makes perfect sense in C++ if you follow the definition for assignment given above: "Take the value stored in the variable n" (1) "add 1 and store the result" (2) "into the variable n." This is shown graphically in Figure 4-1.

Figure 4-1:
The effect of executing the expression n = n + 1 when n starts out as 1.

```
// say n starts out a 1

n = n + 1;           Steps to
                     evaluate
n = 1 + 1;           the expression

n = 2;
```

Initializing a variable at declaration

You can initialize your variable at the time that it's declared by following it with an equals sign and a value:

```
int n = 1;      // declare and initialize variable
```

Forgetting to initialize a variable

Forgetting to initialize a variable before using it is a very common error in C++. So much so that the compiler actually goes to great pains to detect this case and warn you about it. Consider the following statements:

```
int n1, n2 = 0;
n2 = n1 + 1;
cout << "n1 = " << n1 << endl;
cout << "n2 = " << n2 << endl;
```

CodeBlocks generates the following warning when building the program containing this snippet:

```
warning: "n1" is used uninitialized in this function
```

Though it's a really bad idea, you are free to ignore warnings. Executing the program generates the output:

```
n1 = 54
n2 = 55
```

It's easy to see why n2 is equal to 55 given that n1 is 54, but why is n1 equal to 54 in the first place? I could turn the question around and ask, "Why not?" This is an expression of the old adage, "Everyone has to be somewhere." The C++ equivalent is, "Every variable must have a value." If you don't initialize a variable to something, it'll get a random value from memory. In this case, the value 54 was left over from some previous usage.

This initializes only the one variable, so if you write the following compound declaration

```
int n1, n2 = 0;
```

you've initialized n2 but not n1. This is one reason it's not a good idea to declare multiple variables in a single declaration. (See the sidebar "Forgetting to initialize a variable".)

Integer Constants

C++ understands any symbol that begins with a digit and contains only digits to be an *integer constant*. The following are legal constants:

```
123
1
256
```

A constant cannot contain any funny characters. The following is not legal:

```
123Z456
```

The following is legal but doesn't mean what you think:

```
123+456
```

This actually defines the sum of two constants `123` and `456`, or the value `479`.

Normally C++ assumes that constants are decimal (base 10). However, for historical reasons, a number that begins with a 0 is assumed to be octal (base 8). By the same token, a number that starts with `0x` or `0X` is assumed to be hexadecimal. Hexadecimal uses the letters `A` through `F` or `a` through `f` for the digits beyond 9. Thus, `0xFF`, `0377`, and `255` are all equivalent. Don't worry if you don't know what octal or hexadecimal are — we won't be using them in this book.

Don't start a constant with 0 unless you mean it to be in octal.

An integer constant can have certain symbols appended to the end to change its type. You will see the different types of integer constants in Chapter 14.

Expressions

Variables and constants are useful only if you can use them to perform calculations. The term *expression* is C++ jargon for a calculation. You've already seen the simplest expression:

```
int n;                  // declaration
n = 1;                  // expression
```

Expressions always involve variables, constants, and operators. An *operator* performs some arithmetic operation on its arguments. Most operators take two arguments — these are called *binary operators*. A few operators take a single argument — these are the *unary operators*.

All expressions return a value and a type. (Note that `int` is the type of all the expressions described in this chapter.)

Binary operators

A *binary operator* is an operator that takes two arguments. If you can say `var1 op var2`, then `op` must be a binary operator. The most common binary operators are the same simple operations that you learned in grade school. The common binary operators appear in Table 4-1. (This table also includes the unary operators that are described a little later in this chapter.)

Table 4-1	Mathematical Operators in Order of Precedence	
Precedence	*Operator*	*Meaning*
1	- (unary)	Returns the negative of its argument
2	++ (unary)	Increment
2	-- (unary)	Decrement
3	* (binary)	Multiplication
3	/ (binary)	Division
3	% (binary)	Modulo
4	+ (binary)	Addition
4	- (binary)	Subtraction
5	=, *=,%=,+=,-= (special)	Assignment types

The simplest binary is the assignment operator noted by the equals sign. The assignment operator says "take the value on the right-hand side and store at the location on the left-hand side of the operator." (I describe the special assignment operators at the end of this chapter.)

Multiplication, division, addition, subtraction, and modulo are the operators used to perform arithmetic. They work just like the arithmetic operators you learned in grammar school with the following special considerations:

✔ **Multiplication must always be expressly stated and is never implied as it is in algebra.** Consider the following example:

```
int n = 2;                  // declare a variable
int m = 2n;                 // this generates an error
```

The expression above does not assign m the value of 2 times n. Instead, C++ tries to interpret 2n as a variable name. Since variable names can't start with a digit, it generates an error during the build step.

What the programmer meant was:

```
int n = 2;
int m = 2 * n;              // this is OK
```

✔ **Integer division throws away the remainder.** Thus, the following:

```
int n = 13 / 7;             // assigns the value 1 to n
```

Fourteen divided by 7 is 2. Thirteen divided by seven is 1. (You will see decimal variable types that can handle fractions in Chapter 14.)

✔ **The modulo operator returns the remainder after division** (you might not remember modulo):

```
int n = 13 % 7;          // sets n to 6
```

Fourteen modulo seven is zero. Thirteen modulo seven is six.

Decomposing compound expressions

A single expression can include multiple operators:

```
int n = 5 + 100 + 32;
```

When all the operators are the same, C++ evaluates the expression from left to right:

```
5 + 100 + 32
105 + 32
137
```

When different operators are combined in a single expression, C++ uses a property called *precedence*. Precedence is the order that operators are evaluated in a compound expression. Consider the following example:

```
int n = 5 * 100 + 32;
```

What comes first, multiplication or addition? Or is this expression simply evaluated from left to right? Refer back to Table 4-1, which tells you that multiplication has a precedence of 3, which is higher than the precedence of addition which is 4 (smaller values have higher precedence). Thus, multiplication occurs first:

```
5 * 100 + 32
500 + 32
532
```

The order of the operations is overruled by the precedence of the operators. As you can see

```
int n = 32 + 5 * 100;
```

generates the same result:

```
32 + 5 * 100
32 + 500
532
```

But what if you really want 5 times the sum of 100 plus 32? You can override the precedence of the operators by wrapping expressions that you want performed first in parentheses as follows:

```
int n = 5 * (100 + 32);
```

Now the addition is performed before the multiplication:

```
5 * (100 + 32)
5 * 132
660
```

You can combine parentheses to make expressions as complicated as you like. C++ always starts with the deepest nested parentheses it can find and works its way out.

```
(3 + 2) * ((100 / 20) + (50 / 5))
(3 + 2) * (5 + 10)
5 * 15
75
```

You can always divide complicated expressions using intermediate variables. The following is safer:

```
int factor = 3 + 2;
int principal = (100 / 20) + (50 / 5);
int total = factor * principal;
```

Assigning a name to intermediate values also allows the programmer to explain the parts of a complex equation, making it easier for the next guy to understand.

Unary Operators

The *unary operators* are those operators that take a single argument. The unary mathematical operators are -, ++, and –.

The minus operator changes the sign of its argument. A positive number becomes negative, and a negative number becomes positive:

```
int n = 10;
int m = -n;                    // m is now -10
```

The ++ and the -- operators increment and decrement their arguments by one.

Why a separate increment operator?

Why did the authors of C++ think that an increment operator was called for? After all, this operator does nothing more than add 1, which can be done with an assignment expression. The authors of C++ (and its predecessor C) were obsessed with efficiency. They wanted to generate the fastest machine code they possibly could. They knew that most processors have an increment and decrement instruction,

and they wanted the C++ compiler to use that instruction if at all possible. They reasoned that n++ would get converted into an increment instruction while n = n + 1; might not. This type of thing makes very little difference today, but the increment and decrement operators are here to stay. As you will see in Chapters 9 and 10, they get a lot more use than you might think.

The increment and decrement operators are unique in that they come in two versions: a *prefix* and a *postfix* version.

The prefix version of increment is written ++n, while the postfix is written n++.

Both the prefix and postfix increment operators increment their argument by one. The difference is in the value returned. The prefix version returns the value after the increment operation, while the postfix returns the value before the increment. (The same is true of the decrement operator.) This is demonstrated in the following IncrementOperator program:

```cpp
// IncrementOperator - demonstrate the increment operator

#include <cstdio>
#include <cstdlib>
#include <iostream>

using namespace std;

int main(int nNumberofArgs, char* pszArgs[])
{
    // demonstrate the increment operator
    int n;

    // first the prefix
    n = 1;
    cout << "The value of n is    " <<    n << endl;
    cout << "The value of ++n is " << ++n << endl;
    cout << "The value of n afterwards is " << n << endl;
    cout << endl;

    // now the postfix
    n = 1;
    cout << "The value of n is    " <<    n << endl;
    cout << "The value of n++ is " << n++ << endl;
```

```
        cout << "The value of n afterwards is " << n << endl;
        cout << endl;

        // wait until user is ready before terminating program
        // to allow the user to see the program results
        system("PAUSE");
        return 0;
}
```

The output from this program appears as follows:

```
The value of n is    1
The value of ++n is 2
The value of n afterwards is 2

The value of n is    1
The value of n++ is 1
The value of n afterwards is 2

Press any key to continue . . .
```

This example demonstrates both the prefix and postfix increment. In both cases, the variable n is initialized to 1. Notice that the value of n after executing both ++n and n++ is 2. However, the value of ++n was 2 (the value after the increment), while the value of n++ was 1 (the value before the increment).

The Special Assignment Operators

The assignment operator is absolutely critical to any computer language. How else can I store a computed value? However, C++ provides a complete set of extra versions of the assignment operator that seems less critical.

The authors of C++ must have noticed that expressions of the following form were very common:

```
x = x # value;
```

Here # stands for some binary operator. In their perhaps overzealous pursuit of terseness, the authors created a separate assignment for each of the binary operators of the form:

```
x #= value;   // where # is any one of the binary operators
```

Thus, for example

```
n = n + 2;
```

can be written as

```
n += 2;
```

Note: You don't see this all that often, and I present it here primarily for completeness.

Chapter 5

Character Expressions

*C*hapter 4 introduces the concept of the integer variable. This chapter introduces the integer's smaller sibling, the character or `char` (pronounced variously as *care*, *chair*, or as in the first syllable of *char*coal) to us insiders. I have used characters in programs appearing in earlier chapters — now it's time to introduce them formally.

Defining Character Variables

Character variables are declared just like integers except with the keyword `char` in place of `int`:

```
char inputCharacter;
```

Character constants are defined as a single character enclosed in single quotes, as in the following:

```
char letterA = 'A';
```

This may seem like a silly question, but what exactly is "A"? To answer that, I need to explain what it means to encode characters.

Encoding characters

As I mentioned in Chapter 1, everything in the computer is represented by a pattern of ones and zeros that can be interpreted as numbers. Thus, the bit pattern 0000 0001 is the number 1 when interpreted as an integer. However, this same bit pattern means something completely different when interpreted as an instruction by the processor. So it should come as no surprise that the computer encodes the characters of the alphabet by assigning each a number.

Consider the character 'A'. You could assign it any value you want as long as we all agree. For example, you could assign a value of 1 to 'A', if you wanted to. Logically, you might then assign the value 2 to 'B', 3 to 'C', and so on. In this scheme, 'Z' would get the value 26. You might then start over by assigning the value 27 to 'a', 28 to 'b', right down to 52 for 'z'. That still leaves the digits '0' through '9' plus all the special symbols like space, period, comma, slash, semicolon, and the funny characters you see when you press the number keys while holding Shift down. Add to that the unprintable characters like tab and newline. When all is said and done, you could encode the entire English keyboard using numbers between 1 and 127.

I say "you *could*" assign a value for 'A', 'B', and the remaining characters; however, that wouldn't be a very good idea because it has already been done. Sometime around 1963, there was a general agreement on how characters should be encoded in English. The ASCII (American Standard Coding for Information Interchange) character encoding shown in Table 5-1 was adopted pretty much universally except for one company. IBM published its own standard in 1963 as well. The two encoding standards duked it out for about ten years, but by the early 1970s when C and C++ were being created, ASCII had just about won the battle. The char type was created with ASCII character encoding in mind.

Table 5-1	The ASCII Character Set		
Value	*Char*	*Value*	*Char*
0	NULL	64	@
1	Start of Heading	65	A
2	Start of Text	66	B
3	End of Text	67	C
4	End of Transmission	68	D
5	Enquiry	69	E

Value	Char	Value	Char
6	Acknowledge	70	F
7	Bell	71	G
8	Backspace	72	H
9	Tab	73	I
10	Newline	74	J
11	Vertical Tab	75	K
12	New Page; Form Feed	76	L
13	Carriage Return	77	M
14	Shift Out	78	N
15	Shift In	79	O
16	Data Link Escape	80	P
17	Device Control 1	81	Q
18	Device Control 2	82	R
19	Device Control 3	83	S
20	Device Control 4	84	T
21	Negative Acknowledge	85	U
22	Synchronous Idle	86	V
23	End of Transmission	87	W
24	Cancel	88	X
25	End of Medium	89	Y
26	Substitute	90	Z
27	Escape	91	[
28	File Separator	92	\
29	Group Separator	93	]
30	Record Separator	94	^
31	Unit Separator	95	_
32	Space	96	`
33	!	97	a
34	"	98	b
35	#	99	c
36	$	100	d
37	%	101	e

(continued)

Table 5-1 *(continued)*

Value	Char		Value	Char
38	&		102	f
39	'		103	g
40	(		104	h
41	)		105	i
42	*		106	j
43	+		107	k
44	,		108	l
45	=		109	m
46	.		110	n
47	/		111	o
48	0		112	p
49	1		113	q
50	2		114	r
51	3		115	s
52	4		116	t
53	5		117	u
54	6		118	v
55	7		119	w
56	8		120	x
57	9		121	y
58	:		122	z
59	;		123	{
60	<		124	|
61	=		125	}
62	>		126	~
63	?		127	DEL

The first thing that you'll notice is that the first 32 characters are the "unprintable" characters. That doesn't mean that these characters are so naughty that the censor won't allow them to be printed — it means that they don't display as a symbol when printed on the printer (or on the console for that matter). Many of these characters are no longer used or only used in obscure ways. For example, character 25 "End of Medium" was probably printed as the last character before the end of a reel of magnetic tape. That was a big deal in 1963, but today it has limited use. My favorite is character 7, the Bell — this used to ring the bell on the old teletype machines. (The Code::Blocks C++ generates a beep when you display the bell character.)

The characters starting with 32 are all printable with the exception of the last one, 127, which is the Delete character.

Example of character encoding

The following simple program allows you to play with the ASCII character set:

```
// CharacterEncoding - allow the user to enter a
//                     numeric value then print that value
//                     out as a character

#include <cstdio>
#include <cstdlib>
#include <iostream>

using namespace std;

int main(int nNumberofArgs, char* pszArgs[])
{
    // Prompt the user for a value
    int nValue;
    cout << "Enter decimal value of char to print:";
    cin >> nValue;

    // Now print that value back out as a character
    char cValue = (char)nValue;
    cout << "The char you entered was [" << cValue
         << "]" << endl;

    // wait until user is ready before terminating program
    // to allow the user to see the program results
    system("PAUSE");
    return 0;
}
```

This program begins by prompting the user to "Enter decimal value of a char to print". The program then reads the value entered by the user into the int variable nValue.

The program then assigns this value to a char variable cValue.

TIP

The (char) appearing in front of nValue is called a *cast*. In this case, it casts the value of nValue from an int to a char. I could have performed the assignment without the cast as in

```
cValue = nValue;
```

However, the type of the variables wouldn't match: The value on the right of the assignment is an int, while the value on the left is a char. C++ will perform the assignment anyway, but it will generally complain about such conversions by generating a warning during the build step. The cast converts the value in nValue to a char before performing the assignment:

```
cValue = (char)nValue;   // cast nValue to a char before
                         // assigning the value to cValue
```

The final line outputs the character cValue within a set of square brackets.

The following shows a few sample runs of the program. In the first run, I entered the value 65, which Table 5-1 shows as the character 'A':

```
Enter decimal value of char to print:65
The char you entered was [A]
Press any key to continue . . .
```

The second time I entered the value 97, which corresponds to the character 'a':

```
Enter decimal value of char to print:97
The char you entered was [a]
Press any key to continue . . .
```

On subsequent runs, I tried special characters:

```
Enter decimal value of char to print:36
The char you entered was [$]
Press any key to continue . . .
```

The value 7 didn't print anything, but did cause my PC to issue a loud beep that scared the heck out of me.

The value 10 generated the following odd output:

```
Enter decimal value of char to print:10
The char you entered was [
]
Press any key to continue . . .
```

Referring to Table 5-1, you can see that 10 is the newline character. This character doesn't actually print anything but causes subsequent output to start at the beginning of the next line, which is exactly what happened in this case: The closed brace appears by itself at the beginning of the next line when following a newline character.

The `endl` that appears at the end of many of the output commands that you've seen so far generates a newline. It also does a few other things, which you'll see in Chapter 31.

Encoding Strings of Characters

Theoretically, you could print anything you want using individual characters. However, that could get really tedious as the following code snippet demonstrates:

```
cout << 'E' << 'n' << 't' << 'e' << 'r' << ' '
     << 'd' << 'e' << 'c' << 'i' << 'm' << 'a'
     << 'l' << ' ' << 'v' << 'a' << 'l' << 'u'
     << 'e' << ' ' << 'o' << 'f' << ' ' << 'c'
     << 'h' << 'a' << 'r' << ' ' << 't' << 'o'
     << ' ' << 'p' << 'r' << 'i' << 'n' << 't'
     << ':';
```

C++ allows you to encode a sequence of characters by enclosing the string in double quotes:

```
cout << "Enter decimal value of char to print:";
```

I'll have a lot more to say about character strings in Chapter 16.

Special Character Constants

You can code a normal, printable character by placing it in single quotes:

```
char cSpace = ' ';
```

You can code any character you want, whether printable or not, by placing its octal value after a backslash:

```
char cSpace = '\040';
```

A constant appearing with a leading zero is assumed to be octal, also known as base 8.

You can code characters in base 16, hexadecimal, by preceding the number with a backslash followed by a small x as in the following example:

```
char cSpace = '\x20';
```

The decimal value 32 is equal to 40 in base 8 and 20 in base 16. Don't worry if you don't feel comfortable with octal or hexadecimal. C++ provides shortcuts for the most common characters.

C++ provides a name for some of the unprintable characters that are particularly useful. Some of the more common ones are shown in Table 5-2.

Table 5-2	Some of the Special C++ Characters		
Char	*Special Symbol*	*Char*	*Special Symbol*
'	\'	Newline	\n
"	\"	Carriage Return	\r
\	\\	Tab	\t
NULL	\0	Bell	\a

The most common is the newline character, which is nicknamed '\n'. In addition, you must use the backslash if you want to print the single quote character:

```
char cQuote = '\'';
```

Since C++ normally interprets a single quote mark as enclosing a character, you have to precede a single quote mark with a backslash character to tell it, "Hey, this single quote is not enclosing a character, this is the character."

In addition, the character '\\' is a single backslash.

This leads to one of the more unfortunate coincidences in C++. In Windows, the backslash is used in filenames as in the following:

```
C:\\Base Directory\Subdirectory\File Name
```

This is encoded in C++ with each backslash replaced by a pair of backslashes as follows:

```
"C:\\\\Base Directory\\Subdirectory\\File Name"
```

Wide load ahead

By the early 1970s when C and C++ were invented, the 128-character ASCII character set had pretty much beat out all rivals. So it was logical that the `char` type was defined to accommodate the ASCII character set. This character set was fine for English but became overly restrictive when programmers tried to write applications for other European languages.

Fortunately, C and C++ had provided enough room in the `char` for 256 different characters. Standards committees got busy and used the characters between 128 and 255 for characters that occur in European languages but not English, such as umlauts and accented characters. You can see the results of their handy work using the example `CharacterEncoding` program from this chapter: Enter 142 and the program prints out an Ä.

No matter what you do, the `char` variable is just not large enough to handle all of the many different alphabets, such as Cyrillic, Hebrew, Arabic, and Korean — not to mention the many thousands of Chinese kanji symbols. Something had to give.

C++ responded first by introducing the "wide character" of type `wchar_t`. This was intended to implement whatever wide character set that is native to the host operating system. On Windows, that would be the variant of Unicode known as UTF-2 or UTF-16. (Here the 2 stands for two bytes, the size of each wide character, whereas the 16 stands for 16 bits.) However, Macintosh's OS X uses a different variant of Unicode known as UTF-8. Unicode can display not only every alphabet on the planet but also the kanjis used in Chinese and Japanese. The 2009 update to the C++ standard added two further types, `char16_t` and `char32_t`, which implement specifically UTF-16 and UTF-32.

For almost every feature that I describe in this book for handling character variables, there is an equivalent feature for the wide character types; programming Unicode, however, is beyond the scope of a beginning text.

Chapter 6

if I Could Make My Own Decisions

. . . .

In This Chapter

▶ Defining character variables and constants

▶ Encoding characters

▶ Declaring a string

▶ Outputting characters to the console

. . . .

*M*aking decisions is a part of the everyday world. Should I get a drink now or wait for the commercial? Should I take this highway exit to go to the bathroom or else wait for the next? Should I take another step or stop and smell the roses? If I am hungry or I need gas, then I should stop at the convenience store. If it is a weekend and I feel like it, then I can sleep in. See what I mean?

An assistant, even a stupid one, has to be able to make at least rudimentary decisions. Consider the Tire Changing Language in Chapter 1. Even there, the program had to be able to test for the presence of a lug nut to avoid waving a wrench around uselessly in space over an empty bolt, thereby wasting everyone's time.

All computer languages provide some type of decision-making capability. In C++, this is handled primarily by the `if` statement.

The if Statement

The format of the `if` statement is straightforward:

```
if (m > n)    // if m is greater than n...
{
              // ...then do this stuff
}
```

When encountering if, C++ first executes the logical expression contained within the parentheses. In this case, the program evaluates the conditional expression "is m greater than n." If the expression is true, that is, if m truly is greater than n, then control passes to the first statement after the { and continues from there. If the logical expression is not true, control passes to the first statement after the }.

Comparison operators

Table 6-1 shows the different operators that can be used to compare values in logical expressions.

Binary operators have the format expr1 operator expr2.

Table 6-1	The Comparison Operators
Operator	*Meaning*
==	equality; true if the left-hand argument has the same value as the expression on the right
!=	inequality; opposite of equality
>	greater than; true if the left-hand argument is greater than the right
<	less than; true if the left-hand argument is less than the right
>=	greater than or equal to; true if the left argument is greater than or equal to the right
<=	less than or equal to; true if the left argument is less than or equal to the right

Don't confuse the equality operator (==) with the assignment operator (=). This is a common mistake for beginners.

The following BranchDemo program shows how the operators shown in Table 6-1 are used:

```
// BranchDemo - demonstrate the if statement

#include <cstdio>
#include <cstdlib>
#include <iostream>

using namespace std;

int main(int nNumberofArgs, char* pszArgs[])
```

```
{
    // enter operand1 and operand2
    int  nOperand1;
    int  nOperand2;
    cout << "Enter argument 1:";
    cin  >> nOperand1;
    cout << "Enter argument 2:";
    cin  >> nOperand2;

    // now print the results
    if (nOperand1 > nOperand2)
    {
        cout << "Argument 1 is greater than argument 2"
             << endl;
    }
    if (nOperand1 < nOperand2)
    {
        cout << "Argument 1 is less than argument 2"
             << endl;
    }
    if (nOperand1 == nOperand2)
    {
        cout << "Argument 1 is equal to argument 2"
             << endl;
    }

    // wait until user is ready before terminating program
    // to allow the user to see the program results
    system("PAUSE");
    return 0;
}
```

Program execution begins with main() as always. The program first declares two int variables cleverly named nOperand1 and nOperand2. It then prompts the user to "Enter argument 1", which it reads into nOperand1. The process is repeated for nOperand2.

The program then executes a sequence of three comparisons. It first checks whether nOperand1 is less than nOperand2. If so, the program outputs the notification "Argument 1 is less than argument 2". The second if statement displays a message if the two operands are equal in value. The final comparison is true if nOperand1 is greater than nOperand2.

The following shows a sample run of the BranchDemo program:

```
Enter argument 1:5
Enter argument 2:10
Argument 1 is less than argument 2
Press any key to continue . . .
```

Figure 6-1 shows the flow of control graphically for this particular run.

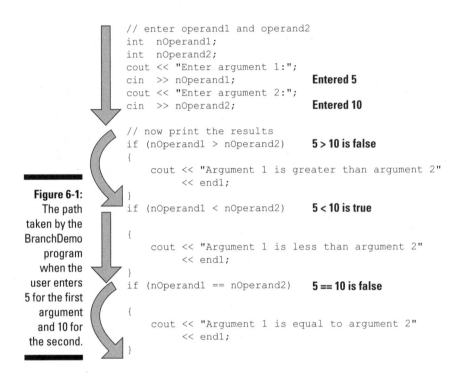

```
// enter operand1 and operand2
int  nOperand1;
int  nOperand2;
cout << "Enter argument 1:";
cin  >> nOperand1;          Entered 5
cout << "Enter argument 2:";
cin  >> nOperand2;          Entered 10

// now print the results
if (nOperand1 > nOperand2)      5 > 10 is false
{
    cout << "Argument 1 is greater than argument 2"
        << endl;
}
if (nOperand1 < nOperand2)      5 < 10 is true

{
    cout << "Argument 1 is less than argument 2"
        << endl;
}
if (nOperand1 == nOperand2)     5 == 10 is false

{
    cout << "Argument 1 is equal to argument 2"
        << endl;
}
```

Figure 6-1:
The path
taken by the
BranchDemo
program
when the
user enters
5 for the first
argument
and 10 for
the second.

The way the BranchDemo program is written, all three comparisons are performed every time. This is slightly wasteful since the three conditions are mutually exclusive. For example, nOperand1 > nOperand2 can't possibly be true if nOperand1 < nOperand2 has already been found to be true. Later in this chapter, I show you how to avoid this waste.

Say "No" to "No braces"

Actually the braces are optional. Without braces, only the first expression after the if statement is conditional. However, it is much too easy to make a mistake this way, as demonstrated in the following snippet:

```
// Can't have a negative age. If age is less than zero...
if (nAge < 0)
    cout << "Age can't be negative; using 0" << endl;
    nAge = 0;

// program continues
```

You may think that if nAge is less than 0, this program snippet outputs a message and resets nAge to zero. In fact, the program sets nAge to zero no matter what its original value. The preceding snippet is equivalent to the following:

```
// Can't have a negative age. If age is less than zero...
if (nAge < 0)
{
    cout << "Age can't be negative; using 0" << endl;
}
    nAge = 0;

// program continues
```

It's clear from the comments and the indent that the programmer really meant the following:

```
// Can't have a negative age. If age is less than zero...
if (nAge < 0)
{
    cout << "Age can't be negative; using 0" << endl;
    nAge = 0;
}

// program continues
```

The C++ compiler can't catch this type of mistake. It's safer just to always supply the braces.

C++ treats all white space the same. It ignores the alignment of expressions on the page.

Always use braces to enclose the statements after an if statement, even if there is only one. You'll generate a lot fewer errors that way.

What else Is There?

C++ allows the program to specify a clause after the keyword else that is executed if the conditional expression is false, as in the following example:

```
if (m > n)    // if m is greater than n...
{
             // ...then do this stuff;...
}
else         // ...otherwise,...
{
             // ...do this stuff
}
```

The `else` clause must appear immediately after the close brace of the `if` clause. In use, the `else` appears as shown in the following snippet:

```
if (nAge < 0)
{
    cout << "Age can't be negative; using 0." << endl;
    nAge = 0;
}
else
{
    cout << "Age of " << nAge << " entered" << endl;
}
```

In this case, if nAge is less than zero, the program outputs the message `"Age can't be negative; using 0."` and then sets nAge to 0. This corresponds to the flow of control shown in the first image in Figure 6-2. If nAge is not less than zero, the program outputs the message `"Age of x entered"`, where *x* is the value of nAge. This is shown in the second image in Figure 6-2.

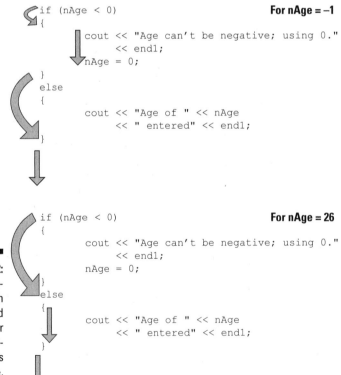

Figure 6-2: Flow of control through an `if` and `else` for two different values of nAge.

Logical expressions: Do they have any value?

At the beginning of this chapter, I called the comparison symbols < and > *operators,* and I described statements containing these operators as *expressions.* But expressions have a value and a type. What is the value and type of an expression like m > n? In C++, the type of this expression is bool (named in honor of George Boole, the inventor of Logic Calculus). Expressions of type bool can have only one of two values: true or else false. Thus, you can write the following:

```
bool bComparison = m > n;
```

For historical reasons, there is a conversion between the numerical types like int and char and bool: A value of 0 is considered the same as false. Any non-zero value is considered the same as true.

Thus, the if statement

```
if (cCharacter)
{
    // execute this code if cCharacter is not NULL
}
```

is the same as

```
if (cCharacter != '\0')
{
    // execute this code if cCharacter is not NULL
}
```

Assigning a true/false value to a character may seem a bit obtuse, but you'll see in Chapter 16 that it has a very useful application.

Nesting if Statements

The braces of an if or an else clause can contain another if statement. These are known as *nested* if statements. The following NestedIf program shows an example of a nested if statement in use.

```
// NestedIf - demonstrate a nested if statement
//
#include <cstdio>
#include <cstdlib>
#include <iostream>

using namespace std;

int main(int nNumberofArgs, char* pszArgs[])
{
```

```
// enter your birth year
int  nYear;
cout << "Enter your birth year: ";
cin  >> nYear;

// Make determination of century
if (nYear > 2000)
{
    cout << "You were born in the 21st century"
         << endl;
}
else
{
    cout << "You were born in ";
    if (nYear < 1950)
    {
        cout << "the first half";
    }
    else
    {
        cout << "the second half";
    }
    cout << " of the 20th century"
         << endl;
}

// wait until user is ready before terminating program
// to allow the user to see the program results
system("PAUSE");
return 0;
}
```

This program starts by asking the user for his birth year. If the birth year is greater than 2000, then the program outputs the string `"You were born in the 21st century"`.

The year 2000 belongs to the 20th century, not the 21st.

If the birth year is not greater than 2000, then the program enters the `else` clause of the outer `if` statement. This clause starts by outputting the string `"You were born in"` before comparing the birth year to 1950. If the birth year is less than 1950, then the program adds the first `"the first half"`. If the birth year is not less than 1950, then the `else` clause of the inner `if` statement is executed, which tacks on the phrase `"the second half"`. Finally, the program adds the concluding phrase `"of the 20th century"` to whatever has been output so far.

In practice, the output of the program appears as follows for three possible values for birth year. First, 2002 produces the following:

```
Enter your birth year: 2002
You were born in the 21st century
Press any key to continue . . .
```

My own birth year of 1956 generates the following:

```
Enter your birth year: 1956
You were born in the second half of the 20th century
Press any key to continue . . .
```

Finally, my father's birth year of 1932 generates the third possibility:

```
Enter your birth year: 1932
You were born in the first half of the 20th century
Press any key to continue . . .
```

I could use a nested if to avoid the unnecessary comparisons in the NestedBranchDemo program:

```
if (nOperand1 > nOperand2)
{
    cout << "Argument 1 is greater than argument 2"
        << endl;
}
else
{
    if (nOperand1 < nOperand2)
    {
        cout << "Argument 1 is less than argument 2"
            << endl;
    }
    else
    {
        cout << "Argument 1 is equal to argument 2"
            << endl;
    }
}
```

This version performs the first comparison just as before. If nOperand1 is greater than nOperand2, this snippet outputs the string "Argument 1 is greater than argument 2". From here, however, control jumps to the final closed brace, thereby skipping the remaining comparisons.

If nOperand1 is not greater than nOperand2, then the snippet performs a second test to differentiate the case that nOperand1 is less than nOperand2 from the case that they are equal in value.

Figure 6-3 shows graphically the flow of control for the NestedBranchDemo program for the same input of 5 and 10 described earlier in the chapter.

```
// enter operand1 and operand2
int   nOperand1;
int   nOperand2;
cout << "Enter argument 1:";
cin  >> nOperand1;                     Entered 5
cout << "Enter argument 2:";
cin  >> nOperand2;                     Entered 10

// now print the results
if (nOperand1 > nOperand2)             5 > 10 is false
{
    cout << "Argument 1 is greater than argument 2"
        << endl;
}
else
{
    if a(nOperand1 < nOperand2)        5 < 10 is true
    {
    cout << "Argument 1 is less than argument 2"
        << endl;
    }
    else
    {
    cout << "Argument 1 is equal to argument 2"
        << endl;
    }
}
```

Figure 6-3: The path taken by the Nested- Branch- Demo program when the user enters 5 and 10 as before.

Performing the test for equality is unnecessary: If nOperand1 is neither greater than nor less than nOperand2, then it must be equal.

Compound Conditional Expressions

The three logical operators that can be used to create what are known as *compound conditional expressions* are shown in Table 6-2.

Table 6-2	The Logical Operators
Operator	*Meaning*
&&	AND; true if the left- and right-hand arguments are true; otherwise, false
||	OR; true if either the left- or right-hand arguments is true; otherwise, false
!	NOT; true if the argument on the right is false; otherwise, false

The programmer is asking two or more questions in a conditional compound expression, as in the following code snippet:

```
// make sure that nArgument is between 0 and 5
if (0 < nArgument && nArgument < 5)
```

Figure 6-4 shows how three different values of nArgument are evaluated by this expression.

Figure 6-4:
The evaluation of the compound expression
`0 < n && n < 5` for three different values of n.

```
0 < nArgument && nArgument < 5
        where nArgument = -1
           0 < -1 && -1 < 5
            false && true
                 false
        where nArgument = 7
            0 < 7 && 7 < 5
             true&&false
                 false
        where nArgument = 2
            0 <2 && 2 < 5
            true && true
                 true
```

By the way, the snippet

```
if (m < nArgument && nArgument < n)
```

is the normal way of coding the expression "if nArgument is between m and n, exclusive". This type of test does not include the end points — that is, this test will fail if nArgument is equal to m or n. Use the <= comparison operator if you want to include the end points.

Short circuit evaluation

Look carefully at a compound expression involving a logical AND like

```
if (expr1 && expr2)
```

If expr1 is false, then the overall result of the compound expression is false, irrespective of the value of expr2. In fact, C++ doesn't even evaluate expr2 if expr1 is false — false && anything is false. This is known as *short circuit evaluation* because it short circuits around executing unnecessary code in order to save time.

The situation is exactly the opposite for the logical OR:

```
if (expr1 || expr2)
```

If expr1 is true, then the overall expression is true, irrespective of the value of expr2.

Short circuit evaluation is a good thing since the resulting programs execute more quickly; however, it can lead to unexpected results in a few cases. Consider the following admittedly contrived case:

```
if (m <= nArgument && nArgument++ <= n)
```

The intent is to test whether nArgument falls into the range [m, n] and to increment nArgument as part of the test. However, short circuit evaluation means that the second test doesn't get executed if m <= nArgument is not true. If the second test is never evaluated, then nArgument doesn't get incremented.

Remember: If you didn't follow that, just remember the following: Don't put an expression that has a side effect like incrementing a variable in a conditional.

Chapter 7

Switching Paths

In This Chapter

▶ Using the `switch` keyword to choose between multiple paths

▶ Taking a `default` path

▶ Falling through from one case to another

*O*ften programs have to decide between a very limited number of options: Either m is greater than n or it's not; either the lug nut is present or it's not. Sometimes, however, a program has to decide between a large number of possible legal inputs. This could be handled by a series of `if` statements, each of which tests for one of the legal inputs. However, C++ provides a more convenient control mechanism for selecting among a number of options known as the `switch` statement.

Controlling Flow with the switch Statement

The `switch` statement has the following format:

```
switch(expression)
{
  case const1:
    // go here if expression == const1
    break;

  case const2:
    // go here if expression == const2
    break;

  case const3:            // repeat as often as you like
    // go here if expression == const3
    break;

  default:
    // go here if none of the other cases match
}
```

Upon encountering the `switch` statement, C++ evaluates `expression`. It then passes control to the case with the same value as `expression`. Control continues from there to the `break` statement. The `break` transfers control to the } at the end of the `switch` statement. If none of the cases match, control passes to the default case.

The default case is optional. If the expression doesn't match any case and no default case is provided, control passes immediately to the }.

Consider the following example code snippet:

```cpp
int nMonth;
cout << "Enter the number of the month: ";
cin  >> nMonth;

switch (nMonth)
{
  case  1:
    cout << "It's January"  << endl;
    break;
  case  2:
    cout << "It's February" << endl;;
    break;
  case  3:
    cout << "It's March"    << endl;;
    break;
  case  4:
    cout << "It's April"    << endl;;
    break;
  case  5:
    cout << "It's May"      << endl;;
    break;
  case  6:
    cout << "It's June"     << endl;;
    break;
  case  7:
    cout << "It's July"     << endl;;
    break;
  case  8:
    cout << "It's August"   << endl;;
    break;
  case  9:
    cout << "It's September"<< endl;;
    break;
  case 10:
    cout << "It's October"  << endl;;
    break;
  case 11:
    cout << "It's November" << endl;;
    break;
```

```
    case 12:
      cout << "It's December" << endl;;
      break;
    default:
      cout << "That's not a valid month" << endl;;

  }
```

I got the following output from the program when inputting a value of 3:

```
Enter the number of the month: 3
It's March
Press any key to continue . . .
```

Figure 7-1 shows how control flowed through the `switch` statement to generate the earlier result of "March."

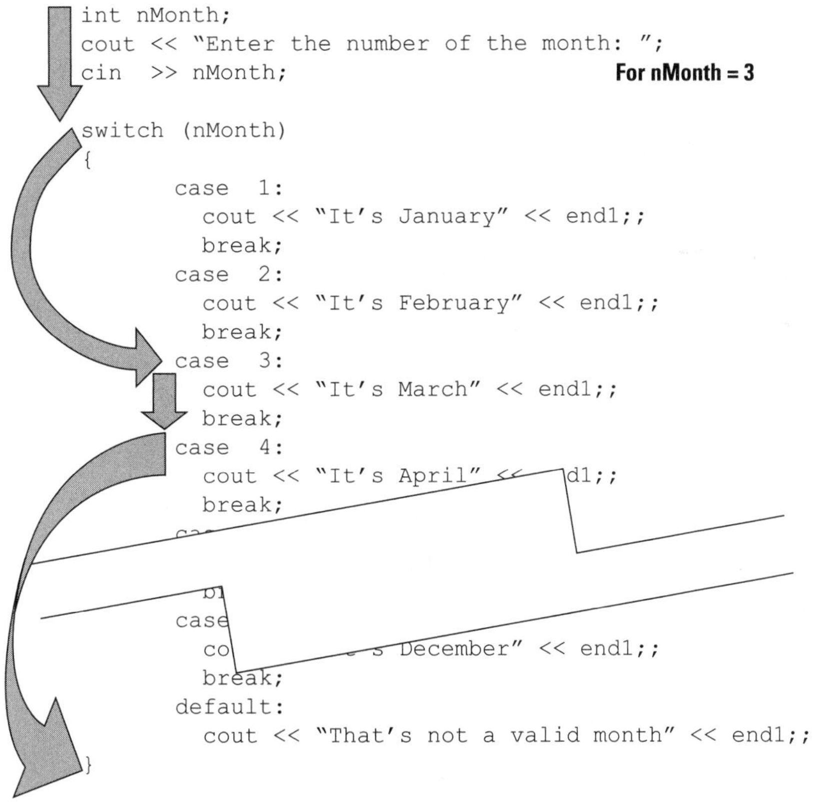

Figure 7-1:
Flow through a `switch` statement listing the months of the year where the operator enters month 3.

```
int nMonth;
cout << "Enter the number of the month: ";
cin  >> nMonth;                            For nMonth = 3

switch (nMonth)
{
    case  1:
      cout << "It's January" << endl;;
      break;
    case  2:
      cout << "It's February" << endl;;
      break;
    case  3:
      cout << "It's March" << endl;;
      break;
    case  4:
      cout << "It's April" << endl;;
      break;

    case
      co          s December" << endl;;
      break;
    default:
      cout << "That's not a valid month" << endl;;
}
```

A `switch` statement is not like a series of `if` statements. For example, only constants are allowed after the `case` keyword (or expressions that can be completely evaluated at build time). You cannot supply an expression after a case. Thus, the following is not legal:

```
// cases cannot be expressions; in general, the
// following is not legal
switch(n)
{
  case m:
    cout << "n is equal to m" << endl;
    break;
  case 2 * m:
    cout << "n is equal to 2m" << endl;
    break;
  case 3 * m:
    cout << "n is equal to 3m" << endl;
}
```

Each of the cases must have a value at build time. The value of m is not known until the program executes.

Control Fell Through: Did I break It?

Just as the default case is optional, the `break` at the end of each case is also optional. Without the `break` statement, however, control simply continues on from one case to the next. Programmers say that control *falls through*. This is most useful when two or more cases are handled in the same way.

For example, C++ may differentiate between upper- and lowercase, but most humans do not. The following code snippet prompts the user to enter a C to create a checking account and an S to create a savings account. However, by providing extra case statements, the snippet handles lowercase c and s the same way:

```
cout << "Enter C to create checking account, "
     << "S to create a saving account, "
     << "and X to exit: ";
cin  >> cAccountType;
switch(cAccountType)
{
  case 'S':           // upper case S
  case 's':           // lower case s
    // creating savings account
    break;

  case 'C':           // upper case C
  case 'c':           // lower case c
```

```
        // create checking account
        break;

    case 'X':            // upper case X
    case 'x':            // lower case x
        // exit code goes here
        break;

    default:
        cout << "I didn't understand that" << endl;
}
```

Implementing an Example Calculator with the switch Statement

The following SwitchCalculator program uses the `switch` statement to implement a simple calculator:

```
// SwitchCalculator - use the switch statement to
//                    implement a calculator

#include <cstdio>
#include <cstdlib>
#include <iostream>

using namespace std;

int main(int nNumberofArgs, char* pszArgs[])
{
    // enter operand1 op operand2
    int  nOperand1;
    int  nOperand2;
    char cOperator;
    cout << "Enter 'value1 op value2'\n"
         << "where op is +, -, *, / or %:" << endl;
    cin >> nOperand1 >> cOperator >> nOperand2;

    // echo what the operator entered
    cout << nOperand1 << " "
         << cOperator << " "
         << nOperand2 << " = ";

    // now calculate the result; remember that the
    // user might enter something unexpected
    switch (cOperator)
    {
```

```
        case '+':
            cout << nOperand1 + nOperand2;
            break;
        case '-':
            cout << nOperand1 - nOperand2;
            break;
        case '*':
        case 'x':
        case 'X':
            cout << nOperand1 * nOperand2;
            break;
        case '/':
            cout << nOperand1 / nOperand2;
            break;
        case '%':
            cout << nOperand1 % nOperand2;
            break;
        default:
            // didn't understand the operator
            cout << " is not understood";
    }
    cout << endl;

    // wait until user is ready before terminating program
    // to allow the user to see the program results
    system("PAUSE");
    return 0;
}
```

This program begins by prompting the user to enter `"value1 op value2"` where *op* is one of the common arithmetic operators +, −, *, / or %. The program then reads the variables nOperand1, cOperator, and nOperand2.

The program starts by echoing back to the user what it read from the keyboard. It follows this with the result of the calculation.

Echoing the input back to the user is always a good programming practice. It gives the user confirmation that the program read his input correctly.

The `switch` on cOperator differentiates between the operations that this calculator implements. For example, in the case that cOperator is `'+'`, the program reports the sum of nOperand1 and nOperand2.

Because `'X'` is another common symbol for multiply, the program accepts `'*'`, `'X'`, and `'x'` all as synonyms for multiply using the case "fall through" feature. The program outputs an error message if cOperator doesn't match any of the known operators.

The output from a few sample runs appears as follows:

```
Enter 'value1 op value2'
where op is +, -, *, / or %:
22 x 6
22 x 6 = 132
Press any key to continue . . .
```

```
Enter 'value1 op value2'
where op is +, -, *, / or %:
22 / 6
22 / 6 = 3
Press any key to continue . . .
```

```
Enter 'value1 op value2'
where op is +, -, *, / or %:
22 % 6
22 % 6 = 4
Press any key to continue . . .
```

```
Enter 'value1 op value2'
where op is +, -, *, / or %:
22 $ 6
22 $ 6 =  is not understood
Press any key to continue . . .
```

Notice that the final run executes the default case of the `switch` statement since the character `'$'` did not match any of the cases.

Chapter 8

Debugging Your Programs, Part I

- -

- -

*Y*ou may have noticed that your programs often don't work the first time you run them. In fact, I have seldom, if ever, written a nontrivial C++ program that didn't have some type of error the first time I tried to execute it.

This leaves you with two alternatives: You can abandon a program that has an error, or you can find and fix the error. I assume that you want to take the latter approach. In this chapter, I first help you distinguish between types of errors and how to avoid errors in the first place. Then you get to find and eradicate two bugs that originally plagued the Conversion program in Chapter 3.

Identifying Types of Errors

Two types of errors exist — those that C++ can catch on its own and those that the compiler can't catch. Errors that C++ can catch are known as *compile-time* or *build-time errors*. Build-time errors are generally easier to fix because the compiler points you to the problem, if you can understand what the compiler's telling you. Sometimes the description of the problem isn't quite right (it's easy to confuse a compiler), but you start to understand better how the compiler thinks as you gain experience.

Errors that C++ can't catch don't show up until you try to execute the program during the process known as *unit testing*. During unit testing, you execute your program with a series of different inputs, trying to find inputs that make it crash. (You don't want your program to crash, of course, but better that you — rather than your user — find and correct these cases.)

The errors that you find by executing the program are known as *run-time errors*. Run-time errors are harder to find than build-time errors because you have no hint of what's gone wrong except for whatever errant output the program might generate.

The output isn't always so straightforward. For example, suppose that the program lost its way and began executing instructions that aren't even part of the program you wrote. (That happens a lot more often than you might think.) An errant program is like a train that's jumped the track — the program doesn't stop executing until it hits something really big. For example, the CPU may just happen to execute a divide by zero — this generates an alarm that the operating system intercepts and uses as an excuse to terminate your program.

An errant program is like a derailed train in another way — once the program starts heading down the wrong path, it *never* jumps back onto the track.

Not all run-time errors are quite so dramatic. Some errant programs stay on the tracks but generate the wrong output (almost universally known as "garbage output"). These are even harder to catch since the output may seem reasonable until you examine it closely.

In this chapter, you will debug a program that has both a compile time and a run-time error — not the "jump off the track and start executing randomly" variety but more of the generate garbage kind.

Avoiding Introducing Errors

The easiest and best way to fix errors is to avoid introducing them into your programs in the first place. Part of this is just a matter of experience, but adopting a clear and consistent programming style helps.

Coding with style

We humans have a limited amount of CPU power between our ears. We need to direct what CPU cycles we do have toward the act of creating a working program. We shouldn't get distracted by things like indentation.

This makes it important that you be consistent in how you name your variables, where you place open and close braces, how much you indent, and so on. This is called your coding style. Develop a style and stick to it. After a while your coding style will become second nature. You'll find that you can code your programs in less time and you can read the resulting programs with less effort if your coding style is clear and consistent. This translates into fewer coding errors.

I recommend that as a beginner you mimic the style you see in this book. You can change it later when you've gained some experience of your own.

When working on a program with several programmers, it's just as important that you all use the same style to avoid a Tower of Babel effect with conflicting and confusing styles. Every project that I've ever worked on had a coding manual that articulated sometimes in excruciating detail exactly how an `if` statement was to be laid out, how far to indent for `case`, and whether to put a blank line after the `break` statements, to name just a few examples.

Fortunately, Code::Blocks can help. The Code::Blocks editor understands C++. It will automatically indent the proper number of spaces for you after an open brace, and it will outdent when you type in the closed brace to align statements properly.

You can run the 'Source code formatter' plug-in that comes with Code::Blocks. With the file you are working on open and the project active, select Plugins➪ Source Code Formatter (AStyle). This will reformat the current file using the standard indention rules.

C++ doesn't care about indention. All whitespace is the same to it. Indention is there to make the resulting program easier to read and understand.

Establishing variable naming conventions

There is more debate about the naming of variables than about how many angels would fit on the head of a pin. I use the following rules when naming variables:

- ✔ **The first letter is lowercase and indicates the type of the variable.** n for `int`, c for `char`, b for `bool`. You'll see others in later chapters. This is very helpful when using the variable because you immediately know its type.

- ✔ **Names of variables are descriptive.** No variables names like x or y. I'm too old — I need something that I can recognize when I try to read my own program tomorrow or next week or next year.

- ✔ **Multiple word names use uppercase at the beginning of each word with no underscores between words.** I save underscores for a particular application, which I describe in Chapter 12.

I expand on these rules in chapters involving other types of C++ objects (such as functions in Chapter 11 and classes in Chapter 19).

Finding the First Error with a Little Help

My first version of the Conversion program appeared as follows (it appears on the enclosed CD-ROM as ConversionError1):

```cpp
//
//   Conversion - Program to convert temperature from
//                Celsius degrees into Fahrenheit:
//                Fahrenheit = Celsius  * (212 - 32)/100 + 32
//
#include <cstdio>
#include <cstdlib>
#include <iostream>
using namespace std;

int main(int nNumberofArgs, char* pszArgs[])
{
    // enter the temperature in Celsius
    int nCelsius;
    cout << "Enter the temperature in Celsius: ";

    // convert Celsius into Fahrenheit values
    int nFahrenheit;
    nFahrenheit = 9/5 * nCelsius + 32;

    // output the results (followed by a NewLine)
    cout << "Fahrenheit value is: ";
    cout << nFahrenheit << endl;

    // wait until user is ready before terminating program
    // to allow the user to see the program results
    system("PAUSE");
    return 0;
}
```

During the build step, I get my first indication that there's a problem — Code::Blocks generates the following warning message:

```
In function 'int main(int char**)':
warning: 'nCelsius' is used uninitialized in this function
=== Build finished: 0 errors, 1 warnings ===
```

How bad can this be? After all, it's just a warning, right? So I decide to push forward and execute the program anyway.

Sure enough, I get the following meaningless output without giving me a chance to enter the Celsius temperature:

```
Enter the temperature in Celsius:
Fahrenheit value is:110
Press any key to continue . . .
```

Referring to the prompt, I can see that I have forgotten to input a value for nCelsius. The program proceeded forward calculating a Fahrenheit temperature based upon whatever garbage happened to be in nCelsius when it was declared.

Adding the following line immediately after the prompt gets rid of the warning and solves the first problem:

```
cin >> nCelsius;
```

The moral to this story is "Pay attention to warnings!" A warning almost always indicates a problem in your program. You shouldn't even start to test your programs until you get a clean build: no errors and no warnings. If that's not possible, at least convince yourself that you understand the reason for every warning generated.

Finding the Run-Time Error

Once all the warnings are gone, it's time to start testing. Good testing requires an organized approach. First, you decide the test data that you're going to use. Next, you determine what output you expect for each of the given test inputs. Then you run the program and compare the actual results with the expected results. What could be so hard?

Formulating test data

Determining what test data to use is part engineering and part black art. The engineering part is that you want to select data such that every statement in your program gets executed at least once. That means every branch of every if statement and every case of every switch statement gets executed at least once.

Having every statement execute at least once is called *full statement coverage* and is considered the minimum acceptable testing criteria. The chance of programming mistakes making it into the field is just too high without executing every statement at least once under test conditions.

This simple program has only one path and contains no branches.

The black art is looking at the program and determining where errors might lie in the calculation. For some reason, I just assume that every test should include the key values of 0 and 100 degrees Celsius. To that, I will add one negative value and one value in the middle between 0 and 100. Before I start, I use a handy-dandy conversion program to look up the equivalent temperature in Fahrenheit, as shown in Table 8-1.

Table 8-1	Test Data for the Conversion Program
Input Celsius	*Resulting Fahrenheit*
0	32
100	212
-40	-40
50	122

Executing the test cases

Running the tests is simply a matter of executing the program and supplying the input values from Table 8-1. The first case generates the following results:

```
Enter the temperature in Celsius: 0
Fahrenheit value is: 32
Press any key to continue . . .
```

So far, so good. The second data case generates the following output:

```
Enter the temperature in Celsius: 100
Fahrenheit value is: 132
Press any key to continue . . .
```

This doesn't match the expected value. Houston, we have a problem.

The value of 132 degrees is not completely unreasonable. That's why it's important to decide what the expected results are before you start. Otherwise, reasonable but incorrect results can slip by undetected.

Seeing what's going on in your program

What could be wrong? I check over the calculations and everything looks fine. I need to get a peek at what's going on in the calculation. A way to get at the internals of your program is to add output statements. I want to print the values going into each of the calculations. I also need to see the intermediate results. To do so, I break the calculation into its parts that I can print. Keep the original expression as a comment so you don't forget where you came from.

This version of the program is included on the enclosed CD-ROM as ConversionError2.

This version of the program includes the following changes:

```
// nFahrenheit = 9/5 * nCelsius + 32;
cout << "nCelsius = " << nCelsius << endl;
int nFactor = 9 / 5;
cout << "nFactor = " << nFactor << endl;
int nIntermediate = nFactor * nCelsius;
cout << "nIntermediate = " << nIntermediate << endl;
nFahrenheit = nIntermediate + 32;
cout << "nFahrenheit = " << nFahrenheit << endl;
```

I display the value of nCelsius to make sure that it got read properly from the user input. Next, I try to display the intermediate results of the conversion calculation in the same order that C++ will. First to go is the calculation 9 / 5, which I save into a variable I name nFactor (the name isn't important). This value is multiplied by nCelsius, the results of which I save into nIntermediate. Finally, this value will get added to 32 to generate the result, which is stored into nFahrenheit.

By displaying each of these intermediate values, I can see what's going on in my calculation. Repeating the error case, I get the following results:

```
Enter the temperature in Celsius: 100
nCelsius = 100
nFactor = 1
nIntermediate = 100
nFahrenheit = 132
Fahrenheit value is: 132
Press any key to continue . . .
```

Right away I see a problem: `nFactor` is equal to 1 and not 9 / 5. Then the problem occurs to me; integer division rounds down to the nearest integer value. Integer 9 divided by integer 5 *is* 1.

I can avoid this problem by performing the multiply before the divide. There will still be a small amount of integer round-off, but it will only amount to a single degree.

Another solution would be to use decimal variables that can retain fractional values. You'll see that solution in Chapter 14.

The resulting formula appears as follows:

```
nFahrenheit = nCelsius * 9/5 + 32;
```

This is the version of the calculation that appears on the CD-ROM in the original Conversion program.

Now rerunning the tests, I get the following:

```
Enter the temperature in Celsius: 0
Fahrenheit value is: 32
Press any key to continue . . .
```

```
Enter the temperature in Celsius: 100
Fahrenheit value is: 212
Press any key to continue . . .
```

```
Enter the temperature in Celsius: -40
Fahrenheit value is: -40
Press any key to continue . . .
```

```
Enter the temperature in Celsius: 50
Fahrenheit value is: 122
Press any key to continue . . .
```

This matches the expected values from Table 8-1.

Notice that, after making the change, I started over from the beginning, supplying all four test cases — not just the values that didn't work properly the first time. Any changes to the calculation invalidate all previous tests.

Part III
Becoming a Functional Programmer

The 5th Wave   By Rich Tennant

"We're researching molecular/digital technology that moves massive amounts of information across binary pathways that interact with free-agent programs capable of making decisions and performing logical tasks. We see applications in really high-end doorbells."

In this part . . .

Now that you've mastered the basics of simple expressions, it's time for you to learn about loops, how to get into them, and, even more importantly, how to get out of them. You'll also see how to break a large program into smaller components that are easier to program. In the last chapter of this part, you'll see some more techniques for debugging your programs.

Chapter 9

while Running in Circles

*D*ecision making is a fundamental part of almost every program you write, which I initially emphasize in Chapter 1. However, another fundamental feature that is clear — even in the simple Lug Nut Removal algorithm — is the ability to loop. That program turned the wrench in a loop until the lug nut fell off, and it looped from one lug nut to the other until the entire wheel came off. This chapter introduces you to two of the three looping constructs in C++.

Creating a while Loop

The `while` loop has the following format:

```
while (expression)
{
    // stuff to do in a loop
}

// continue here once expression is false
```

When a program comes upon a `while` loop, it first evaluates the expression in the parentheses. If this expression is `true`, then control passes to the first line inside the {. When control reaches the }, the program returns back to the expression and starts over. Control continues to cycle through the code in the braces until `expression` evaluates to `false` (or until something else breaks the loop — more on that a little later in this chapter).

The following Factorial program demonstrates the `while` loop:

```
Factorial(N) = N * (N-1) * (N-2) * ... * 1
```

```cpp
//
//  Factorial - calculate factorial using the while
//
//             construct.
//
#include <cstdio>
#include <cstdlib>
#include <iostream>
using namespace std;

int main(int nNumberofArgs, char* pszArgs[])
{
    // enter the number to calculate the factorial of
    int nTarget;
    cout << "This program calculates factorial.\n"
         << "Enter a number to take factorial of: ";
    cin  >> nTarget;

    // start with an accumulator that's initialized to 1
    int nAccumulator = 1;
    int nValue = 1;
    while (nValue <= nTarget)
    {
        cout << nAccumulator << " * "
             << nValue << " equals ";
        nAccumulator = nAccumulator * nValue;
        cout << nAccumulator << endl;
        nValue++;
    }

    // display the result
    cout << nTarget << " factorial is "
         << nAccumulator << endl;

    // wait until user is ready before terminating program
    // to allow the user to see the program results
    system("PAUSE");
    return 0;
}
```

The program starts by prompting the user for a target value. The program reads this value into nTarget. The program then initializes both nAccumulator and nValue to 1 before entering the loop.

(Pay attention — this is the interesting part.) The program compares nValue to nTarget. Assume that the user had entered a target value of 5. On the first loop, the question becomes, "Is 1 less than or equal to 5?" The answer is obviously `true`, so control flows into the loop. The program outputs the value of `nAccumulator` (1) and `nValue` (also 1) before multiplying `nAccumulator` by `nValue` and storing the result back into `nAccumulator`.

The last statement in the loop increments `nValue` from 1 to 2.

That done, control passes back up to the `while` statement where `nValue` (now 2) is compared to `nTarget` (still 5). "Is 2 less than or equal to 5?" Clearly, yes; so control flows back into the loop. `nAccumulator` is now set to the result of `nAccumulator` (1) times `nValue` (2). The last statement increments `nValue` to 3.

This cycle of fun continues until `nValue` reaches the value 6, which is no longer less than or equal to 5. At that point, control passes to the first statement beyond the closed brace `}`. This is shown graphically in Figure 9-1.

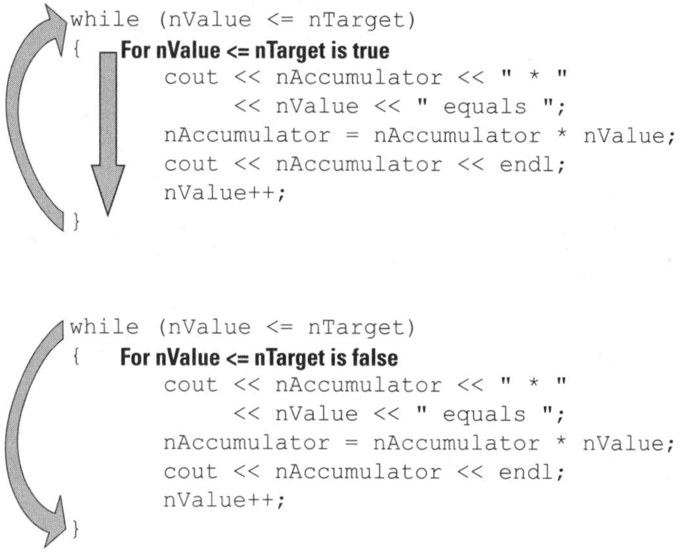

Figure 9-1:
Control continues to cycle through the body of a `while` loop until the conditional expression evaluates to false.

```
while (nValue <= nTarget)
{   For nValue <= nTarget is true
        cout << nAccumulator << " * "
            << nValue << " equals ";
        nAccumulator = nAccumulator * nValue;
        cout << nAccumulator << endl;
        nValue++;
}
```

```
while (nValue <= nTarget)
{   For nValue <= nTarget is false
        cout << nAccumulator << " * "
            << nValue << " equals ";
        nAccumulator = nAccumulator * nValue;
        cout << nAccumulator << endl;
        nValue++;
}
```

The actual output from the program appears as follows for an input value of 5:

```
This program calculates factorial.
Enter a number to take factorial of: 5
1 * 1 equals 1
1 * 2 equals 2
2 * 3 equals 6
6 * 4 equals 24
24 * 5 equals 120
5 factorial is 120
Press any key to continue . . .
```

You are not guaranteed that the code within the braces of a `while` loop is executed at all: If the conditional expression is false the first time it's evaluated, control passes around the braces without ever diving in. Consider, for example, the output from the Factorial program when the user enters a target value of 0:

```
This program calculates factorial.
Enter a number to take factorial of: 0
0 factorial is 1
Press any key to continue . . .
```

No lines of output are generated from within the loop because the condition "Is `nValue` less than or equal to 0" was false even for the initial value of 1. The body of the `while` loop was never executed.

Breaking out of the Middle of a Loop

Sometimes the condition that causes you to terminate a loop doesn't occur until somewhere in the middle of the loop. This is especially true when testing user input for some termination character. C++ provides these two control commands to handle this case:

- ✔ `break` exits the inner most loop immediately.

- ✔ `continue` passes control back to the top of the loop.

The following Product program demonstrates both `break` and `continue`. This program multiplies positive values entered by the user until the user enters a negative number. The program ignores zero.

```cpp
//
//   Product - demonstrate the use of break and continue.
//
#include <cstdio>
#include <cstdlib>
#include <iostream>
using namespace std;

int main(int nNumberofArgs, char* pszArgs[])
{
    // enter the number to calculate the factorial of
    cout << "This program multiplies the numbers\n"
         << "entered by the user. Enter a negative\n"
         << "number to exit. Zeroes are ignored.\n"
         << endl;

    int nProduct = 1;
    while (true)
    {
```

```
        int nValue;
        cout << "Enter a number to multiply: ";
        cin  >> nValue;
        if (nValue < 0)
        {
            cout << "Exiting." << endl;
            break;
        }
        if (nValue == 0)
        {
            cout << "Ignoring zero." << endl;
            continue;
        }

        // multiply accumulator by this value and
        // output the result
        cout << nProduct << " * " << nValue;
        nProduct *= nValue;
        cout << " is " << nProduct << endl;
    }

    // wait until user is ready before terminating program
    // to allow the user to see the program results
    system("PAUSE");
    return 0;
}
```

The program starts out with an initial value of nProduct of 1. The program then evaluates the logical expression true to see if it's true. It is.

There aren't too many rules that hold in C++ without exception, but here's one: true is always true.

The program then enters the loop to prompt the user for another value to multiply times nProduct, the accumulated product of all numbers entered so far. If the value entered is negative, then the program outputs the phrase "Exiting." before executing the break, which passes control out of the loop.

If the value entered is not negative, control passes to the second if statement. If nValue is equal to zero, then the program outputs the messages "Ignoring zero." before executing the continue statement which passes control back to the top of the loop to allow the user to enter another value.

If nValue is neither less than zero nor zero, then control flows down to where nValue is multiplied by nProduct using the special assignment operator (see Chapter 4 if you don't remember this one):

```
nProduct *= nValue;
```

Why is "break" necessary?

You might be tempted to wonder why `break` is really necessary. What if I had coded the loop in the Product example program as

```
int nProduct = 1;
int nValue = 1;
while (nValue > 0)
{
    cout << "Enter a number to multiply: ";
    cin  >> nValue;

    cout << nProduct << " * " << nValue;
    nProduct *= nValue;
    cout << " is " << nProduct << endl;
}
```

You might think that as soon as the user enters a negative value for `nValue`, the expression `nValue > 0` is no longer true and control immediately exits the loop — unfortunately, this is not the case.

The problem is that the logical expression is only evaluated at the beginning of each pass through the loop. Control doesn't immediately fly out of the body of the loop as soon as the condition ceases to be true. An `if` statement followed by a `break` allows me to move the conditional expression into the body of the loop where the value of `nValue` is assigned.

This expression is the same as:

```
nProduct = nProduct * nValue;
```

The output from a sample run from this program appears as follows:

```
This program multiplies the numbers
entered by the user. Enter a negative
number to exit. Zeroes are ignored.

Enter a number to multiply: 2
1 * 2 is 2
Enter a number to multiply: 5
2 * 5 is 10
Enter a number to multiply: 0
Ignoring zero.
Enter a number to multiply: 3
10 * 3 is 30
Enter a number to multiply: -1
Exiting.
Press any key to continue . . .
```

Nested Loops

The body of a loop can itself contain a loop in what is known as *nested loops*. The inner loop must execute to completion during each time through the outer loop.

I have created a program that uses nested loops to create a multiplication table of the form:

```
     0    1    2    3    4    5    6    7    8    9
 0  0*0  0*1  0*2  0*3  0*4  0*5  0*6  0*7  0*8  0*9
 1  1*0  1*1  1*2  1*3  1*4  1*5  1*6  1*7  1*8  1*9
 2  2*0  2*1  2*2  2*3  2*4  2*5  2*6  2*7  2*8  2*9
//... and so on...
```

You can see that for row 0, the program will need to iterate from column 0 through column 9. The program will repeat the process for row 1 and again for row 2 and so on right down to row 9. This implies the need for two loops: an inner loop to iterate over the columns and a second outer loop to iterate over the rows. Each position in the table is simply the row number times the column number.

This is exactly how the following NestedLoops program works:

```cpp
//
//  NestedLoops - this program uses a nested loop to
//                calculate the multiplication table.
//
#include <cstdio>
#include <cstdlib>
#include <iostream>
using namespace std;

int main(int nNumberofArgs, char* pszArgs[])
{
    // display the column headings
    int nColumn = 0;
    cout << "    ";
    while (nColumn < 10)
    {
        // set the display width to two characters
        // (even for one digit numbers)
        cout.width(2);

        // now display the column number
        cout << nColumn << " ";

        // increment to the next column
        nColumn++;
    }
    cout << endl;

    // now go loop through the rows
    int nRow = 0;
```

```
while (nRow < 10)
{
    // start with the row value
    cout << nRow << " - ";

    // now for each row, start with column 0 and
    // go through column 9
    nColumn = 0;
    while(nColumn < 10)
    {
        // display the product of the column*row
        // (use 2 characters even when product is
        // a single digit)
        cout.width(2);
        cout << nRow * nColumn << " ";

        // go to next column
        nColumn++;
    }

    // go to next row
    nRow++;
    cout << endl;
}

// wait until user is ready before terminating program
// to allow the user to see the program results
system("PAUSE");
return 0;
}
```

The first section creates the column headings. This section initializes `nColumn` to 0. It then iterates through `nColumn` printing out its value separated by a space until `nColumn` reaches 10. At this point, the program exits the first loop and then tacks a new line on the end to finish the row. This is shown graphically in Figure 9-2.

Executing just this section alone generates the following output:

```
 0  1  2  3  4  5  6  7  8  9
```

This program demonstrates an unfair advantage that I have. The expression `cout.width(2)` sets the display width to two columns — C++ will pad a space on the left for single-digit numbers. I know it's cheating to make use of a feature that I don't present to the reader until Chapter 31, but it's very difficult to get the columns to line up without resorting to fixed-width output.

The second set of loops, the nested loops, starts at `nRow` equal to 0. The program prints out the row number followed by a dash before launching into a second loop that starts `nColumn` at 0 again and iterates it back up to 9. For each pass through this inner loop, the program sets the output width to two spaces and then displays `nRow * nColumn` followed by a space.

```
// display the column headings
int nColumn = 0;
while (nColumn < 10)
{
        // now display the column number
        cout << nColumn << " ";

        // increment to the next column
        nColumn++;
}
//go to the next row
cout << endl;
```

Figure 9-2:
The first loop outputs the column headings.

Output: 0 1 2 3 4 5 6 7 8 9

The display width resets itself each time you output something, so it's necessary to set it back to two each time before outputting a number.

The program outputs a newline to move output to the next row each time it increments `nRow`. This is shown graphically in Figure 9-3.

The output from this program appears as follows:

```
      0   1   2   3   4   5   6   7   8   9
0 -   0   0   0   0   0   0   0   0   0   0
1 -   0   1   2   3   4   5   6   7   8   9
2 -   0   2   4   6   8  10  12  14  16  18
3 -   0   3   6   9  12  15  18  21  24  27
4 -   0   4   8  12  16  20  24  28  32  36
5 -   0   5  10  15  20  25  30  35  40  45
6 -   0   6  12  18  24  30  36  42  48  54
7 -   0   7  14  21  28  35  42  49  56  63
8 -   0   8  16  24  32  40  48  56  64  72
9 -   0   9  18  27  36  45  54  63  72  81
Press any key to continue . . .
```

There is nothing magic about 0 through 9 in this table. I could just have easily created a 12 x 12 multiplication table (or any other combination) by changing the comparison expression in the three `while` loops. However, for anything larger than 10 x 10, you will need to increase the minimum width to accommodate the three-digit products. Use `cout.width(3)`.

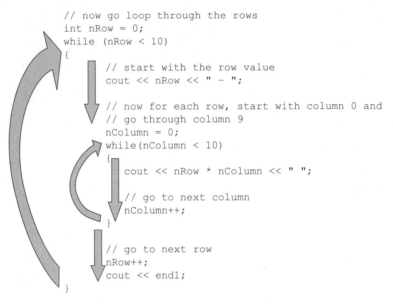

```
// now go loop through the rows
int nRow = 0;
while (nRow < 10)
{
    // start with the row value
    cout << nRow << " - ";

    // now for each row, start with column 0 and
    // go through column 9
    nColumn = 0;
    while(nColumn < 10)
    {
        cout << nRow * nColumn << " ";

        // go to next column
        nColumn++;
    }

    // go to next row
    nRow++;
    cout << endl;
}
```

Figure 9-3:
The inner
loop iterates
from left to
right across
the col-
umns, while
the outer
loop iterates
from top
to bottom
down the
rows.

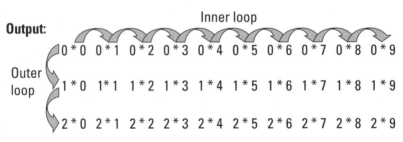

Output:

Inner loop

0*0 0*1 0*2 0*3 0*4 0*5 0*6 0*7 0*8 0*9

Outer
loop

1*0 1*1 1*2 1*3 1*4 1*5 1*6 1*7 1*8 1*9

2*0 2*1 2*2 2*3 2*4 2*5 2*6 2*7 2*8 2*9

Chapter 10

Looping for the Fun of It

● ●

In This Chapter

▶ Introducing the `for` loop

▶ Reviewing an example ForFactorial program

▶ Using the comma operator to get more done in a single `for` loop

● ●

*T*he most basic of all control structures is the `while` loop, which is the topic of Chapter 9. This chapter introduces you its sibling, the `for` loop. Though not quite as flexible, the `for` loop is actually the more popular of the two — it has a certain elegance that is hard to ignore.

The for Parts of Every Loop

If you look again at the examples in Chapter 9, you'll notice that most loops have four essential parts. (This feels like breaking down a golf swing into its constituent parts.)

✔ **The setup:** Usually the setup involves declaring and initializing an `increment` variable. This generally occurs immediately before the `while`.

✔ **The test expression:** The expression within the `while` loop that will cause the program to either execute the loop or exit and continue on. This always occurs within the parentheses following the keyword `while`.

✔ **The body:** This is the code within the braces.

✔ **The increment:** This is where the increment variable is incremented. This usually occurs at the end of the body.

In the case of the Factorial program, the four parts looked like this:

```
int nValue = 1;           // the setup
while (nValue <= nTarget) // the test expression
{                         // the body
    cout << nAccumulator << " * "
```

```
        << nValue << " equals ";
    nAccumulator = nAccumulator * nValue;
    cout << nAccumulator << endl;
    nValue++;                     // the increment
}
```

The for loop incorporates these four parts into a single structure using the keyword for:

```
for(setup; test expression; increment)
{
    body;
}
```

The flow is shown graphically in Figure 10-1.

1. As the CPU comes innocently upon the for keyword, control is diverted to the setup clause.

2. Once the setup has been performed, control moves over to the test expression.

3. (a) If the test expression is true, control passes to the body of the for loop.

   (b) If the test expression is false, control passes to the next statement after the closed brace.

4. Once control has passed through the body of the loop, the CPU is forced to perform a U-turn back up to the increment section of the loop.

   That done, control returns to the test expression and back to Step 3.

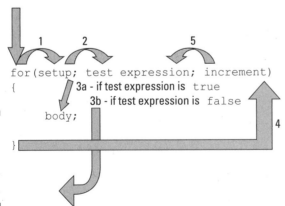

Figure 10-1:
The flow in
and around
the for
loop.

This `for` loop is completely equivalent to the following `while` loop:

```
setup;
while(test expression)
{
    body;

    increment;
}
```

Looking at an Example

The following example program is the Factorial program written as a `for` loop (this program appears on the enclosed CD-ROM as ForFactorial):

```
//
//  ForFactorial - calculate factorial using the for
//                 construct.
//
#include <cstdio>
#include <cstdlib>
#include <iostream>
using namespace std;

int main(int nNumberofArgs, char* pszArgs[])
{
    // enter the number to calculate the factorial of
    int nTarget;
    cout << "This program calculates factorial.\n"
         << "Enter a number to take factorial of: ";
    cin  >> nTarget;

    // start with an accumulator that's initialized to 1
    int nAccumulator = 1;
    for(int nValue = 1; nValue <= nTarget; nValue++)
    {
        cout << nAccumulator << " * "
             << nValue << " equals ";
        nAccumulator = nAccumulator * nValue;
        cout << nAccumulator << endl;
    }

    // display the result
    cout << nTarget << " factorial is "
```

```
        << nAccumulator << endl;

    // wait until user is ready before terminating program
    // to allow the user to see the program results
    system("PAUSE");
    return 0;
}
```

The logic of this ForFactorial program is virtually identical to its older
Factorial twin: The program prompts the user to enter a number to take the
factorial of. It then initializes nAccumulator to 1 before entering the loop
that calculates the factorial.

ForFactorial creates an increment variable, nValue, that it initializes to 1
in the setup clause of the for statement. That done, the program compares
nValue to nTarget, the value entered by the user in the test expression
section of the for. If nValue is less than or equal to nTarget, control enters
the body of the loop where nAccumulator is multiplied by nValue.

That done, control flows back up to the increment section of the for loop.
This expression, nValue++, increments nValue by 1. Flow then moves to
the test expression, where nValue is compared with nTarget and the
process repeated until eventually nValue exceeds the value of nTarget. At
that point, control passes to the next statement after the closed brace.

The output from this program appears as follows:

```
This program calculates factorials of user input.
Enter a negative number to exit
Enter number: 5
5 factorial is 120
Enter number: 6
6 factorial is 720
Enter number: -1
Press any key to continue . . .
```

All four sections of the for loop are optional. An empty setup, body, or
increment section has no effect; that is, it does nothing. (That makes sense.)
An empty test expression is the same as true. (This is the only thing that
would make sense — if it evaluated to false, then the body of the for loop
would never get executed, and the result would be useless.)

A variable defined within the setup section of a for loop is only defined within
the for loop. It is no longer defined once control exits the loop.

Getting More Done with the Comma Operator

There is a seemingly useless operator that I haven't mentioned (up until now, that is) known as the comma operator. It appears as follows:

```
expression1, expression2;
```

This says execute `expression1` and then execute `expression2`. The resulting value and type of the overall expression is the same as that of `expression2`. Thus, I could say something like the following:

```
int i;
int j;
i = 1, j = 2;
```

Why would I ever want to do such a thing, you ask? Answer: You wouldn't except when writing `for` loops.

The following CommaOperator program demonstrates the comma operator in combat. This program calculates the products of pairs of numbers. If the operator enters N, the program outputs 1 * N, 2 * N-1, 3 * N-2, and so on, all the way up to N * 1. (This program doesn't do anything particularly useful. You'll see the comma operator used to effect when discussing arrays in Chapter 15.)

```
//
//   CommaOperator - demonstrate how the comma operator
//                   is used within a for loop.
//
#include <cstdio>
#include <cstdlib>
#include <iostream>
using namespace std;

int main(int nNumberofArgs, char* pszArgs[])
{
    // enter a target number
    int nTarget;
    cout << "Enter maximum value: ";
    cin  >> nTarget;
```

```
for(int nLower = 1, nUpper = nTarget;

        nLower <= nTarget; nLower++, nUpper--)
{
    cout << nLower << " * "
         << nUpper << " equals "
         << nLower * nUpper << endl;
}

// wait until user is ready before terminating program
// to allow the user to see the program results
system("PAUSE");
return 0;
}
```

The program first prompts the operator for a target value, which is read into nTarget. It then moves to the for loop. However, this time not only do you want to increment a variable from 1 to nTarget, you also want to decrement a second variable from nTarget down to 1.

Here the setup clause of the for loop declares a variable nLower that it initializes to 1 and a second variable nTarget that gets initialized to nTarget. The body of the loop displays nLower, nUpper, and the product nLower * nTarget. The increment section increments nLower and decrements nUpper.

The output from the program appears as follows:

```
Enter maximum value: 15
1 * 15 equals 15
2 * 14 equals 28
3 * 13 equals 39
4 * 12 equals 48
5 * 11 equals 55
6 * 10 equals 60
7 * 9 equals 63
8 * 8 equals 64
9 * 7 equals 63
10 * 6 equals 60
11 * 5 equals 55
12 * 4 equals 48
13 * 3 equals 39
14 * 2 equals 28
15 * 1 equals 15
Press any key to continue . . .
```

In this example run, I entered 15 as the target value. You can see how nLower increments in a straight line from 1 to 15, while nUpper makes its way from 15 down to 1.

Actually, the output from this program is mildly interesting: No matter what you enter, the value of the product increases rapidly at first as nLower increments from 1. Fairly quickly, however, the curve flattens out and asymptotically approaches the maximum value in the middle of the range before heading back down. The maximum value for the product always occurs when nLower and nUpper are equal.

Could I have made the earlier for loop work without using the comma operator? Absolutely. I could have taken either variable, nLower or nUpper, out of the for loop and handled them as separate variables. Consider the following code snippet:

```
nUpper = nTarget;
for(int nLower = 1; nLower <= nTarget; nLower++)
{
    cout << nLower << " * "
         << nUpper << " equals "
         << nLower * nUpper << endl;
    nUpper--;
}
```

This version would have worked just as well.

The for loop can't do anything that a while loop cannot do. In fact, any for loop can be converted into an equivalent while loop. However, because of its compactness, you will see the for loop a lot more often.

Up to and including this chapter, all of the programs have been one monolithic whole stretching from the opening brace after main() to the corresponding closing brace. This is okay for small programs, but it would be really cool if you could divide your program into smaller bites that could be digested separately. That is the goal of the next chapter on functions.

Chapter 11

Functions, I Declare!

· ·

In This Chapter

▶ Breaking programs down into functions

▶ Writing and using functions

▶ Returning values from a function

▶ Passing values to a function

▶ Providing a function prototype declaration

· ·

The programs you see prior to this chapter are small enough and simple enough to write in one sequence of instructions. Sure, there have been branches using `if` statements and looping with `while` and `for` loops, but the entire program was in one place for all to see.

Real-world programs aren't usually that way. Programs that are big enough to deal with the complexities of the real world are generally too large to write in one single block of C++ instructions. Real-world programs are broken into modules called *functions* in C++. This chapter introduces you to the wonderful world of functions.

Breaking Your Problem Down into Functions

Even the Tire Changing Program from Chapter 1 was too big to write in a single block. I only tackled the problem of removing the lug nuts. I didn't even touch the problem of jacking up the car, removing the wheel, getting the spare out, and so on.

In fact, suppose that I were to take the lug nut removing code and put it into a module that I call something fiendishly clever, like RemoveLugNuts(). (I add the parentheses to follow C++ grammar.) I could bundle up similar modules for the other functions.

The resulting top-level module for changing a tire might look like the following:

```
1. Grab spare tire;
2. RaiseCar();
3. RemoveLugNuts();   // we know what this does
4. ReplaceWheel();
5. AttachLugNuts();   // inverse of RemoveLugNuts()
6. LowerCar();
```

Only the first statement is actually an instruction written in Tire Changing Language. Each of the remaining statements is a reference to a module somewhere. These modules consist of sequences of statements written in Tire Changing Language (including possible references to other, simpler modules).

Imagine how this program is executed: The tire changing processor starts at statement 1. First it sees the simple instruction Grab spare tire, which it executes without complaint (it always does exactly what you tell it to do). It then continues on to statement 2.

Statement 2, however, says, "Remember where you're at and go find the set of instructions called RaiseCar(). Once you've finished there, come back here for further instructions." In similar fashion, Statements 3 through 6 also direct the friendly mechanically inclined processor off to separate sets of instructions.

Understanding How Functions Are Useful

There are several reasons for breaking complex problems up into simpler functions. The original reason that a function mechanism was added to early programming languages was the Holy Grail of reuse. The idea was to create functions that could be reused in multiple programs. For example, factorial is a common mathematical procedure. If I rewrote the Factorial program as a function, I could invoke it from any program in the future that needs to calculate a factorial. This form of reuse allows code to be easily reused from different programs as well as from different areas within the same program.

Once a function mechanism was introduced, however, people discovered that breaking up large problems into simpler, smaller problems brought with it further advantages. The biggest advantage has to do with the number of things that a person can think about at one time. This is often referred to as the "Seven Plus or Minus Two" Rule. That's the number of things that a person can keep active in his mind at one time. Almost everyone can keep at least five objects in their active memory, but very few can keep more than nine objects active in their consciousness at one time.

You will have no doubt noticed that there are a lot of details to worry about when writing C++ code. A C++ module quickly exceeds the nine-object upper limit as it increases in size. Such functions are hard to understand and therefore to write and to get working properly.

It turns out to be much easier to think of the top-level program in terms of high-level functionality, much as I did in the tire changing example at the beginning of this chapter. This example divided the act of changing a tire into six steps, implemented in five functions.

Of course, I still have to implement each of these functions, but these are much smaller problems than the entire problem of changing a tire. For example, when implementing `RaiseCar()`, I don't have to worry about tires or spares, and I certainly don't have to deal with the intricacies of loosening and tightening lug nuts. All I have to think about in that function is how to get the car off the ground.

In computer nerd-speak, we say that these different functions are written at different *levels of abstraction*. The Tire Changing program is written at a very high level of abstraction; the `RemoveLugNuts()` function in Chapter 1 is written at a low level of abstraction.

Writing and Using a Function

Like so many things, functions are best understood by example. The following code snippet shows the simplest possible example of creating and invoking a function:

```
void someFunction()
{
    // do stuff
    return;
}

int main(int nNumberofArgs, char* pszArgs[])
{
    // do something

    // now invoke someFunction()
    someFunction();

    // keep going here once control returns
}
```

This example contains all the critical elements necessary to create and invoke a function:

1. **The declaration:** The first thing is the declaration of the function. This appears as the name of the function with a type in front followed by a set of open and closed parentheses. In this case, the name of the function is someFunction(), and its return type is void. (I'll explain what that last part means in the "Returning things" section of this chapter.)

2. **The definition:** The declaration of the function is followed by the definition of what it does. This is also called the body of the function. The body of a function always starts with an open brace and ends with a closed brace. The statements inside the body are just like those within a loop or an if statement.

3. **The return:** The body of the function contains zero or more return statements. A return returns control to immediately after the point where the function was invoked. Control returns automatically if it ever reaches the final closed brace of the function body.

4. **The call:** A function is called by invoking the name of the function followed by open and closed parentheses.

The flow of control is shown in Figure 11-1.

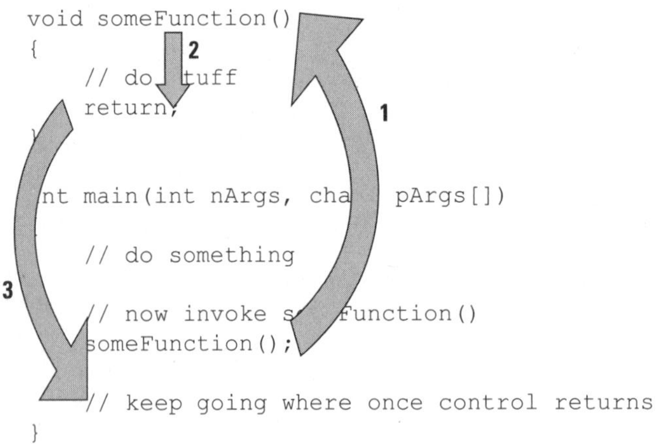

Figure 11-1: Invoking a function passes control to the module. Control returns to immediately after the call.

```
void someFunction()
{
    // do stuff
    return;                    1
}

int main(int nArgs, char pArgs[])
{
    // do something

    // now invoke someFunction()
    someFunction();

    // keep going where once control returns
}
```

Returning things

Functions often return a value to the caller. Sometimes this is a calculated value — a function like factorial() might return the factorial of a number. Sometimes this value is an indication of how things went — this is usually known as an *error return*. So the function might return a zero if everything went OK, and a non-zero if something went wrong during the execution of the function.

To return a value from a function, you need to make two changes:

1. Replace void with the type of value you intend to return.

2. Place the value to return after the keyword return. C++ does not allow you to return from a function by running into the final closed brace if the return type is other than void.

The keyword void is C++-ese for "nothing." Thus a function declared with a return type of int returns an integer. A function declared with a return type of void returns nothing.

Reviewing an example

The following FunctionDemo program uses the function sumSequence() to sum a series of numbers entered by the user at the keyboard. This function is invoked repeatedly until the user enters a zero length sequence.

```
//
//    FunctionDemo - demonstrate how to use a function
//                   to simplify the logic of the program.
//
#include <cstdio>
#include <cstdlib>
#include <iostream>
using namespace std;


//
// sumSequence() - return the sum of a series of numbers
//                 entered by the user. Exit the loop
//                 when the user enters a negative
//                 number.
int sumSequence()
{
    // create a variable into which we will add the
    // numbers entered by the user
    int nAccumulator = 0;

    for(;;)
    {
        // read another value from the user
        int nValue;
        cout << "Next: ";
        cin  >> nValue;

        // exit if nValue is negative
        if (nValue < 0)
        {
            break;
        }
```

```
            // add the value entered to the accumulated value
            nAccumulator += nValue;
        }

    // return the accumulated value to the caller
    return nAccumulator;
}

int main(int nNumberofArgs, char* pszArgs[])
{
    cout << "This program sums sequences of numbers.\n"
         << "Enter a series of numbers. Entering a\n"
         << "negative number causes the program to\n"
         << "print the sum and start over with a new\n"
         << "sequence. "
         << "Enter two negatives in a row to end the\n"
         << "program." << endl;

    // stay in a loop getting input from the user
    // until he enters a negative number
    for(;;)
    {
        // accumulate a sequence
        int nSum = sumSequence();

        // if the sum is zero...
        if (nSum == 0)
        {
            // ...then exit the program
            break;
        }

        // display the result
        cout << "Sum = " << nSum << endl;
    }

    // wait until user is ready before terminating program
    // to allow the user to see the program results
    system("PAUSE");
    return 0;
}
```

First, concentrate on the `main()` program. After outputting rather verbose instructions to the user, the program enters a `for` loop.

A `for` loop whose conditional expression is empty (as in `for(;;)`) will loop forever unless something within the body of the loop causes control to exit the loop (or until Hell freezes over).

The first non-comment line within this loop is the following:

```
int nSum = sumSequence();
```

This expression passes control to the sumSequence() function. Once control returns, the declaration uses the value returned by sumSequence() to initialize nSum.

The function sumSequence() first initializes nAccumulator to zero. It then prompts the user for value from the keyboard. If the number entered is not negative, it is added to the value in nAccumulator, and the user is prompted for another value in a loop. As soon as the user enters a negative number, the function breaks out of the loop and returns the value accumulated in nAccumulator to the caller.

The following is a sample run from the FunctionDemo program:

```
This program sums sequences of numbers.
Enter a series of numbers. Entering a
negative number causes the program to
print the sum and start over with a new
sequence. Enter two negatives in a row to end the
program.
Next: 5
Next: 15
Next: 20
Next: -1
Sum = 40
Next: 1
Next: 2
Next: 3
Next: 4
Next: -1
Sum = 10
Next: -1
Press any key to continue . . .
```

Passing Arguments to Functions

Functions that do nothing but return a value are of limited value because the communication is one-way — from the function to the caller. Two-way communication requires *function arguments*, which I discuss next.

Function with arguments

A function argument is a variable whose value is passed to the function during the call. The following FactorialFunction converts the previous factorial operation into a function:

```cpp
//
//  FactorialFunction - rewrite the factorial code as
//                a separate function.
//
#include <cstdio>
#include <cstdlib>
#include <iostream>
using namespace std;

//
// factorial - return the factorial of the argument
//             provided. Returns a 1 for invalid arguments
//             such as negative numbers.
int factorial(int nTarget)
{
    // start with an accumulator that's initialized to 1
    int nAccumulator = 1;
    for (int nValue = 1; nValue <= nTarget; nValue++)
    {
        nAccumulator *= nValue;
    }

    return nAccumulator;
}

int main(int nNumberofArgs, char* pszArgs[])
{
    cout << "This program calculates factorials"
         << " of user input.\n"
         << "Enter a negative number to exit" << endl;

    // stay in a loop getting input from the user
    // until he enters a negative number
    for (;;)
    {
        // enter the number to calculate the factorial of
        int nValue;

        cout << "Enter number: ";
        cin  >> nValue;

        // exit if the number is negative
        if (nValue < 0)
```

```
        {
            break;
        }

        // display the result
        int nFactorial = factorial(nValue);
        cout << nValue << " factorial is "
             << nFactorial << endl;
    }

    // wait until user is ready before terminating program
    // to allow the user to see the program results
    system("PAUSE");
    return 0;
}
```

The declaration of `factorial()` includes an argument `nTarget` of `int`.
Looking ahead, you can see that this is intended to be the value to calculate
the factorial of. The return value of the function is the calculated factorial.

In `main()`, the program prompts the user for a value, which it stores in
`nValue`. If the value is negative, the program terminates. If not, it calls
`factorial()` passing the value of `nValue`. The program stores the returned
value in `nFactorial`. It then outputs both values before returning to prompt
the user for a new value.

Functions with multiple arguments

A function can have multiple arguments by separating them by commas.
Thus, the following function returns the product of two integer arguments:

```
int product(int nValue1, int nValue2)
{
    return nValue1 * nValue2;
}
```

Exposing main ( )

Now the truth can be told: The "keyword" `main()` from our standard template is nothing more than a function — albeit a function with strange arguments, but a function nonetheless.

Overloading function names

C++ allows the programmer to assign the same name to two or more functions if the functions can be distinguished by either the number or types of arguments. This is called *function overloading*. Consider the following example functions:

```cpp
void someFunction()
{
    // ...perform some function
}
void someFunction(int nValue)
{
    // ...perform some other function
}
void someFunction(char cValue)
{
    // ...perform a function on characters
}

int main(int nNumberofArgs, char* pszArgs[])
{
    someFunction();     // call the first function
    someFunction(10);   // call the second function
    someFunction('a');  // now the third function
    return 0;
}
```

By comparing each of the preceding calls with the declarations, it is clear which function is meant by each call. Because of this, C++ aficionados include the type of arguments with the name of the function in what is called the function's *extended name* or *signature*. Thus, the extended names of the three functions are, in fact, different: `someFunction()`, `someFunction(int)`, and `someFunction(char)`.

Warning: Notice that the return type is not part of the extended name and cannot be used to differentiate functions.

When a program is built, C++ adds some boilerplate code that executes before your program ever gains control. This code sets up the environment in which your program will operate. For example, this boilerplate code opens the default input and output channels and attaches them to cin and cout.

After the environment has been established, the C++ boilerplate code calls the function main(), thereby beginning execution of your code. When your program finishes, it returns from main(). This enables the C++ boilerplate to clean up a few things before terminating the program and handing control back over to the operating system.

Defining Function Prototype Declarations

There's a little more to the previous program examples than meets the eye. Consider the second program, FactorialFunction, for example. During the build process, the C++ compiler scanned through the file. As soon as it came upon the `factorial()` function, it made a note in an internal table somewhere in the function's extended name and its return type. This is how the compiler was able to understand what I was talking about when I invoked the `factorial()` function later on in `main()` — it saw that I was trying to call a function, and it said, "Let me look in my table of defined functions for one called `factorial()`. Aha, here's one!"

In this case, the function was defined and the types and number of arguments matched perfectly, but that isn't always the case. What if I had invoked the function not with an integer but with something that could be converted into an integer? Suppose I had called the function as follows:

```
factorial(1.1);
```

That's not a perfect match, 1.1 is not an integer, but C++ knows how to convert 1.1 into an integer. So it *could* make the conversion and use `factorial(int)` to complete the call. The question is, *does* it?

The answer is "Yes." C++ will generate a warning in some cases to let you know what it's doing, but it will generally make the necessary type conversions to the arguments to use the functions that it knows about.

Note: I know that I haven't discussed the different variable types and won't until Chapter 14, but the argument I am making is fairly generic. You will also see in Chapter 14 how to avoid warnings caused by automatic type conversions.

What about a call like the following:

```
factorial(1, 2);
```

There is no conversion that would allow C++ to lop off an argument and use the `factorial(int)` function to satisfy this call, so C++ generates an error in this case.

The only way C++ can sort out this type of thing is if it sees the function declaration before it sees the attempt to invoke the function. This means each function must be declared before it is used.

I know what you're thinking (I think): C++ could be a little less lazy and look ahead for function declarations that occur later on before it gives up and starts generating errors, but the fact is that it doesn't. It's just one of those things, like my crummy car; you learn to live with it.

So does that mean you have to define all of your functions before you can use them? No. C++ allows you to declare a function without a body in what is known as a *prototype declaration*.

A prototype declaration creates an entry for the function in the table I was talking about. It fills in the extended name, including the number and type of the arguments, and the return type. C++ leaves the definition of the function, the function body, empty until later.

In practice, a prototype declaration appears as follows:

```
// the prototype declaration
int factorial(int nTarget);

int main(int nNumberofArgs, char* pszArgs[])
{
    cout << "The factorial of 10 is "
         << factorial(10) << endl;

    return 0;
}

// the definition of the factorial(int) function;
// this satisfies our promise to provide a definition
// for the prototype function declaration above
int factorial(int nTarget)
{
    // start with an accumulator that's initialized to 1
    int nAccumulator = 1;
    for (int nValue = 1; nValue <= nTarget; nValue++)
    {
        nAccumulator *= nValue;
    }

    return nAccumulator;
}
```

The prototype declaration tells the world (or at least that part of the world after the declaration) that `factorial()` takes a single integer argument and returns an integer. That way, C++ can check the call in `main()` against the declaration to see whether any type conversions need to take place or whether the call is even possible.

The prototype declaration also represents a promise to C++ to provide a complete definition of `factorial(int)` somewhere else in the program. In this case, the full definition of `factorial(int)` follows right after `main()`.

It is common practice to provide prototype declarations for all functions defined within a module. That way, you don't have to worry about the order in which they are defined. I'll have more to say about this topic in the next chapter.

Chapter 12

Dividing Programs into Modules

· ·

In This Chapter

▶ Breaking programs down into functions

▶ Writing and using functions

▶ Returning values from a function

▶ Passing values to a function

▶ Providing a function prototype declaration

· ·

*I*n Chapter 11, I show you how to divide a complex problem into a number of separate functions; it is much easier to write and get a number of smaller functions to work than one large, monolithic program. Oftentimes, however, you may want to reuse the functions you create in other applications. For example, I could imagine reusing the `factorial()` function I created in Chapter 11 in the future.

One way to reuse such functions is to copy-and-paste the source code for the `factorial()` function into my new program. However, it would be a lot easier if I could put the function in a separate file that I could then link into future applications. Breaking programs into separate source code modules is the subject of this chapter.

Breaking Programs Apart

The programmer can break a single program into separate source files generally known as *modules*. These modules are compiled into machine code by the C++ compiler separately and then combined during the build process to generate a single program.

The process of combining separately compiled modules into a single program is called *linking*.

Breaking programs into smaller, more manageable pieces has several advantages. First, breaking a program into smaller modules reduces the compile time. Code::Blocks takes only a few seconds to gobble up and digest the programs that appear in this book. Very large programs can take quite a while, however. I have worked on projects that took most of the night to rebuild.

In addition, recompiling all of the source code in the project just because one or two lines change is extremely wasteful. It's much better to recompile just the module containing the change and then relink it into all of the unchanged modules to create a new executable with the change. (The updated module may contain more than just the one changed function but not that many more.)

Second, it's easier to comprehend and, therefore, easier to write and debug a program that consists of a number of well thought out but quasi-independent modules, each of which represents a logical grouping of functions. A large, single source module full of all the functions that a program might use quickly becomes hard to keep straight.

Third is the much vaunted specter of reuse. A module full of reusable functions that can be linked into future programs is easier to document and maintain. A change in the module to fix some bug is quickly incorporated into other executables that use that module.

Finally, there's the issue of working together as a team. Two programmers can't work on the same module (at least not very well). An easier approach is to assign one set of functions contained in one module to a programmer while assigning a different set of functions in a different module to a second programmer. The modules can be linked together when ready for testing.

Breaking Up Isn't That Hard to Do

I can't really include a large program in a book like this . . . well, I could, but there wouldn't be enough left for anything else. I will use the FactorialFunction demo from Chapter 11 as my example large-scale program. In this section, I will create the FactorialModule project that separates the program into several source modules. To do this, I will perform the following steps:

1. Create the FactorialModule project.

   This is no different than creating any of the other project files up to this point in the book.

2. Create the `Factorial.cpp` file to contain the factorial function.

3. Create the `Factorial.h` include file (whatever that is) to be used by all modules that want to call.

4. Update `main.cpp` to use the `factorial()` function.

Creating Factorial.cpp

The initial console application project created by Code::Blocks has only one source file, `main.cpp`. The next step is to create a second source file that will contain the factorial function.

Follow these steps to create `factorial.cpp` containing the `factorial()` function:

1. Select File⇨New⇨File.

Code::Blocks responds by opening the window shown in Figure 12-1 showing the different types of files you can add.

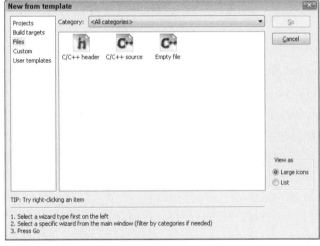

Figure 12-1:
The New
File wizard
provides
you help
in adding
source files
to your
project.

2. Select C/C++ Source and then click Go.

This opens up a box warning that you are about to enter the mysterious and dangerous Source File Wizard.

3. Click Next.

This will open the Source File Wizard.

4. Click the ... next to the Filename with Full Path prompt.

A File Open dialog box appears, allowing you to navigate to a different folder if you want to keep your source files in different directories. But don't make it any more complicated than it has to be.

5. Enter `factorial.cpp` as the name of the source file and click Save.

6. **You want this file added to all executables that you create, so select All for the build targets.**

When you are finished, the dialog box should look like Figure 12-2.

Figure 12-2:
The C/C++
Source
File dialog
box lets
you enter
the name
of the new
module,
facto-
rial.
cpp.

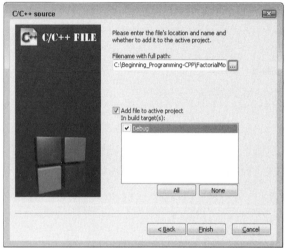

7. **Click Finish to create `Factorial.cpp` and add it to the Project.**

The project file includes the list of all source files that it takes to build your program.

8. **Update `factorial.cpp` as follows:**

```
//
// factorial - this module includes the factorial function
//
#include <cstdio>
#include <cstdlib>
#include <iostream>
using namespace std;
#include "factorial.h"
//
// factorial - return the factorial of the argument
//             provided. Returns a 1 for invalid arguments
//             such as negative numbers.
int factorial(int nTarget)
{
    // start with an accumulator that's initialized to 1
    int nAccumulator = 1;
    for (int nValue = 1; nValue <= nTarget; nValue++)
    {
```

```
        nAccumulator *= nValue;
    }

    return nAccumulator;
}
```

The first four lines are part of the standard template used for all C++ source files in this book. The next line is the `factorial.h` include file, which I discuss further later in this chapter. This is followed by the `factorial()` function much as it appeared in Chapter 11.

Include files don't follow the same grammar rules as C++. For example, unlike other statements in C++, the `#include` must start in column 1 and doesn't require a semicolon at the end.

Don't try to compile `factorial.cpp`, as you haven't created `factorial.h` yet.

Creating an #include file

The next step in the process is to create an include file. Okay, what's an include file?

As I discuss in Chapter 11, the prototype declaration describes the functions to be called by providing the number and types of arguments and the type of the return value. Every function that you invoke must have a prototype declaration somewhere before the call.

It is possible to list out the prototype declarations manually for each function you intend to use, but fortunately that isn't necessary. Instead C++ allows the same dummy who created the function to create an include file that contains the function's prototype declarations. This file can then be included in the source files of the modules where the functions are called.

There are (at least) two ways to include these prototypes. One way is to copy the contents of the include file and paste them into the module where the calls are made. This isn't a very good idea, however. For one thing, it is really laborious. For another, if the prototype declaration for any one of the functions in the include file is changed, the programmer will have to go through every place the include file is used, delete the old one, and repaste in the new file.

Rather than do that, C++ includes a preprocessor that understands very few instructions. Each of these instructions starts with a pound sign (#) in column 1 followed immediately by a command. (Preprocessor commands also end at the end of the line and don't require a semicolon.)

The most common preprocessor command is `#include "filename.h"`. This command copies and pastes the contents of `filename.h` at the point of the `#include` to create what is known as an *intermediate source file.* The preprocessor then passes this intermediate source file on to the C++ compiler for processing. This process is shown graphically in Figure 12-3.

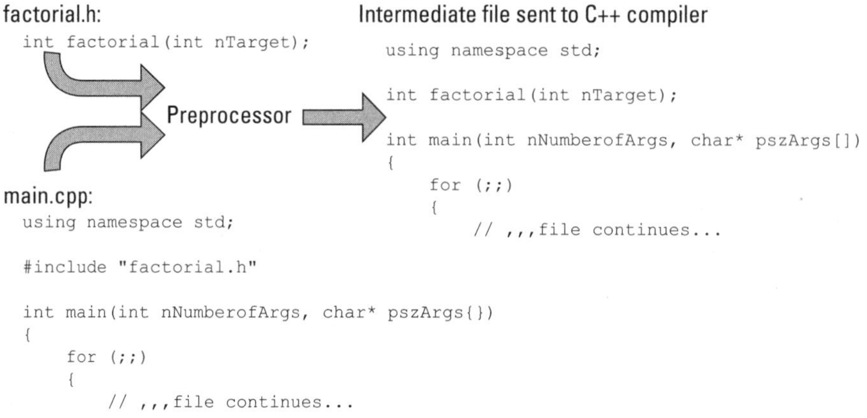

Figure 12-3:
The preprocessor inserts the contents of an include file at the point of the `#include` command before passing the results to the C++ compiler.

```
factorial.h:                                  Intermediate file sent to C++ compiler
  int factorial(int nTarget);                    using namespace std;

                                                  int factorial(int nTarget);

                         Preprocessor             int main(int nNumberofArgs, char* pszArgs[])
                                                  {
                                                      for (;;)
main.cpp:                                             {
  using namespace std;                                   // ,,,file continues...

  #include "factorial.h"

  int main(int nNumberofArgs, char* pszArgs{})
  {
      for (;;)
      {
          // ,,,file continues...
```

Including #include files

The Code::Blocks wizard makes creating an include file painless. Just execute the following steps:

1. **Select File**⇨**New**⇨**File.**

   Code::Blocks responds by opening the window shown in Figure 12-1 just as before. This time you're creating an include file.

2. **Select Include File and then click Go.**

3. **In the next window that warns you're about to enter the Include File Wizard, click Next.**

4. **Click the ... next to the Filename with Full Path prompt.**

   A File Open dialog box appears.

5. **Enter `factorial.h` as the name of the include file and click Save.**

6. **You want this file added to all executables that you create, so select All for the build targets.**

   When you are finished, the dialog box should look like Figure 12-4.

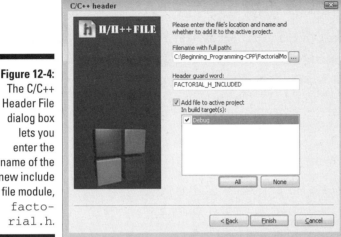

Figure 12-4:
The C/C++
Header File
dialog box
lets you
enter the
name of the
new include
file module,
facto-
rial.h.

7. **Click Finish to create an empty include file that looks like the following:**

```
#ifndef FACTORIAL_H_INCLUDED
#define FACTORIAL_H_INCLUDED




#endif // FACTORIAL_H_INCLUDED
```

8. **Edit the include file by adding the prototype for the `factorial()` function as follows:**

```
#ifndef FACTORIAL_H_INCLUDED
#define FACTORIAL_H_INCLUDED

int factorial(int nTarget);

#endif // FACTORIAL_H_INCLUDED
```

9. **Click File Save.**

You're done!

Notice that the include file has been added to the project description in the Management tab of Code::Blocks. This indicates that Code::Blocks will automatically rebuild the application if the include file changes.

Why include `factorial.h` in `factorial.cpp`? After all, `factorial()` doesn't require a prototype of itself. You do this as a form of error checking. C++ will generate an error message when compiling `factorial.cpp` if the prototype declaration in `factorial.h` does not match the definition of the function. This ensures that the prototype declaration being used by other source code modules matches the function definition.

Creating main.cpp

You're almost there: Open `main.cpp` and edit it to look like the following:

```cpp
//
//   FactorialModule - rewrite the factorial code as
//                     a separate function in its own module.
//
#include <cstdio>
#include <cstdlib>
#include <iostream>
using namespace std;

#include "factorial.h"

int main(int nNumberofArgs, char* pszArgs[])
{
    cout << "This program calculates factorials"
         << " of user input.\n"
         << "Enter a negative number to exit" << endl;

    // stay in a loop getting input from the user
    // until he enters a negative number
    for (;;)
    {
        // enter the number to calculate the factorial of
        int nValue;

        cout << "Enter number: ";
        cin  >> nValue;

        // exit if the number is negative
        if (nValue < 0)
        {
            break;
        }

        // display the result
        int nFactorial = factorial(nValue);
        cout << nValue << " factorial is "
             << nFactorial << endl;
    }

    // wait until user is ready before terminating program
    // to allow the user to see the program results
    system("PAUSE");
    return 0;
}
```

This version of `main.cpp` looks identical to the FactorialFunction version except that the definition of the `factorial()` function has been removed and the `#include "factorial.h"` added.

Building the result

Now you can build the program (by selecting Build⇨Build). Notice in the output messages that the compiler now compiles two files, `main.cpp` and `factorial.cpp`. This is then followed by a single link step.

When executed, the output from this version is indistinguishable from earlier versions as demonstrated by the following test output:

```
This program calculates factorials of user input.
Enter a negative number to exit
Enter number: 5
5 factorial is 120
Enter number: 6
6 factorial is 720
Enter number: -1
Press any key to continue . . .
```

Using the Standard C++ Library

Now you can see why the standard C++ template includes the directives

```
#include <cstdio>
#include <cstdlib>
#include <iostream>
```

These include files contain the prototype declarations for functions provided by C++ as part of its standard library of routines (like `cin >>`, for example).

Notice that the standard C++ library include files are included in angle brackets (`<>`), while I included my user-defined include file in quotes (`""`). The only difference between the two is that C++ looks for files contained in quotes starting with the "current" directory (the directory containing the project file), while C++ begins searching for bracketed files in the C++ include file directories.

The online help files (at `www.cppreference.com/wiki/`) are a good source of information about the functions that make up the Standard C++ Library.

Variable Scope

Variables are also assigned a storage type depending upon where and how they are defined, as shown in the following snippet:

```
int nGlobalVariable;
void fn()
{
    int nLocalVariable;
    static int nStaticVariable = 1;

    nStaticVariable = 2;
}
```

Variables defined within a function like nLocalVariable don't exist until control passes through the declaration. In addition, nLocalVariable is only defined within fn() — the variable ceases to exist when control exits the fn() function.

By comparison, the variable nGlobalVariable is created when the program begins execution and exists as long as the program is running. All functions have access to nGlobalVariable all the time.

We say that nLocalVariable has *local scope,* and nGlobalVariable has *global scope*.

The keyword static can be used to create a sort of mishling — something between a global and a local variable. The static variable nStaticVariable is created when execution reaches the declaration the first time that function fn() is called. Unlike nLocalVariable, however, nStaticVariable is not destroyed when program execution returns from the function. Instead, it retains its value from one call to the next.

In this example, nStaticVariable is initialized to 1 the first time that fn() is called. The function changes its value to 2. nStaticVariable retains the value 2 on every subsequent call — it is not reinitialized once it has been created. The initialization portion of the declaration is ignored every subsequent time that fn() is called after the first time.

However, the scope of nStaticVariable is still local to the function. Code outside of fn() does not have access to nStaticVariable.

Global variables are useful for holding values that you want all functions to have access to. Static variables are most useful for counters — for example, if you want to know how many times a function is called. However, most variables are of the plain ol' local variety.

Chapter 13

Debugging Your Programs, Part 2

In This Chapter
- ▶ Debugging a multifunction program
- ▶ Performing a unit test
- ▶ Using predefined preprocessor commands during debug

T his chapter expands upon the debugging techniques introduced in Chapter 8 by showing you how to create debugging functions that allow you to navigate your errors more quickly.

C++ functions represent further opportunities both to excel and to screw up. On the downside are the errors that are possible only when your program is divided into multiple functions. However, dividing your programs into functions allows you to examine, test, and debug each function without regard to how the function is being used in the outside program. This allows you to create a much more solid program.

Debugging a Dys-Functional Program

To demonstrate how dividing a program into functions can make the result easier to read and maintain, I created a version of the SwitchCalculator program in which the calculator operation has been split off as a separate function (which it would have been in the first place if I had only known about functions back then). Unfortunately, I introduced an error during the process that didn't show up until performing testing.

The following listing appears on the enclosed CD-ROM as CalculatorError1:

```
// CalculatorError1 - the SwitchCalculator program
//                    but with a subtle error in it
//
#include <cstdio>
#include <cstdlib>
```

```cpp
#include <iostream>
using namespace std;
// prototype declarations
int calculator(char cOperator, int nOper1, int nOper2);

int main(int nNumberofArgs, char* pszArgs[])
{
    // enter operand1 op operand2
    int  nOper1;
    int  nOper2;
    char cOperator;
    cout << "Enter 'value1 op value2'\n"
         << "where op is +, -, *, / or %:" << endl;
    cin >> nOper1 >> cOperator >> nOper2;

    // echo what the user entered followed by the
    // results of the operation
    cout << nOper1 << " "
         << cOperator << " "
         << nOper2 << " = "
         << calculator(cOperator, nOper1, nOper2)
         << endl;

    // wait until user is ready before terminating program
    // to allow the user to see the program results
    system("PAUSE");
    return 0;
}

// calculator -return the result of the cOperator
//             operation performed on nOper1 and nOper2
int calculator(char cOperator, int nOper1, int nOper2)
{
    int nResult = 0;
    switch (cOperator)
    {
        case '+':
            nResult = nOper1 + nOper2;
        case '-':
            nResult = nOper1 - nOper2;
            break;
        case '*':
        case 'x':
        case 'X':
            nResult = nOper1 * nOper2;
            break;
        case '/':
            nResult = nOper1 / nOper2;
            break;
```

```
        case '%':
            nResult = nOper1 % nOper2;
            break;
        default:
            // didn't understand the operator
            cout << " is not understood";
    }
    return nResult;
}
```

The beginning of this program starts the same as its SwitchCalculator precursor except for the addition of the prototype declaration for the newly created `calculator()` function. Notice how much cleaner `main()` is here: It prompts the user for input and then echoes the output along with the results from `calculator()`. Very clean.

The `calculator()` function is also simpler than before since all it does is perform the computation specified by `cOperator`. Gone is the irrelevant code that prompts the user for input and displays the results.

All that's left to do is test the results.

Performing unit level testing

Breaking a program down into functions not only allows you to write your program in pieces, but also it allows you to test each function in your program separately. In this functional version of the SwitchCalculator program, I need to test the `calculator()` function by providing all possible inputs (both legal and illegal) to the function.

First, I generate a set of test cases for `calculator()`. Clearly, I need a test for each case in the switch statement. I will also need some boundary conditions, like "how does the function respond when asked to divide by zero?" Table 13-1 outlines some of the cases I need to test.

Table 13-1	Test Cases for calculator() Showing Expected and Actual Results				
Operator	*Operand1*	*Operand2*	*Expected Result*	*Actual Result*	*Explanation*
+	10	20	30		Simple case
–	20	10	10		Simple case

(continued)

Table 13-1 *(continued)*

Operator	Operand1	Operand2	Expected Result	Actual Result	Explanation
–	10	20	–10		Generate a negative number
*	10	20	200		Simple case
*	10	–5	–50		Try with a negative argument
x	10	20	200		Use the other form of multiply operator
/	20	10	2		Simple case
/	10	0	Don't care as long error generated and program doesn't crash		Try divide by zero
%	23	10	3		Simple case
%	20	10	0		Generate a zero result
%	23	–10	3		Try modulo with a negative number
y	20	10	Don't care as long as error generated and program doesn't crash		Illegal input

It turns out that I'm lucky in this case — the calling function `main()` allows me to provide any input to the function that I want. I can send each of these test cases to `calculator()` without modifying the program. That isn't usually the case — very often the function is only invoked from the main program in certain ways. In these cases, I must write a special test module that puts the function under test through its paces by passing it the various test cases and recording the results.

Why do you need to write extra debug code? What do you care if the function doesn't handle a case properly if that case never occurs in the program? You care because you don't know how the function will be used in the future. Once written, a function tends to take on a life of its own beyond the program that it was written for. A useful function might be used in dozens of different programs that invoke the function in all sorts of different ways that you may not have thought of when you first wrote the function.

The following shows the results for the first test case:

```
Enter 'value1 op value2'
where op is +, -, *, / or %:
10 + 20
10 + 20 = -10
Press any key to continue . . .
```

Already something seems to be wrong. What now?

Outfitting a function for testing

Like most functions, `calculator()` doesn't perform any I/O of its own. This makes it impossible to know for sure what's going on within the function. I addressed this problem in Chapter 8 by adding output statements in key places within the program. Of course, in Chapter 8, you didn't know about functions, but now you do.

It turns out that it's easier to create an error function that prints out everything you might want to know. You can then just copy and paste calls to this test function in key spots. This is quicker and less error prone than making up a unique output statement for each different location.

C++ provides some help in creating and calling such debug functions. The preprocessor defines several special symbols shown in Table 13-2.

Table 13-2	Predefined Symbols Useful in Creating Debug Functions	
Symbol	**Type**	**Value**
__LINE__	int	The line number within the current source code module
__FILE__	const char*	The name of the current module
__DATE__	const char*	The date that the module was compiled (not the current date)
__TIME__	const char*	The time that the module was compiled (not the current time)
__FUNCTION__	const char*	The name of the current function (GCC only)
__PRETTY_FUNCTION__	const char*	The extended name of the current function (GCC only)

You haven't seen the type const char*. You will in Chapter 16. You'll have to take my word for now that this is the type of a character string contained in double quotes like "Stephen Davis is a great guy".

You can see how the predefined preprocessor commands from Table 13-2 are used in the following version of the calculator() function outfitted with calls to a newly created debugger function printErr() (the following code segment is taken from the program CalculatorError2, which is on the enclosed CD-ROM):

```
void printErr(int nLN, char cOperator, int nOp1, int nOp2)
{
    cout << "On line " << nLN
         << ": \'" << cOperator
         << "\' operand 1 = " << nOp1
         << " and operand 2 = " << nOp2
         << endl;
}

// calculator -return the result of the cOperator
//             operation performed on nOper1 and nOper2
int calculator(char cOperator, int nOper1, int nOper2)
{
```

```
    printErr(__LINE__, cOperator, nOper1, nOper2);
    int nResult = 0;
    switch (cOperator)
    {
        case '+':
            printErr(__LINE__, cOperator, nOper1, nOper2);
            nResult = nOper1 + nOper2;
        case '-':
            printErr(__LINE__, cOperator, nOper1, nOper2);
            nResult = nOper1 - nOper2;
            break;
        case '*':
        case 'x':
        case 'X':
            printErr(__LINE__, cOperator, nOper1, nOper2);
            nResult = nOper1 * nOper2;
            break;
        case '/':
            printErr(__LINE__, cOperator, nOper1, nOper2);
            nResult = nOper1 / nOper2;
            break;
        case '%':
            printErr(__LINE__, cOperator, nOper1, nOper2);
            nResult = nOper1 % nOper2;
            break;
        default:
            // didn't understand the operator
            cout << " is not understood";
    }
    return nResult;
}
```

The `printErr()` function displays the value of the operator and the two operands. It also displays the line number that it was called from. The line number is provided by the C++ preprocessor in the form of the __LINE__ symbol. Printing the line number with the error messages tells me how to differentiate the debug output from the program's normal output.

You can see how this works in practice by examining the output from this newly outfitted version of the program:

```
Enter 'value1 op value2'
where op is +, -, *, / or %:
10 + 20
On line 50: '+' operand 1 = 10 and operand 2 = 20
On line 55: '+' operand 1 = 10 and operand 2 = 20
On line 58: '+' operand 1 = 10 and operand 2 = 20
10 + 20 = -10
Press any key to continue . . .
```

Figure 13-1 shows the display of the program within the CodeBlocks editor including the line numbers along the left side of the display.

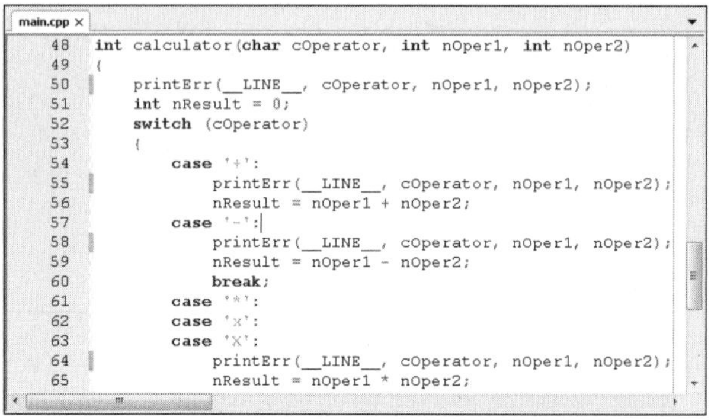

Figure 13-1: The view of the calcu-lator() function in the CodeBlocks editor show-ing the line numbers.

```
main.cpp ×
48   int calculator(char cOperator, int nOper1, int nOper2)
49   {
50       printErr(__LINE__, cOperator, nOper1, nOper2);
51       int nResult = 0;
52       switch (cOperator)
53       {
54           case '+':
55               printErr(__LINE__, cOperator, nOper1, nOper2);
56               nResult = nOper1 + nOper2;
57           case '-':
58               printErr(__LINE__, cOperator, nOper1, nOper2);
59               nResult = nOper1 - nOper2;
60               break;
61           case '*':
62           case 'x':
63           case 'X':
64               printErr(__LINE__, cOperator, nOper1, nOper2);
65               nResult = nOper1 * nOper2;
```

Immediately after I input "10 + 20" followed by the Enter key, the program calls the printErr() function from line 50. That's correct since this is the first line of the function. Checking the values, you can see that the input appears to be correct: cOperator is '+', nOper1 is 10, and nOper2 is 20 just as you expect.

The next call to printErr() occurred from line 55, which is the first line of the addition case, again just as expected. The values haven't changed, so everything seems okay.

The next line is completely unexpected. For some reason, printErr() is being called from line 58. This is the first line of the subtraction case. For some reason, control is falling through from the addition case directly into the subtraction case.

And then I see it! The break statement is missing at the end of the addition case. The program is calculating the sum correctly but then falling through into the next case and overwriting that value with the difference.

First, I add the missing break statement. I do not remove the calls to print-Err() — there may be other bugs in the function, and I'll just end up putting them back. There's no point in removing these calls until I am convinced that the function is working properly.

Returning to unit test

The updated program generates the following output for the addition test case:

```
Enter 'value1 op value2'
where op is +, -, *, / or %:
10 + 20
```

```
On line 49: '+' operand 1 = 10 and operand 2 = 20
On line 54: '+' operand 1 = 10 and operand 2 = 20
10 + 20 = 30
Press any key to continue . . .
```

This matches the expected results from Table 13-1. Continuing through the
test cases identified in this table, everything matches until I get to the case of
10 / 0 to which I get the output shown in Figure 13-2. The output from the
printErr() shows that the input is being read properly, but the program
crashes soon after line 68.

It's pretty clear that the program is, in fact, dying on line 69 when it performs
division by zero. I need to add a test to intercept that case and not perform
the division if the value of nOper2 is zero.

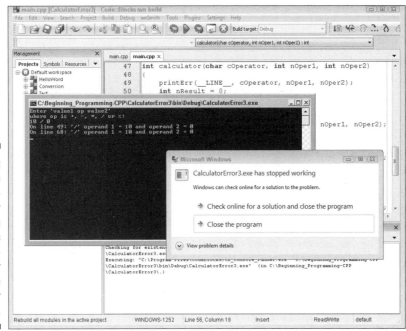

Figure 13-2:
The
Calculator-
Error
program
terminates
with a mys-
terious error
message
when I enter
'10 / 0'.

Of course, this begs the question: What value should I return from the function if nOper2 is zero? The "Expected Result" case in Table 13-1 says that we
don't care what gets returned when dividing by zero as long as the program
doesn't crash. That being the case, I decide to return 0. However, I need to
document this case in the comments to the function.

With that addition to the function, I start testing again from the top.

You need to restart back at the beginning of your test cases each time you modify the function.

The function generates the expected results in every case. Now I can remove the printErr() functions. The completed calculator() function (included in the CalculatorError4 program on the enclosed CD-ROM) appears as follows:

```cpp
// calculator -return the result of the cOperator
//           operation performed on nOper1 and nOper2
//           (In the case of division by zero or if it
//           cannot understand the operator, the
//           function returns a zero.)
int calculator(char cOperator, int nOper1, int nOper2)
{
    int nResult = 0;
    switch (cOperator)
    {
        case '+':
            nResult = nOper1 + nOper2;
            break;
        case '-':
            nResult = nOper1 - nOper2;
            break;
        case '*':
        case 'x':
        case 'X':
            nResult = nOper1 * nOper2;
            break;
        case '/':
            if (nOper2 != 0)
            {
                nResult = nOper1 / nOper2;
            }
            break;
        case '%':
            nResult = nOper1 % nOper2;
            break;
        default:
            // didn't understand the operator
            cout << " is not understood";
    }
    return nResult;
}
```

This version of the calculator() function does not suffer from the error that made the original version incapable of adding properly. In addition, this updated version includes a test in the division case: If nOper2, the divisor, is zero, the function does not perform a division that would cause the program to crash but leaves the value of nResult its initial value of 0.

Part IV
Data Structures

The 5th Wave   By Rich Tennant

"This should unstick the keys a little."

In this part . . .

So far you've been limited to just integer and character variables. Fortunately, C++ defines a rich set of variable types, including that most feared of concepts, the C++ pointer. (Don't worry if you don't know what I'm talking about, you will soon.) I wrap up this part with another discussion of debugging.

Chapter 14

Other Numerical Variable Types

*T*he programs so far have limited themselves to variables of type int with just a few chars thrown in. Integers are great for most calculations — more than 90 percent of all variables in C++ are of type int. Unfortunately, int variables aren't adapted to every problem. In this chapter, you will see both variations of the basic int as well as other types of intrinsic variables. An *intrinsic type* is one that's built into the language. In Chapter 19, you will see how the programmer can define her own variable types.

Some programming languages allow you to store different types of data in the same variable. These are called *weakly typed* languages. C++, by contrast, is a *strongly typed* language — it requires you to declare the type of data the variable is to store. A variable, once declared, cannot change its type.

The Limitations of Integers in C++

The int variable type is the C++ version of an integer. As such, int variables suffer the same limitations as their counting integer equivalents in mathematics do.

Integer round-off

It isn't that an integer expression can't result in a fractional value. It's just that an int has no way of storing the fractional piece. The processor lops off the part to the right of the decimal point before storing the result. (This lopping off of the fractional part of a number is called *truncation*.)

Consider the problem of calculating the average of three numbers. Given three int variables — nValue1, nValue2, and nValue3 — their average is given by the following expression:

```
int nAverage = (nValue1 + nValue2 + nValue3)/3;
```

Suppose that nValue1 equals 1, nValue2 equals 2, and nValue3 equals 2 — the sum of this expression is 5. This means that the average is 5 /3 or either 1 2/3 or 1.666, depending upon your personal preference. But that's not using integer math.

Because all three variables are integers, the sum is assumed to be an integer as well. And because 3 is also an integer, you guessed it, the entire expression is taken to be an integer. Thus, given the same values of 1, 2, and 2, C++ will calculate to the unreasonable but logical result of 1 for the value of nAverage (3, 4, and 5 divided by 3 are all 1; 6 divided by 3 is 2).

The problem is much worse in the following mathematically equivalent formulation:

```
int nAverage = nValue1/3 + nValue2/3 + nValue3/3;
```

Plugging in the same values of 1, 2, and 2, the resulting value of nAverage is now 0 (talking about logical but unreasonable). To see how this can occur, consider that 1/2 truncates to 0, 2/3 truncates to 0, and 2/3 truncates to 0. The sum of 0, 0, and 0 is (surprise!) 0.

You can see that there are times when integer truncation is completely unacceptable.

Limited range

A second problem with the int variable type is its limited range. A normal int can store a maximum value of 2,147,483,647 and a minimum value of –2,147,483,648 — that's roughly from positive 2 billion to negative 2 billion for a total range of 4 billion.

That's on a modern PC, Mac, or other common processor. If you have a much older machine, the int may not be nearly so expansive in its range. I will have a little more to say about that later in this chapter.

Two billion is a very large number — plenty big enough for most applications. That's why the int is useful. But it's not large enough for some applications, including computer technology. In fact, your computer probably executes faster than 2 GHz (gigahertz), depending on how old your computer is (2 GHz is two billion cycles per second). A single strand of fiber cable (the kind that's strung back and forth from one side of the country to the other) can carry way more than 2 billion bits per second. I won't even start on the number of stars in the Milky Way.

A Type That "doubles" as a Real Number

The limitations of the int variable are unacceptable in some applications. Fortunately, C++ understands decimal numbers that have a fractional part. (Mathematicians call these *real numbers*.) In C++, decimal numbers are called *floating point numbers* or simply *floats*. This is because the decimal point can float around from left to right to handle fractional values.

Floating point variables come in two basic flavors in C++. The small variety is declared using the keyword float as follows:

```
float fValue1;        // declare a floating point
float fValue2 = 1.5;  // initialize it at declaration
```

Oddly enough, the standard floating point variable in C++ is its larger sibling, the double precision floating point or simply double. You declare a double precision floating point as follows:

```
double dValue1;
double dValue2 = 1.5;
```

Because the native floating point type for C++ is the double, I generally avoid using float. The float does take up less memory, but this is not an issue for most applications. I will stick with double for the remainder of this book. In addition, when I say "floating point variable," you can assume that I'm talking about a variable of type double.

Solving the truncation problem

To see how the double fixes our truncation problem, consider the average of three floating point variables dValue1, dValue2, and dValue3 given by the formula

```
double dAverage = dValue1/3.0 + dValue2/3.0 + dValue3/3.0;
```

Assume, once again, the initial values of 1.0, 2.0, and 2.0. This renders the above expression equivalent to

```
double dAverage = 1.0/3.0 + 2.0/3.0 + 2.0/3.0;
```

which is, in turn, equivalent to

```
double dAverage = 0.333... + 0.6666... + 0.6666...;
```

resulting in a final value of

```
double dAverage = 1.666...;
```

I have written the preceding expressions as though there were an infinite number of sixes after the decimal point. In fact, this isn't the case. The accuracy of a double is limited to about 14 significant digits. The difference between 1.666666666666 and 1 2/3 is small, but not zero. I will have more to say about this a little later in this chapter.

When an integer is not an integer

C++ assumes that a number followed by a decimal point is a floating point constant. Thus, it takes 2.5 to be a floating point. This decimal point rule is true even if the value to the right of the decimal point is zero. Thus, 3.0 is also a floating point. The distinction to you and me between 3 and 3.0 is small, but not to C++.

Actually, you don't have to put anything on the right of the decimal point. Thus 3. is also a double. However, it's considered good style to include the 0 after the decimal point for floating point constants.

Computer geeks will be interested to know that the internal representations of 3 and 3.0 are totally different (yawn). More importantly, the constant int 3 is subject to int rules, whereas 3.0 is subject to the rules of floating point arithmetic.

Thus, you should try to avoid expressions like the following:

```
double dValue = 1.0;
double dOneThird = dValue/3;
```

Technically this is what is known as a *mixed mode* expression because dValue is a double, while 3 is an int. C++ is not a total idiot — it knows what you want in a case like this, so it will convert the 3 to a double and per-form floating point arithmetic.

We say that C++ *promotes* the int 3 to a double.

C++ will also allow you to assign a floating point result to an `int` variable:

```
int nValue = dValue / 3.0;
```

Assigning a `double` to an `int` is known as a *demotion*.

Some C++ compilers generate a warning when promoting a variable, but Code::Blocks/gcc does not. All C++ compilers generate a warning (or error) when demoting a result due to the loss of precision.

You should get in the habit of avoiding mixed mode arithmetic. If you have to change the type of an expression, do it explicitly using a caste as in the following example:

```
void fn(int nArg)
{
    // calculate one third of nArg; use a caste to
    // promote it to a floating point
    double dOneThird = (double)nArg / 3.0;

    // ...function continues on
```

I am using the naming convention of starting double precision double variables with the letter d. That is merely a convention. You can name your variables any way you like — C++ doesn't care.

Discovering the limits of double

Floating point variables come with their own limitations. They cannot be used to count things, they take longer to process, they consume more memory, and they also suffer from round-off error (though not nearly as bad as `int`). Now, consider each one of these problems in turn.

Counting

You can't use a floating point variable in an application where counting is important. In C++, you can't say that there are 7.0 characters in my first name. Operators involved in counting don't work on floating point variables. In particular, the auto-increment (++) and auto-decrement (−) operators are strictly verboten on `double`.

Calculation speed

Computers can perform integer arithmetic faster than floating point arithmetic. Historically, this difference was significant. In the 1980s, a CPU without a floating point processor to help it along took about 1,000 times longer to perform a floating point division than it did to perform an integer division.

Fortunately, floating point processors have been built into CPUs for many years now, so the difference in performance is not nearly so significant. I wrote the following loop just as a simple example, first using integer arithmetic:

```
int nValue1 = 1, nValue2 = 2, nValue3 = 2;
for (int i = 0; i < 1000000000; i++)
{
    int nAverage = (nValue1 + nValue2 + nValue3) / 3;
}
```

This loop took about 5 seconds to execute on my laptop. I then executed the same loop in floating point:

```
double dValue1 = 1, dValue2 = 2, dValue3 = 2;
for (int i = 0; i < 1000000000; i++)
{
    double dAverage = (dValue1 + dValue2 + dValue3) / 3.0;
}
```

This look took about 21 seconds to execute on the same laptop. Calculating an average 1 billion times in a little over 20 seconds ain't shabby, but it's still four times slower than its integer equivalent.

Consume more memory

Table 14-2 shows the amount of memory consumed by a single variable of each type. On a PC or Macintosh, an `int` consumes 4 bytes, whereas a `double` takes up 8 bytes. That doesn't sound like much and, in fact, it isn't; but if you had a few million of these things you needed to keep in memory . . . well, it still would be a great number. But if you had a few hundred million, then the difference would be considerable.

This is another way of saying, unless you need to store a heck of a lot of objects, don't worry about the difference in memory taken by one type versus another. Instead, pick the variable type based upon your needs.

If you do just happen to be programming an application that needs to manipulate the age of every human on the planet at one time, then you may want to lean toward the smaller `int` (or one of the other integer types I discuss in this chapter) based upon the amount of memory it consumes.

Loss of accuracy

A double variable has about 16 significant digits of accuracy. Consider that a mathematician would express the number 1/3 as 0.333..., where the ellipses indicate that the threes go on forever. The concept of an infinite series makes sense in mathematics, but not in computing. A computer only has a finite amount of memory and a finite amount of accuracy.

C++ can correct for round-off error in a lot of cases. For example, on output if a variable is 0.99999999999999, C++ will just assume that it's really 1.0 and display it accordingly. However, C++ can't correct for all floating point round-off errors, so you need to be careful. For example, you can't be sure that 1/3 + 1/3 + 1/3 is equal to 1.0:

```
double d1 = 23.0;
double d2 = d1 / 7.0;
if (d1 == (d2 * 7.0))
{
    cout << "Did we get here?" << endl;
}
```

You might think that this code snippet would always display the `"Did we get here?"` string, but surprisingly it does not. The problem is that 23 / 7 cannot be expressed exactly in a floating point number. Something is lost. Thus, `d2 * 7` is very close to 23, but is not exactly equal.

Rather than looking for exact equality between two floating point numbers, you should be asking, "Is d2 * 7 vanishingly close to d1 in value?" You can do that as follows:

```
double d1 = 23.0;
double d2 = d1 / 7.0;

// Is d2 * 7.0 within delta of d1?
double difference = (d2 * 7.0) - d1;
double delta = 0.00001;
if (difference < delta && difference > -delta)
{
    cout << "Did we get here?" << endl;
}
```

This code snippet calculates the difference between `d1` and `d2 * 7.0`. If this difference is less than some small delta, the code calls it a day and says that `d1` and `d2 * 7` are essentially equal.

Not so limited range

The largest number that a double can store is roughly 10 to the 38th power. That's a 1 with 38 zeroes after it; that eats the puny 2 billion maximum size for an `int` for breakfast. That's even more than the national debt (at least, at the time of this writing). I'm almost embarrassed to call this a limit, but I suppose there are applications where 38 zeroes aren't enough.

Remember that only the first 16 digits are significant. The remaining 22 digits are noise having already succumbed to standard floating point round-off error.

Variable Size — the "long" and "short" of It

C++ allows you to expand on integer variable types by adding the following descriptors on the front: const, unsigned, short, or else long. Thus, you could declare something like the following:

```
unsigned long int ulnVariable;
```

A const variable cannot be modified. All numbers are implicitly const. Thus, 3 is of type const int, while 3.0 is a const double, and '3' is a const char.

An unsigned variable can take on non-negative values only; however, it can handle a number roughly twice as large as its signed sibling. Thus, an unsigned int has a range of 0 to 4 billion (as opposed to the regular signed int's range of –2 billion to 2 billion).

C++ allows you to declare a short int and a long int. For example, a short int takes less space but has a more limited range than a regular int, whereas a long int takes more storage and has a significantly larger range.

The int is assumed. Thus, the following two declarations are both accepted and completely equivalent:

```
long int lnVar1;   // declare a long int
long lnVar2;       // also a long int; int is assumed
```

The C++ 2009 Standard even defines a long long int and a long double. The Code::Blocks/gcc that comes on the enclosed CD-ROM understands what these are, but not all compilers do. These are just like long int and double, respectively, only more so — more accuracy and larger range.

Not all combinations are allowed. For example, unsigned can be applied only to the counting types int and char. Table 14-1 shows the legal combinations and their meaning along with how to declare a constant of that type.

Table 14-1	The Common C++ Variable Types	
Type	*Declaring a Constant*	*What It Is*
int	1	A simple counting number, either positive or negative.
unsigned int	1U	A non-negative counting number.

Type	Declaring a Constant	What It Is
short int	---	A potentially smaller version of the int. It uses less memory but has a more limited range.
long int	1L	A potentially larger version of the int. It may use more memory but has a larger range. There is no difference between long and int on the Code::Blocks/gcc compiler.
long long int	1LL	A potentially even larger version of the int.
float	1.0F	A single precision real number.
double	1.0	A double precision real number.
long double	---	A potentially larger floating point number. On the PC, long double is the native size for numbers internally to the numeric processor.
char	'c'	A single char variable stores a single character. Not suitable for arithmetic.
wchar_t	L'c'	A wide character. Used to store larger character sets such as Chinese kanji symbols. Also known as UTF or Unicode.

How far do numbers range?

It may seem odd, but the C++ standard doesn't actually say exactly how big a number each of the data types can accommodate. The standard addresses only the relative size of each variable type. For example, it says that the maximum long int is at least as large as the maximum int.

The authors of C++ weren't trying to be mysterious. They wanted to allow the compiler to implement the absolute fastest code possible for the base machine. The standard was designed to work for all different types of processors running different operating systems.

In fact, the standard size of an int has changed over the past decades. Before 2000, the standard int on most PCs was 2 bytes and had a range of plus or minus 64,000. Some time around 2000, the basic word size on the Intel processors changed to 32 bits. Most compilers changed to the default int of today that's 4 bytes and has a range of plus or minus 2 billion.

Table 14-2 provides the size and range of each variable type on the Code::Blocks/gcc compiler provided on the enclosed CD-ROM (and most other compilers meant for an Intel processor running on a 32-bit operating system).

Table 14-2	Range of Numeric Types in Code::Blocks/gcc		
Type	**Size [bytes]**	**Accuracy**	**Range**
short int	2	exact	−32,768 to 32,767
int	4	exact	−2,147,483,648 to 2,147,483,647
long int	4	exact	−2,147,483,648 to 2,147,483,647
long long int	8	exact	−9,223,372,036,854,775,808 to 9,223,372,036,854,775,807
float	4	7 digits	+/− 3.4028 * $10^{+/-38}$
double	8	16 digits	+/− 1.7977 * $10^{+/-308}$
long double	12	19 digits	+/−1.1897 * $10^{+/-4932}$

Attempting to calculate a number that is beyond the range of a variable's type is known as an *overflow*. The C++ standard generally leaves the results of an overflow undefined. That's another way that the inventors of C++ wanted to leave the language flexible so that the machine code generated would be as fast as possible.

On the PC, a floating point overflow generates an exception that, if not handled, will cause your program to crash. (I don't discuss exception handling until Chapter 32.) As bad as that sounds, an integer overflow is even worse — C++ generates an incorrect result without complaint.

Types of Constants

I mentioned the const declaration earlier in this chapter and again in Table 14-1, but I would like to take a minute to expand upon constants now.

A *constant value* is an explicit number or character such as 1 or 0.5 or 'c'. Constant values cannot be changed, that is, they cannot appear on the left-hand side of an assignment statement. Every constant value has a type. The type of 1 is const int. The type of 0.5 is const double. Table 14-1 explains how to declare constant values with different types. For example, 1L is of type const long.

A variable can be declared constant using the const keyword:

```
const double PI = 3.14159;   // declare a constant variable
```

A const variable must be initialized when it is declared since you will not get another chance in the future — just like a constant value, a const variable cannot appear on the left-hand side of an assignment statement.

It is common practice to declare const variables using all capitals. Multiple words within a variable name are divided by an underscore as in TWO_PI. As always, this is just convention — C++ doesn't care.

It may seem odd to declare a variable and then say that it can't be changed. Why bother? Largely because a carefully named constant can make a program a lot easier to understand. Consider the following two equivalent expressions:

```
double dC = 6.28318 * dR;   // what does this mean?
double dCircumference = TWO_PI * dRadius; // this is a lot
                            // easier to understand
```

It should be a lot clearer to the reader of this code that the second expression is multiplying the radius by 2π to calculate the circumference.

Passing Different Types to Functions

Floating point variables and variables of different size are passed to function in the same way that int variables are as demonstrated in the following code snippet. This example snippet passes the value of the variable dArg along with the const double 0.0 to the function maximumFloat().

```
// maximumFloat - return the larger of two floating
//                point arguments
double maximumFloat(double d1, double d2)
{
    if (d1 > d2)
    {
        return d1;
    }
    return d2;
}

void otherFunction()
{
    double dArg = 1.0;
    double dNonNegative = maximumFloat(dArg, 0.0);
    // ...function continues...
```

I discuss functions in Chapter 11.

Overloading function names

The type of the arguments are part of the extended name of the function. Thus, the full name of the earlier example function is maximumFloat (double, double). In Chapter 11, you see how to differentiate between two functions by the number of arguments. You can also differentiate between two functions by the type of the arguments, as shown in the following example:

```
double maximum(double d1, double2);
int    maximum(int n1, int n2);
```

When declared this way, it's clear that the call maximum(1, 2) refers to maximum(int, int), while the call maximum(3.0, 4.0) refers to maximum(double, double).

Defining functions that have the same name but different arguments is called *function overloading*.

Sometimes the programmer's intentions start to get a little obscure, but you can even differentiate by the signedness and length as well:

```
int maximum(int n1, int n2);
long maximum(long l1, long l2);
unsigned maximum(unsigned un1, unsigned un2);
```

Fortunately, this is rarely necessary in practice.

Mixed mode overloading

The rules can get really weird when the arguments don't line up exactly. Consider the following example code snippet:

```
double maximum(double d1, double d2);
int    maximum(int n1, int n2);

void otherFunction()
{
    // which function is invoked by the following?
    double dNonNegative = maximum(dArg, 0);
    // ...function continues...
```

const arguments are a constant problem

Since C++ passes the value of the argument, you cannot differentiate by const-ness. Consider the following call to see why:

```
double maximum(double d1, double d2);

void otherFunction()
{
    double dArg = 2.0;
    double dNonNegative = maximum(dArg, 0.0);
```

What actually gets passed to maximum() are the values 2.0 and 0.0. The maximum() function can't tell whether these values came from a variable like dArg or a constant like 0.0.

You *can* declare the arguments of a function to be const. Such a declaration means that you cannot change the argument's value within the function. This is demonstrated in the following implementation of maximum(double, double):

```
double maximum(const double d1, const double d2)
{
    double dResult = d1;
    if (d2 > dResult)
    {
        dResult = d2;
    }

    // the following would be illegal
    d1 = 0.0; d2 = 0.0

    return dResult;
}
```

The assignment to d1 and d2 is not allowed because both have been declared const and therefore are not changeable.

What is not legal is the following:

```
// these two functions are not different enough to be
    distinguished
double maximum(double d1, double d2);
double maximum(const double d1, const double d2);

void otherFunction()
{
    double dArg = 2.0;

    // C++ doesn't know which one of the above functions to call
    double dNonNegative = maximum(dArg, 0.0);
```

C++ has no way of differentiating between the two when you make the call. I have more to say about const arguments in Chapter 17.

Here, the arguments don't line up exactly with either declaration. There is no `maximum(double, int)`. C++ could reasonably take any one of the following three options:

- Promote the 0 to a `double` and call `maximum(double, double)`.
- Demote the double to an `int` and invoke `maximum(int, int)`.
- Throw up its electronic hands and report a compiler error.

The general rule is that C++ will promote arguments in order to find a match but will not automatically demote an argument. However, you can't always count on this rule. In this case, Code::Blocks generates an error that the call is ambiguous. That is, the third option wins.

My advice is to not rely on C++ to figure out what you mean by making the necessary conversions explicit:

```
void otherFunction(int nArg1, double dArg2)
{
    // use an explicit cast to make sure that the
    // proper function is called
    double dNonNegative = maximum((double)nArg1, dArg2);
```

Now it is clear that I mean to call `maximum(double, double)`.

Chapter 15

Arrays

*T*he variables declared so far have been of different types with different sizes and capabilities. Even so, each variable has been capable of holding only a single value at a time. If I wanted to hold three numbers, I had to declare three different variables. The problem is that there are times when I want to hold a set of numbers that are somehow closely related. Storing them in variables with names that bear some similarity of spelling like nArg1, nArg2, and so on may create associations in my mind but not for poor, ignorant C++.

There is another class of variable known as the *array* that can hold a series of values. Arrays are the subject of this chapter and the next chapter. (Here I present arrays in general. In the next chapter, I look at the particular case of the character array.)

What Is an Array?

If you are mathematically inclined and were introduced to the concept of the array in high school or college, you may want to skim this section.

You may think of a variable as a truck. There are small trucks, like a short int, capable of holding only a small value; and there are larger trucks, like a long double, capable of holding astoundingly large numbers. However, each of these trucks can hold only a single value.

Each truck has a unique designator. Perhaps you give your vehicles names, but even if you don't, each has a license plate that uniquely describes each of your vehicles, at least within a given state.

This works fine for a single family. Even the largest families don't have so many cars that this arrangement gets confusing. But think about an auto rental agency. What if they referred to their cars solely by a license plate number or some other ID? (Boy, just thinking about that Hertz!)

After filling out the myriad forms — including deciding whether I want the full insurance coverage and whether I'm too lazy to fill it up with gas before I bring it back — the guy behind the counter says, "Your car is QZX123." Upon leaving the building and walking to the parking lot, I look over a sea of cars that rival a Wal-Mart parking lot. Exactly where is QZX123?

That's why the guy behind the counter actually says something quite differ-ent. He says something to the effect, "Your car is in slot B11." This means that I am to skip past row A directly to row B and then start scanning down the line for the eleventh car from the end. The numbers are generally painted on the pavement to help me out, but even if they weren't, I could probably figure out which car he meant.

Several things have to be true in order for this system to work:

✔ The slots have to be numbered in order (B2 follows B1 and comes imme-diately before B3), ideally with no breaks or jumps in the sequence.

✔ Each slot is designed to hold a car (a given parking slot may be empty, but the point is that I would never find a house in a parking slot).

✔ The slots are equally spaced (being equally spaced means that I can jump ahead and guess about where B50 is without walking along from B1 through B49, checking each one).

That's pretty much the way arrays work. I can give a series of numbers a single name. I refer to individual numbers within the series by index. So the variable x may refer to a whole series of whole numbers, $x(1)$ would be the first number in the series, $x(2)$ the second, and so on, just like the cars at the rental agency.

Declaring an Array

To declare an array in C++, you must provide the name, type, and number of elements in the array. The syntax is as follows:

```
int nScores[100];
```

This declares an array of 100 integers and gives them the name nScores.

TIP

It is common practice to use the same naming convention for arrays as for non-arrays but to use the plural form. That makes sense because nScores refers to 100 integer values.

Indexing into an Array

You must provide an index to access a specific element within the array. An index must be a counting type (like int), as demonstrated here:

```
nScores[11] = 10;
```

This is akin to the way that rental cars are numbered. However, unlike humans, C++ numbers its arrays starting with 0. Thus, the first score in the array nScores is nScores[0].

So how does this work exactly? I will return to the rental car lot one more time (for the last time, I promise). Figure 15-1 shows how rental cars typically number their parking lots. The first car in row B carries the designation B1. To find B11, I simply move my gaze ten cars to the right.

Figure 15-1:
Cars in a rental car lot are typically numbered sequentially starting with 1 to make them easier to find.

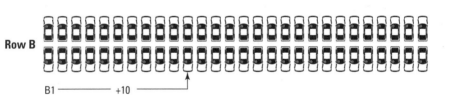

C++ does a similar thing. To execute the statement nScores[11] = 10, C++ starts with the address of the first element in nScores. It then moves to the right 11 spaces and stores a 10 at that location. This is shown graphically in Figure 15-2. (I say a lot more about what it means to "take the address of the first element" in the next three chapters. Please just accept the statement for now.)

Figure 15-2:
C++ calcu-
lates the
location of
`nScores`
`[11]` by
moving over
11 `int`
slots from
the begin-
ning of the
`nScores`
array.

`nScores[11] = 10;`

`nScores:`

											10	

+0   +1   +2   +3   +4   +5   +6   +7   +8   +9   +10   +11   +12

+11

The fact that C++ starts counting at zero leads to a point that always confuses beginners. The statement

```
int nScores[100];
```

declares 100 scores, which are numbered from 0 to 99. The expression

```
nScores[100] = 0;  // this is an error
```

zeroes out the first element *beyond* the end of the array. The last element in the array is `nScores[99]`. The C++ compiler will not catch this error and will happily access this non-element, which very often leads to the program accessing some other variable by mistake. This type of error is very hard to find because the results are so unpredictable.

Looking at an Example

The following example averages a set of scores and then displays that average. However, unlike earlier demonstrations, this program retains the scores' input in an array that it can then output along with the average.

```
//
//   ArrayDemo - demonstrate the use of an array
//               to accumulate a sequence of numbers
//
#include <cstdio>
#include <cstdlib>
```

```cpp
#include <iostream>

using namespace std;

// displayArray - displays the contents of the array
//                of values of length nCount
void displayArray(int nValues[100], int nCount)
{
    for(int i = 0; i < nCount; i++)
    {
        cout.width(3);
        cout << i << " - " << nValues[i] << endl;
    }
}

// averageArray - averages the contents of an array
//                of values of length nCount
int averageArray(int nValues[100], int nCount)
{
    int nSum = 0;
    for(int i = 0; i < nCount; i++)
    {
        nSum += nValues[i];
    }
    return nSum / nCount;
}

int main(int nNumberofArgs, char* pszArgs[])
{
    int nScores[100];
    int nCount;

    // prompt the user for input
    cout << "This program averages a set of scores\n"
         << "Enter scores to average\n"
         << "(enter a negative value to terminate input"
         << endl;
    for(nCount = 0; nCount < 100; nCount++)
    {
        cout << "Next: ";
        cin >> nScores[nCount];
        if (nScores[nCount] < 0)
        {
            break;
        }
    }

    // now output the results
    cout << "Input terminated." << endl;
    cout << "Input data:" << endl;
```

```
    displayArray(nScores, nCount);
    cout << "The average is "
        << averageArray(nScores, nCount)
        << endl;

    // wait until user is ready before terminating program
    // to allow the user to see the program results
    system("PAUSE");
    return 0;
}
```

This program starts at the beginning of main() by prompting the user for a series of integer values. The program saves each of the numbers that the user inputs into the array nScores in a loop. The program exits the loop as soon as the user enters a negative number.

Notice that this program keeps track of the number of values entered in the variable nCount. The program will exit the loop after 100 entries whether or not the user enters a negative number — because that's all the room the program has for storing values. You should always make sure that you don't over-run the end of an array.

Once the user has either entered a negative value or 100 values in a row, the program exits the loop. Now the nScores array contains all of the numbers entered, and nCount contains a count of the number of values that are stored in the array.

The program then calls the function displayArray() to echo to the user the values entered. Finally, the function averageArray() returns the integer average of the numbers entered.

The displayAverage() function iterates through the values in the array passed it, displaying each value in turn. The averageArray() function works by also iterating through the array nValues, accumulating the sum of each element in a local variable nSum. The function returns nSum / nCount, which is the average of the values in nValues.

In practice, the output of the program appears as follows:

```
This program averages a set of scores
Enter scores to average
(enter a negative value to terminate input
Next: 10
Next: 20
Next: 30
Next: 40
Next: 50
```

```
Next: -1
Input terminated.
Input data:
   0 - 10
   1 - 20
   2 - 30
   3 - 40
   4 - 50
The average is 30
Press any key to continue . . .
```

Initializing an Array

Like any other variable, an array starts out with an indeterminate value if you don't initialize it. The only difference is that unlike a simple variable, which contains only one undetermined value, an array starts out with a whole lot of unknown values:

```
int nScores[100];   // none of the values in nScores
                    // known until you initialize them
```

You can initialize the elements of an array with a loop as follows:

```
int nScores[100];   // declare the array and then...
for (int i = 0; i < 100; i++) // ...initialize it
{
    nScores[i] = 0;
}
```

You can also initialize an array when you declare it by including the initial values in braces after the declaration. For a small array, this is easy:

```
int nCount[5] = {0, 1, 2, 3, 4};
```

Here I initialized the value of nCount[0] to 0, nCount[1] to 1, nCount[2] to 2, and so on. If there are more elements than numbers in the list, C++ pads the list with zeros. Thus, in the following case:

```
int nCount[5] = {1};
```

the first element (nCount[0]) is set to 1. Every other element gets initialized to zero. You can use this to initialize a large array to zero as well:

```
int nScores[100] = {0};
```

This not only declares the array but initializes every element in the array to zero.

By the same token, you don't have to provide an array size if you have an initializer list — C++ will just count the number of elements in the list and make the array that size:

```
int nCount[] = {1, 2, 3, 4, 5};
```

This declares nCount to be 5 elements large because that's how many values there are in the initializer list.

Arrays are useful for holding small to moderate amounts of data. (Really large amounts of data require a database of some sort.) By far, the most common type of array is the character array, which is the subject of the next chapter.

Chapter 16

Arrays with Character

· ·

In This Chapter

▶ Introducing the `null` terminated character array

▶ Creating an ASCIIZ array variable

▶ Examining two example ASCIIZ manipulation programs

▶ Reviewing some of the most common built-in ASCIIZ library functions

· ·

Chapter 15 introduced the concept of arrays. The example program collected values into an integer array, which was then passed to a function to display and a separate function to average. However, as useful as an array of integers might be, far and away the most common type of array is the character array. Specifically something known as the *ASCIIZ character array,* which is the subject of this chapter.

The ASCII-Zero Character Array

Arrays have an inherent problem: You can never know by just looking at the array how many values are actually stored in it. Knowing the size of an array is not enough. That tells you how many values the array *can* hold, not how many it actually *does* hold. The difference is like the difference between how much gas your car's tank can hold and how much gas it actually has. Even if your tank holds 20 gallons, you still need a gas gauge to tell you how much is in it.

For a specific example, the ArrayDemo program in Chapter 15 allocated enough room in `nScores` for 100 integers, but that doesn't mean the user actually entered that many. He might have entered a lot fewer.

There are essentially two ways of keeping track of the amount of data in an array:

- ✔ **Keep a count of the number of values in a separate int variable.** This is the technique used by the ArrayDemo program. The code that read the user input kept track of the number of entries in nCount. The only problem is that the program had to pass nCount along to every function to which it passed the nScores array. The array was not useful without knowing how many values it stored.

- ✔ **Use a special value in the array as an indicator of the last element used.** By convention, this is the technique used for character arrays in C++.

Look back at the table of legal ASCII characters in Chapter 5. You'll notice that one character in particular is not a legal character: '\0'. This character is also known as the null character. It is the character with a numerical value of zero. A program can use the null character as the end of a string of characters since it can never be entered by the user. This means that you don't have to pass a separate count variable around — you can always tell the end of the string by looking for a null.

The designers of C and C++ liked this feature so well that they settled on it as the standard for character strings. They even gave it a name: the *ASCII-zero* array or *ASCIIZ* for short.

The null character has another advantageous property. It is the only character whose value is considered false in a comparison expression (such as in a loop or an if statement).

Remember from Chapter 9 that 0 or null is considered false. All other values evaluate to true.

This makes writing loops that manipulate ASCIIZ strings even easier, as you will see in the following examples.

Declaring and Initializing an ASCIIZ Array

I could declare an ASCIIZ character array containing my first name as follows:

```
char szMyName[8] = {'S', 't', 'e', 'p',
                    'h', 'e', 'n', '\0'};
```

Actually, the 8 is redundant. C++ is smart enough to count the number of characters in the initialization string and just make the array that big. Thus, the following is completely equivalent to the previous example:

```
char szMyName[] = {'S', 't', 'e', 'p',
                   'h', 'e', 'n', '\0'};
```

The only problem with this is that it's awfully clumsy. I have to type a lot more than just the seven characters that make up my name. (I had to type about five keystrokes for every character in my name — that's a lot of overhead.) ASCIIZ strings are so common in C++ that the language provides a shorthand option:

```
char szMyName[] = "Stephen";
```

These two initialization statements are completely equivalent. In fact, a string contained in double quotes is nothing more than an array of constant characters terminated with a `null`.

The string `"Stephen"` consists of eight characters — don't forget to count the terminating `null`.

Looking at an Example

Let's take the simple case of displaying a string. You know by now that C++ understands how to display ASCIIZ strings just fine, but suppose it didn't. What would a function designed to display a string look like? The following DisplayASCIIZ program shows one example:

```
//
//  DisplayASCIIZ - display an ASCIIZ string one character
//                  at a time as an example of ASCIIZ
//                  manipulation
//
#include <cstdio>
#include <cstdlib>
#include <iostream>
using namespace std;


// displayString - display an ASCIIZ string one character
//                 at a time
void displayString(char szString[])
{
```

```
        for(int index = 0; szString[index] != '\0'; index++)
        {
            cout << szString[index];
        }
    }

    int main(int nNumberofArgs, char* pszArgs[])
    {
        char szName1[] = {'S', 't', 'e', 'p',
                          'h', 'e', 'n', '\0'};
        char szName2[] = "Stephen";

        cout << "Output szName1: ";
        displayString(szName1);
        cout << endl;

        cout << "Output szName2: ";
        displayString(szName2);
        cout << endl;

        // wait until user is ready before terminating program
        // to allow the user to see the program results
        system("PAUSE");
        return 0;
    }
```

The displayString() function is the key to this demonstration program.
This function iterates through the array of characters passed to it using the
variable index. However, rather than rely on a separate variable containing
the number of characters in the array, this function loops until the character
at szString[index] is the null character, '\0'. As long as the current
character is not a null character, the loop outputs it to the display.

The main() function creates two versions of my name, first using dis-
crete characters for szName1 and then a second time using the shortcut
"Stephen" for szName2. The function then displays both strings using the
displayString() function both to show that the function works and to
demonstrate the equivalence of the two strings.

The output from the program appears as follows:

```
Output szName1: Stephen
Output szName2: Stephen
Press any key to continue . . .
```

Notice that szName1 and szName2 display identically (since they are the
same).

Constant character problems

Technically "Stephen" is not of type `char[]`, that is, "array of characters" — it's of type `const char[]`, that is "array of const characters." The difference is that you cannot modify the characters in an array of constant characters. Thus, you could do the following:

```
char cT = "Stephen"[1];   // fetch the second character, the 't'
```

But you could not modify it by putting it on the left-hand side of an equal sign:

```
"Stephen"[1] = 'x';       // replace the 't' with an 'x'
```

This pickiness about `const` doesn't normally make a difference, but it can cause C++ consternation when declaring arguments to a function. For example, in the DisplayASCIIZ demo program, I could not say `displayString("Stephen")` because `displayString()` is declared to accept an array of characters (`char[]`), where "Stephen" is an array of `const` characters (`const char[]`).

I can solve this problem by simply declaring `displayString()` as follows:

```
void displayString(const char szString[]);
```

The function works because `displayString()` never tries to modify the `szString` array passed to it.

Don't worry if this discussion of `const` versus non-`const` variables leaves you confused — you'll get another chance to see this in action in Chapter 18.

Looking at a More Detailed Example

Displaying a string of characters is fairly simple. What about a little bit tougher example? The following program concatenates two strings that it reads from the keyboard.

To concatenate two strings means to tack one onto the end of the other. For example, the result of concatenating "abc" with "DEF" is "abcDEF".

Before you examine the program, think about how you could go about concatenating a string, call it szSource, onto the end of another one called szTarget.

First, you need to find the end of the szTarget string (see the top of Figure 16-1). Once you've done that, you copy characters from szSource one at a time into szTarget until you reach the end of the szSource string (as demonstrated at the bottom of Figure 16-1). Make sure that the result has a final null on the end, and you're done.

Figure 16-1:
To concatenate, the function must do the following:
(a) First, find the terminating `null` of the target string; (b) Then copy characters from the source to the target until the terminating `null` on the source is encountered.

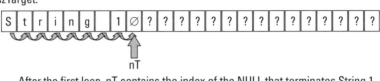

szTarget:

After the first loop, nT contains the index of the NULL that terminates String 1.

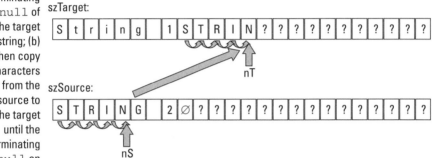

szTarget:

szSource:

The following assignment transfers a character from szSource to szTarget starting at the terminating NULL:

```
szTarget[nT] = szSource[nS];
```

That's exactly how the `concatenateString()` function works in the ConcatenateString example program.

```cpp
//
//  ConcatenateString - demonstrate the manipulation of
//                      ASCIIZ strings by implementing a
//                      concatenate function
//
#include <cstdio>
#include <cstdlib>
#include <iostream>
using namespace std;


// concatenateString - concatenate one string onto the
//                      end of another
void concatenateString(char szTarget[],
                const char szSource[])
{
    // first find the end of the target string
    int nT;
    for(nT = 0; szTarget[nT] != '\0'; nT++)
    {
    }
```

```
    // now copy the contents of the source string into
    // the target string, beginning at 'nT'
    for(int nS = 0; szSource[nS] != '\0'; nT++, nS++)
    {
        szTarget[nT] = szSource[nS];
    }

    // add the terminator to szTarget
    szTarget[nT] = '\0';
}

int main(int nNumberofArgs, char* pszArgs[])
{
    // Prompt user
    cout << "This program accepts two strings\n"
         << "from the keyboard and outputs them\n"
         << "concatenated together.\n" << endl;

    // input two strings
    cout << "Enter first string: ";
    char szString1[256];
    cin.getline(szString1, 256);

    cout << "Enter the second string: ";
    char szString2[256];
    cin.getline(szString2, 256);

    // now concatenate one onto the end of the other
    cout << "Concatenate first string onto the second"
         << endl;
    concatenateString(szString1, szString2);

    // and display the result
    cout << "Result: <"
         << szString1
         << ">" << endl;

    // wait until user is ready before terminating program
    // to allow the user to see the program results
    system("PAUSE");
    return 0;
}
```

The concatenateString() function accepts two strings, szTarget and szSource. Its goal is to tack szSource onto the end of szTarget.

The function assumes that the szTarget array is large enough to hold both strings tacked together. It has no way of checking to make sure that there is enough room. More on that a little later in this chapter

Notice that the target argument is passed first and the source second. This may seem backwards, but it really doesn't matter — either argument can be the source or the target. It's just a C++ convention that the target goes first.

In the first `for` loop, the function iterates through `szTarget` by incrementing the index `nT` until `szTarget[nT] == '\0'`, that is, until `nT` points to the terminating `null` character. This corresponds to the situation at the top of Figure 16-1.

The function then enters a second loop in which it copies each character from `szSource` into `szTarget` starting at `nT` and moving forward. This corresponds to the bottom of Figure 16-1.

This example shows a situation when using the comma operator in a `for` loop is justified.

Since the `for` loop terminates before it copies the terminating `null` from `szSource`, the function must add the terminating `null` onto the result before returning.

The `main()` program prompts the user to enter two strings, each terminated with a newline. The program then concatenates the two strings by calling the new `concatenateString()` function and displays the results.

The expression `cin >> string;` stops inputting at the first white space. The `getline()` function used in the example program reads input from the keyboard just like `cin >> string;`, but it reads an entire line up to the newline at the end. It does not include the newline in the character string that it returns. Don't worry about the strange syntax of the call to `getline()` — I cover that in Chapter 23.

The results of a sample run of the program appear as follows:

```
This program accepts two strings
from the keyboard and outputs them
concatenated together.

Enter first string: String 1
Enter the second string: STRING 2
Concatenate first string onto the second
Result: <String 1STRING 2>
Press any key to continue . . .
```

Note that the second argument to `concatenateString()` is actually declared to be a `const char[]` (pronounced "array of constant characters"). That's because the function does not modify the source string. Declaring it to be an array of constant characters allows you to call the function passing it a constant string as in the following call:

```
concatenateString(szString, "The End");
```

Foiling hackers

How does the `concatenateString()` function in the earlier example program know whether there is enough room in `szTarget` to hold both the source and target strings concatenated together? The answer is that it doesn't.

This is a serious bug. If a user entered enough characters before pressing Enter, he could overwrite large sections of data or even code. In fact, this type of fixed buffer overwrite bug is one of the ways that hackers gain control of PCs through a browser to plant virus code.

In the following corrected version, `concatenateString()` accepts an additional argument: the size of the `szTarget` array. The function checks the index nT against this number to make sure that it does not write beyond the end of the target array.

The program appears as ConcatenateNString on the enclosed CD-ROM:

```
// concatenateString - concatenate one string onto the
//                      end of another (don't write beyond
//                      nTargetSize)
void concatenateString(char szTarget[],
                       int  nTargetSize,
                 const char szSource[])
{
    // first find the end of the target string
    int nT;
    for(nT = 0; szTarget[nT] != '\0'; nT++)
    {
    }

    // now copy the contents of the source string into
    // the target string, beginning at 'nT' but don't
    // write beyond the nTargetSize'th element (- 1 to
    // leave room for the terminating null)
    for(int nS = 0;
            nT < (nTargetSize - 1) && szSource[nS] != '\0';
            nT++, nS++)
    {
        szTarget[nT] = szSource[nS];
    }

    // add the terminator to szTarget
    szTarget[nT] = '\0';
}
```

The first part of the function starts out exactly the same, incrementing through `szTarget` looking for the terminating `null`. The difference is in the second loop. This `for` loop includes two terminating conditions. Control exits the loop if either of the following is true:

✔ szSource[nS] is the null character, meaning that you've gotten to the final character in szSource.

✔ nT is greater than or equal to nTargetSize - 1 meaning that you've exhausted the space available in szTarget (- 1 because you have to leave room for the terminating null at the end).

This extra check is irritating but necessary to avoid overrunning the array and producing a program that can crash in strange and mysterious ways.

Do I Really Have to Do All That Work?

C++ doesn't provide much help with manipulating strings in the language itself. Fortunately, the standard library includes a number of functions for manipulating these strings that save you the trouble of writing them yourself. Table 16-1 shows the most common of these functions.

Table 16-1   Common ASCIIZ String Manipulation Functions

Function	Description
isalpha(char c)	Returns a true if the character is alphabetic ('A' through 'Z' or 'a' through 'z').
isdigit(char c)	Returns a true if the character is a digit ('0' through '9').
isupper(char c)	Returns a true if the character is an upper-case alphabetic.
islower(char c)	Returns a true if the character is a lower-case alphabetic.
isprint(char c)	Returns a true if the character is printable.
isspace(char c)	Returns a true if the character is a form of white space (space, tab, newline, and so on).
strlen(char s[])	Returns the number of characters in a string (not including the terminating null).
strcmp(char s1[], char s2[])	Compares two strings. Returns 0 if the strings are identical. Returns a 1 if the first string occurs later in the dictionary than the second. Returns a –1 otherwise.
strncpy(char target[], char source[], int size)	Copies the source string into the target string but not more than 'size' characters.

Function	Description
`strncat(char target[], char source[], int size)`	Concatenates the source string onto the end of the target string for a total of not more than 'size' characters.
`tolower(char c)`	Returns the lowercase version of the character passed to it. Returns the current character if it is already lowercase or has no uppercase equivalent (such as a digit).
`toupper(char c)`	Returns the uppercase version of the character passed to it.

The following example program uses the `toupper()` function to convert a string entered by the user into all caps:

```
//
//   ToUpper - convert a string input by the user to all
//             upper case.
//
#include <cstdio>
#include <cstdlib>
#include <iostream>
using namespace std;


// toUpper - convert every character in an ASCIIZ string
//           to uppercase
void toUpper(char szTarget[], int  nTargetSize)
{
    for(int nT = 0;
            nT < (nTargetSize - 1) && szTarget[nT] != '\0';
            nT++)
    {
        szTarget[nT] = toupper(szTarget[nT]);
    }
}

int main(int nNumberofArgs, char* pszArgs[])
{
    // Prompt user
    cout << "This program accepts a string\n"
         << "from the keyboard and echoes the\n"
         << "string in all caps.\n" << endl;

    // input two strings
    cout << "Enter string: ";
    char szString[256];
    cin.getline(szString, 256);
```

```
        // now convert the string to all uppercase
        toUpper(szString, 256);

        // and display the result
        cout << "All caps version: <"
             << szString
             << ">" << endl;

        // wait until user is ready before terminating program
        // to allow the user to see the program results
        system("PAUSE");
        return 0;
    }
```

The `toUpper()` function follows a pattern that will quickly become old hat for you: It loops through each element in the ASCIIZ string using a `for` loop. The loop terminates if either the size of the string is exhausted or the program reaches the terminating `null` character.

The function passes each character in the string to the standard C++ library `toupper()` function. It stores the character returned by the function back into the character array.

It is not necessary to first test to make sure that the character is lowercase using `islower()` — both the `tolower()` and the `toupper()` functions return the character passed to them if the character has no lower- or uppercase equivalent.

The `main()` function simply prompts the user to enter a string. The program reads the input string by calling `getline()`. It then converts whatever it reads to uppercase by calling `toUpper()` and then displays the results.

The following shows the results of a sample run:

```
This program accepts a string
from the keyboard and echoes the
string in all caps.

Enter string: This is a string 123!@#.
All caps version: <THIS IS A STRING 123!@#.>
Press any key to continue . . .
```

Notice that the input string includes uppercase characters, lowercase characters, digits, and symbols. The lowercase characters are converted to uppercase in the output string, but the uppercase characters, digits, and symbols are unchanged.

In this chapter, you've seen how to handle ASCIIZ strings as a special case of character arrays. In practice, many of the standard functions rely on something known as a *pointer*. In the next two chapters, you'll see how pointers work. I will then return to these same example functions and implement them using pointers to demonstrate the elegance of the pointer solution.

Chapter 17

Pointing the Way to C++ Pointers

*T*his chapter introduces the powerful concept of *pointers.* By that I don't mean specially trained dogs that point at birds but rather variables that point at other variables in memory. I start with an explanation of computer addressing before getting into the details of declaring and using pointer variables. This chapter wraps up with a discussion of something known as the heap and how we can use it to solve a problem that I slyly introduced in the last chapter.

But don't think the fun is over when this chapter ends. The next chapter takes the concept of pointers one step further. In fact, in one way or another, pointers will reappear in almost every remaining chapter of this book.

It may take you a while before you get comfortable with the concept of pointer variables. Don't get discouraged. You may have to read through this chapter and the next a few times before you grasp all of the subtleties.

What's a Pointer?

A *pointer* is a variable that contains the address of another variable in the computer's internal memory. Before you can get a handle on that statement, you need to understand how computers address memory.

The details of computer addressing on the Intel processor in your PC or Macintosh are quite complicated and much more involved than you need to worry about in this book. I will use a very simple memory model in these discussions.

Every piece of random access memory (RAM) has its own, unique address. For most computers, including Macintoshes and PCs, the smallest address-able piece of memory is a byte.

A byte is 8 bits and corresponds to a variable of type `char`.

An address in memory is exactly like an address of a house, or would be if the following conditions were true:

✔ Every house is numbered in order.

✔ There are no skipped or duplicated numbers.

✔ The entire city consists of one long street.

So, for example, the address of a particular byte of memory might be 0x1000. The next byte after that would have an address of 0x1001. The byte before would be at 0x0FFF.

I don't know why, but, by convention, memory addresses are always expressed in hexadecimal. Maybe it's so that non-programmers will think that computer addressing is really complicated.

Declaring a Pointer

A `char` variable is designed to hold an ASCII character, an `int` an integer number, and a `double` a floating point number. Similarly, a pointer variable is designed to hold a memory address. You declare a pointer variable by adding an asterisk (*) to the end of the type of the object that the pointer points at, as in the following example:

```
char* pChar;    // pointer to a character
int*  pInt;     // pointer to an int
```

A pointer variable that has not otherwise been initialized contains an unknown value. You can initialize a pointer variable with the address of a variable of the same type using the ampersand (&) operator:

```
char cSomeChar = 'a';
char* pChar;
pChar = &cSomeChar;
```

In this snippet, the variable `cSomeChar` has some address. For argument's sake, let's say that C++ assigned it the address 0x1000. (C++ also initialized that location with the character `'a'`.) The variable `pChar` also has a location of its own, perhaps 0x1004. The value of the expression &cSomeChar is 0x1000, and its type is char* (read "pointer to char"). So the assignment on the third line of the snippet example stores the value 0x1000 in the variable pChar. This is shown graphically in Figure 17-1.

Figure 17-1:
The layout
of cSome
Char and
pChar in
memory
after their
declaration
and initial-
ization, as
described in
the text.

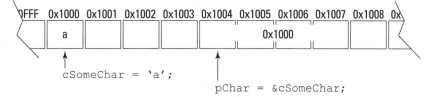

Take a minute to really understand the relationship between the figure and the three lines of C++ code in the snippet. The first declaration says, "go out and find a 1-byte location in memory, assign it the name cSomeChar, and initialize it to 'a'." In this example, C++ picked the location 0x1000.

The next line says, "go out and find a location large enough to hold the address of a char variable and assign it the name pChar." In this example, C++ assigned pChar to the location 0x1004.

In Code::Blocks, all addresses are 4 bytes in length irrespective of the size of the object being pointed at — a pointer to a char is the same size as a pointer to a double. The real world is similar — the address of a house looks the same no matter how large the house is.

The third line says, "assign the address of cSomeChar (0x1000) to the variable pChar." Figure 17-1 represents the state of the program after these three statements.

"So what?" you say. Here comes the really cool part demonstrated in the following expression:

```
*pChar = 'b';
```

This line says, "store a 'b' at the char location pointed at by pChar." This is demonstrated in Figure 17-2. To execute this expression, C++ first retrieves the value stored in pChar (that would be 0x1000). It then stores the character 'b' at that location.

Figure 17-2:
The steps
involved in
executing
*pChar
= 'b'.

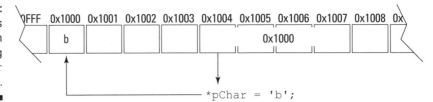

$$*pChar = 'b';$$

The * when used as a binary operator means "multiply"; when used as a unary operator, * means "find the thing pointed at by." Similarly & has a meaning as a binary operator (though I didn't discuss it), but as a unary operator, it means "take the address of."

So what's so exciting about that? After all, I could achieve the same effect by simply assigning a 'b' to cSomeChar directly:

```
cSomeChar = 'b';
```

Why go through the intermediate step of retrieving its address in memory? Because there are several problems that can be solved only with pointers. I discuss two common ones in this chapter. I'll describe a number of problems that are most easily solved with pointers in subsequent chapters.

Passing Arguments to a Function

There are two ways to pass arguments to a function: either by value or by reference. Now, consider both in turn.

Passing arguments by value

In Chapter 11, I write that arguments are passed to functions by value, meaning that it is the value of the variable that gets passed to the function and not the variable itself.

The implications of this become clear in the following snippet (taken from the PassByReference example program on the enclosed CD-ROM):

```cpp
void fn(int nArg1, int nArg2)
{
    // modify the value of the arguments
    nArg1 = 10;
    nArg2 = 20;
}

int main(int nNumberofArgs, char* pszArgs[])
{
    // initialize two variables and display their values
    int nValue1 = 1;
    int nValue2 = 2;

    // now try to modify them by calling a function
    fn(nValue1, nValue2);

    // what is the value of nValue1 and nValue2 now?
    cout << "nValue1 = " << nValue1 << endl;
    cout << "nValue2 = " << nValue2 << endl;

    return 0;
}
```

This program declares two variables, nValue1 and nValue2, initializes them to some known value, and then passes their value to a function fn(). This function changes the value of its arguments and simply returns.

> **Question:** What is the value of nValue1 and nValue2 in main() after the control returns from fn()?

> **Answer:** The value of nValue1 and nValue2 remain unchanged at 1 and 2, respectively.

To understand why, examine carefully how C++ handles memory in the call to fn(). C++ stores local variables (like nValue1 and nValue2) in a special area of memory known as the *stack*. Upon entry into the function, C++ figures out how much stack memory the function will require and then reserves that amount. Say, for argument's sake, that in this example, the stack memory carved out for main() starts at location 0x1000 and extends to 0x101F. In this case, nValue1 might be at location 0x1000 and nValue2 at location 0x1004.

An int takes up 4 bytes in Code::Blocks. See Chapter 14 for details.

As part of making the call to fn(), C++ first stores the values of each argument on the stack starting at the rightmost argument and working its way to the left.

The last thing that C++ stores as part of making the call is the return address so that the function knows where to return to after it is complete.

For reasons that have more to do with the internal workings of the CPU, the stack "grows downward," meaning that the memory used by fn() will have addresses smaller than 0x1000. Figure 17-3 shows the state of memory at the point that the computer processor reaches the first statement in fn(). C++ stored the second argument to the function at location 0x0FF4 and the first argument at 0x0FF0.

Remember that this is just a possible layout of memory. I don't know (or care) that any of these are in fact the actual addresses used by C++ in this or any other function call.

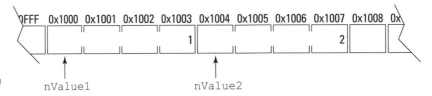

nValue1   nValue2

Figure 17-3: A possible layout of memory immediately after entering the function fn(int, int).

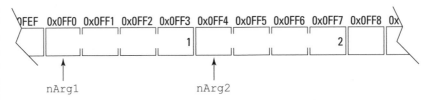

nArg1   nArg2

Layout in memory immediately after making the call:
fn(nValue1, nValue2)

The function fn(int, int) contains two statements:

```
nArg1 = 10;
nArg2 = 20;
```

Figure 17-4 shows the contents of memory immediately after these two state-ments are executed. Pretty simple, really — the value of nArg1 has changed to 10 and nArg2 to 20 just as you would expect. The main point of this dem-onstration, however, is the fact that changing the value of nArg1 and nArg2 has no effect on the original variables back at nValue1 and nValue2.

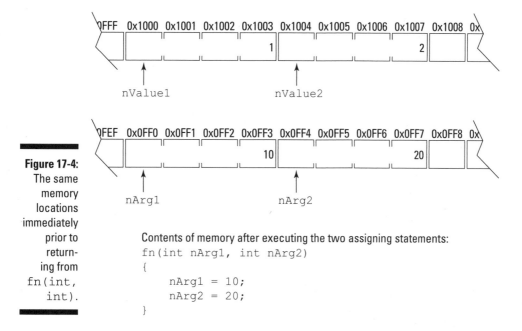

Figure 17-4: The same memory locations immediately prior to return-ing from fn(int, int).

Contents of memory after executing the two assigning statements:
```
fn(int nArg1, int nArg2)
{
        nArg1 = 10;
        nArg2 = 20;
}
```

Passing arguments by reference

So what if I wanted the changes made by fn() to be permanent? I could do this by passing not the value of the variables but their address. This is dem-onstrated by the following snippet (also taken from the PassByReference example program):

```
// fn(int*, int*) - this function takes its arguments
//                     by reference
void fn(int* pnArg1, int* pnArg2)
{
    // modify the value of the arguments
    *pnArg1 = 10;
    *pnArg2 = 20;
}
```

```
int main(int nNumberofArgs, char* pszArgs[])
{
    // initialize two variables and display their values
    int nValue1 = 1;
    int nValue2 = 2;

    fn(&nValue1, &nValue2);

    return 0;
}
```

Notice first that the arguments to fn() are now declared not to be integers but pointers to integers. The call to fn(int*, int*) passes not the value of the variables nValue1 and nValue2 but their address.

In this example, the value of the expression &nValue1 is 0x1000, and the type is int* (which is pronounced "pointer to int").

The state of memory upon entry into this function is shown in Figure 17-5.

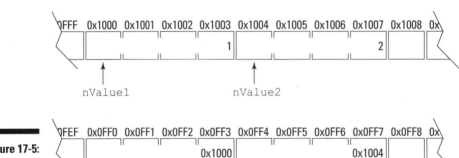

Figure 17-5: The content of memory after the call to fn (int*, int*).

Layout in memory immediately after making the call:
fn(&nValue1, &nValue2)

The function fn(int*, int*) now stores its values at the locations pointed at by its arguments:

```
*pnArg1 = 10;
*pnArg2 = 20;
```

This first statement says "store the value 10 at the int location passed to me in the argument pnArg1." This stores a 10 at location 0x1000, which happens to be the variable nValue1. This is demonstrated graphically in Figure 17-6.

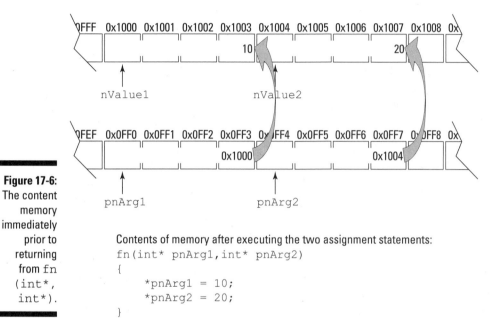

Figure 17-6: The content memory immediately prior to returning from fn (int*, int*).

Contents of memory after executing the two assignment statements:

```
fn(int* pnArg1,int* pnArg2)
{
     *pnArg1 = 10;
     *pnArg2 = 20;
}
```

Putting it together

The complete PassByReference program appears as follows:

```
//
//   PassByReference - demonstrate passing arguments to a
//                     function both by value and by
//                     reference.
//
#include <cstdio>
#include <cstdlib>
#include <iostream>
using namespace std;

// fn(int, int) - demonstrate a function that takes two
//                arguments and modifies their value
void fn(int nArg1, int nArg2)
{
```

```
        // modify the value of the arguments
    nArg1 = 10;
    nArg2 = 20;
}

// fn(int*, int*) - this function takes its arguments
//                  by reference
void fn(int* pnArg1, int* pnArg2)
{
    // modify the value of the arguments
    *pnArg1 = 10;
    *pnArg2 = 20;
}

int main(int nNumberofArgs, char* pszArgs[])
{
    // initialize two variables and display their values
    int nValue1 = 1;
    int nValue2 = 2;
    cout << "The value of nArg1 is " << nValue1 << endl;
    cout << "The value of nArg2 is " << nValue2 << endl;

    // now try to modify them by calling a function
    cout << "Calling fn(int, int)" << endl;
    fn(nValue1, nValue2);
    cout << "Returned from fn(int, int)" << endl;
    cout << "The value of nArg1 is " << nValue1 << endl;
    cout << "The value of nArg2 is " << nValue2 << endl;

    // try again by calling a function that takes
    // addresses as arguments
    cout << "Calling fn(int*, int*)" << endl;
    fn(&nValue1, &nValue2);
    cout << "Returned from fn(int*, int*)" << endl;
    cout << "The value of nArg1 is " << nValue1 << endl;
    cout << "The value of nArg2 is " << nValue2 << endl;

    // wait until user is ready before terminating program
    // to allow the user to see the program results
    system("PAUSE");
    return 0;
}
```

The following is the output from this program:

```
The value of nArg1 is 1
The value of nArg2 is 2
Calling fn(int, int)
Returned from fn(int, int)
The value of nArg1 is 1
```

```
The value of nArg2 is 2
Calling fn(int*, int*)
Returned from fn(int*, int*)
The value of nArg1 is 10
The value of nArg2 is 20
Press any key to continue . . .
```

This program declares the variables nValue1 and nValue2 and initializes them to 1 and 2, respectively. The program then displays their value just to make sure. Next, the program calls the fn(int, int), passing the value of the two variables. That function modifies the value of its arguments, but this has no effect on nValue1 and nValue2 as demonstrated by the fact that their value is unchanged after control returns to main().

The second call passes not the value of nValue1 and nValue2 but their address to the function fn(int*, int*). This time, the changes to pnArg1 and pnArg2 are retained even after control returns to main().

Notice that there is no confusion between the overloaded functions fn(int, int) and fn(int*, int*). The types of the arguments are easily distinguished.

Playing with Heaps of Memory

One of the problems addressed in Chapter 16 was that of fixed-size arrays. For example, the concatenate() function concatenated two ASCIIZ strings into a single string. However, the function had to be careful not to overrun the target array in the event that there wasn't enough room to hold the combined string. This problem would have gone away if concatenate() could have allocated a new array that was guaranteed to be large enough to hold the concatenated string.

That's a great idea, but how big should I make this target array — 256 bytes, 512 bytes? There's no right answer since there's no way to know at compile time how big to make the target array so that it has enough room to hold all possible concatenated strings. You can't know for sure until runtime how much memory you will need.

Do you really need a new keyword?

C++ provides an extra area in memory just for this purpose, known by the somewhat cryptic name of the *heap*. A programmer can allocate any amount of memory off of the heap using the keyword new, as in the following example snippet:

```
char* pArray = new char[256];
```

This example carves a block of memory large enough to hold 256 characters off of the heap. The new keyword returns a pointer to the newly created array. Unlike other variables, heap memory is not allocated until runtime, which means the array size is not limited to constants that are determined at compile time — they can also be variables that are computed at runtime.

It may seem odd that the argument to new is an array while what is returned is a pointer. I will have a lot more to say about the relationship between pointers and arrays in the next chapter.

Thus, I could have said something like the following:

```
int nSizeOfArray = someFunction();
char* pArray = new char[nSizeOfArray];
```

Here the size of the array is computed by someFunction(). Obviously this computation can't occur until the program is actually executing. Whatever value someFunction() returns is used as the size of the array to be allocated in the next statement.

A more practical example is the following code snippet that makes a copy of an ASCIIZ string (assuming you consider copying a string as practical):

```
int nLength = strlen(pszString) + 1;
char* pszCopy = new char[nLength];
strncpy(pszCopy, nLength, pszString);
```

The first statement calls the string function strlen(), which returns the length of the string passed it not including the terminating NULL character. The + 1 adds room for the terminating NULL. The next statement allocates room for the copy off of the heap. Finally, the third string uses the string function strncpy() to copy the contents of pszString into pszCopy. By calculating how big an array you need to store the copy, you are guaranteed that pszCopy is large enough to hold the entire string.

Don't forget to clean up after yourself

Allocating memory off of the heap is a neat feature, but it has one very big danger in C++: If you allocate memory off of the heap, you must remember to return it.

You return memory to the heap using the delete keyword as in the following:

```
char* pArray = new char[256];

// ...use the memory all you want...

// now return the memory block to the heap
delete[] pArray;
pArray = NULL;
```

The `delete[]` keyword accepts a pointer that has been passed to you from the new keyword and restores that memory to the heap.

Use `delete[]` to return an array. Use `delete` (without the open and closed brackets) when returning a single object to the heap.

If you don't return heap memory when you are done with it, your program will slowly consume memory and eventually slow down more and more as the operating system tries to fulfill its apparently insatiable gluttony. Eventually, the program will come to a halt when the O/S can no longer satisfy its requests for memory.

Returning the same memory to the heap twice is not quite as bad. That causes the program to crash almost immediately. It is considered good programming practice to zero out a pointer once you have deleted the memory block that it points to for two very good reasons:

- **Deleting a pointer that contains a NULL has no effect.**
- **NULL is never a valid address.** Trying to access memory at the NULL location will always cause your program to crash immediately, which will tip you off that there is a problem and make it a lot easier to find.

You don't have to delete memory if your program will exit soon — all heap memory is restored to the operating system when a program terminates. However, returning memory that you allocate off the heap is a good habit to get into.

Looking at an example

The following ConcatenateHeap program is a version of the `concatenate()` function that allocates its memory off of the heap:

```
//
//  ConcatenateHeap - similar to ConcatenateString except
//                    this version stores the concatenated
//                    string in memory allocated from the
//                    heap so that we are guaranteed
//                    that the target array is always
//                    large enough
//
```

```cpp
#include <cstdio>
#include <cstdlib>
#include <iostream>
#include <cstring>
using namespace std;


// concatenateString - concatenate two strings together
//                      into an array allocated off of the
//                      heap
char* concatenateString(const char szSrc1[],
                        const char szSrc2[])
{
    // allocate an array of sufficient length
    int nTargetSize = strlen(szSrc1) + strlen(szSrc2) + 1;
    char* pszTarget = new char[nTargetSize];

    // first copy the first string into the target
    int nT;
    for(nT = 0; szSrc1[nT] != '\0'; nT++)
    {
        pszTarget[nT] = szSrc1[nT];
    }

    // now copy the contents of the second string onto
    // the end of the first
    for(int nS = 0; szSrc2[nS] != '\0'; nT++, nS++)
    {
        pszTarget[nT] = szSrc2[nS];
    }

    // add the terminator to szTarget
    pszTarget[nT] = '\0';

    // return the results to the caller
    return pszTarget;
}

int main(int nNumberofArgs, char* pszArgs[])
{
    // Prompt user
    cout << "This program accepts two strings\n"
         << "from the keyboard and outputs them\n"
         << "concatenated together.\n" << endl;

    // input two strings
    cout << "Enter first string: ";
    char szString1[256];
    cin.getline(szString1, 256);

    cout << "Enter the second string: ";
    char szString2[256];
    cin.getline(szString2, 256);
```

```
        // now concatenate one onto the end of the other
        cout << "Concatentate second string onto the first"
             << endl;
        char* pszT = concatenateString(szString1, szString2);

        // and display the result
        cout << "Result: <"
             << pszT
             << ">" << endl;

        // return the memory to the heap
        delete[] pszT;
        pszT = NULL;

        // wait until user is ready before terminating program
        // to allow the user to see the program results
        system("PAUSE");
        return 0;
}
```

This program includes the #include file cstring to gain access to the strlen() function. The concatenateString() function is similar to the earlier versions, except that it returns the address of a block of heap memory containing the concatenated string rather than modify either of the strings passed to it.

Declaring the arguments as const means that the function promises not to modify them. This allows the function to be called with a const string as in the following snippet:

```
char* pFullName = concatenateString("Mr. ", pszName);
```

The string "Mr. " is a const character array in the same sense that 1 is a const integer.

The first statement within concatenateString() calculates the size of the target array by calling strlen() on both source strings and adding 1 for the terminating null.

The next statement allocates an array of that size off of the heap using the new keyword.

The two for loops work exactly like those in the earlier concatenate examples by copying first szSrc1 into the pszTarget array and then szSrc2 before tacking on the final terminating null.

The function then returns the address of the pszTarget array to the caller.

The main() function works the same as in the earlier Concatenate program by prompting the user for two strings and then displaying the concatenated result. The only difference is that this version returns the pointer returned by concatenateString() to the heap before terminating by executing the following snippet:

```
delete pszT;
pszT = NULL;
```

The output from running this program is indistinguishable from its earlier cousins:

```
This program accepts two strings
from the keyboard and outputs them
concatenated together.

Enter first string: this is a string
Enter the second string: THIS IS ALSO A STRING
Concatentate second string onto the first
Result: <this is a stringTHIS IS ALSO A STRING>
Press any key to continue . . .
```

The subject of C++ pointers is too vast to be handled in a single chapter. The next chapter examines the relationship between arrays and pointers, a topic I glossed over in the final example programs in this chapter.

Chapter 18

Taking a Second Look at C++ Pointers

In This Chapter

▶ Defining operations on a pointer

▶ Comparing pointer addition with indexing an array

▶ Extending arithmetic to different types of pointers

▶ Sorting out constant pointers from pointers to constants

▶ Reading the arguments to a program

Chapter 17 introduced the concept of a pointer variable as a variable designed to contain the address of another variable. I even went so far as to suggest a couple of uses for pointer variables. However, you've only begun to see the myriad ways that pointer variables can be used to do some pretty cool stuff and really confuse you at times as well.

This chapter examines carefully the relationship between pointers and arrays, a topic that I brushed over in the last chapter.

Pointers and Arrays

Some of the same operators applicable to integers are applicable to pointer types. This section examines the implications of this to both pointers and the array types studied so far.

Operations on pointers

Table 18-1 lists the three fundamental operations that are defined on pointers.

Table 18-1	Three Operations Defined on Pointer Type Variables	
Operation	*Result*	*Meaning*
`pointer + offset`	pointer	Calculate the address of the object offset entries from the pointer
`pointer++`	pointer	Move the pointer over one entry
`pointer2 - pointer1`	offset	Calculate the number of entries between pointer2 and ponter1

Although not listed in Table 18-1, operations that are related to addition, such as `pointer += offset`, are also defined. Subtraction is defined as well, since it is merely a variation on addition.

The simple memory model used to explain pointers in Chapter 17 will work here to explain how these operations work. Consider an array of 32 one-byte characters called `cArray`. If the first byte of this array is stored at address 0x1000, then the last location will be at 0x101F. While `cArray[0]` will be at 0x1000, `cArray[1]` will be at 0x1001, `cArray[2]` at 0x1002, and so forth.

Now assume a pointer `pArray` is located at location 0x1100. After executing the expression

```
pArray = &cArray[0];
```

the pointer `pArray` will contain the value 0x1000 (see Figure 18-1). By the way, you read this as "`pArray` gets the address of `cArray` sub 0."

Adding a value n to `pArray` generates the address of `cArray[n]`. For example, consider the case where n equals 2. In that case, `pArray + 2` generates the address 0x1002, which is the address of `cArray[2]`. This correspondence is demonstrated in Table 18-2. Figure 18-2 shows this graphically.

Table 18-2	The Correspondence between Pointer Offsets and Array Elements	
Offset	*Result*	*Corresponds to...*
+ 0	0x1000	`cArray[0]`
+ 1	0x1001	`cArray[1]`
+ 2	0x1002	`cArray[2]`
...	...	. . .
+ n	0x1000 + n	`cArray[n]`

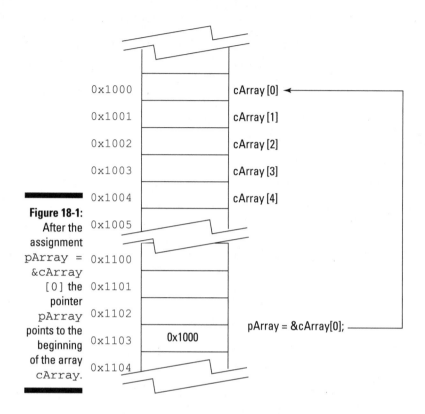

Figure 18-1:
After the assignment
pArray = &cArray [0] the pointer pArray points to the beginning of the array cArray.

Pointer addition versus indexing into an array

The claim

```
pArray = &cArray[0];
*(pArray + 2) = 'c';
```

is the same as

```
cArray[2] = 'c';
```

Before you can respond to this claim, I need to explain how to read the first code snippet. Take it one step at a time. You already know to read the first expression: pArray = &cArray[0] means "pArray gets the address of cArray sub 0."

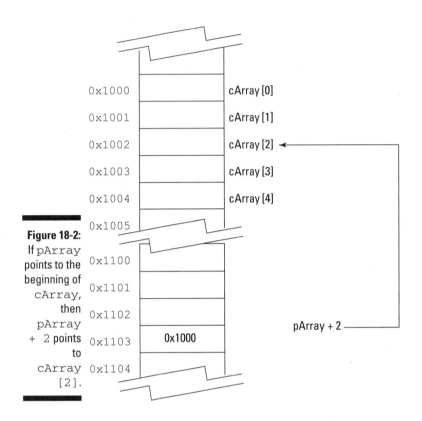

0x1000   cArray [0]

0x1001   cArray [1]

0x1002   cArray [2]

0x1003   cArray [3]

0x1004   cArray [4]

Figure 18-2:
If `pArray` points to the beginning of `cArray`, then `pArray + 2` points to `cArray [2]`.

To interpret the second expression, remember that `pArray + 2` generates the value 0x1002, and it is of type `char*`. `*(pArray + 2)` on the left-hand side of an assignment operator says, "store a `'c'` in the `char` pointed at by `pArray + 2`." This is demonstrated graphically in Figure 18-3.

The parentheses around `*(pArray + 2)` are necessary because unary `*` has higher precedence than addition. The expression `*pArray + 2` retrieves the character pointed at by `pArray` and adds 2 to it. Adding the parentheses forces the addition to occur first and the unary operator to be applied to the result.

In fact (here comes the kicker), the correspondence between the two forms of expression is so strong that C++ considers `cArray[n]` nothing more than a shorthand for `*(pArray + n)` where `pArray` points to the first element in `cArray`:

```
cArray[n] is interpreted as *(&cArray[0] + n)
```

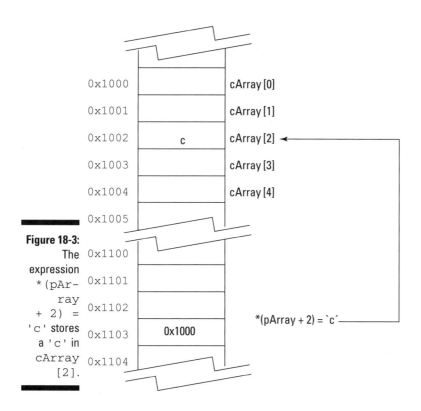

0x1000		cArray [0]
0x1001		cArray [1]
0x1002	c	cArray [2]
0x1003		cArray [3]
0x1004		cArray [4]
0x1005		
0x1100		
0x1101		
0x1102		
0x1103	0x1000	*(pArray + 2) = `c´
0x1104		

Figure 18-3: The expression `*(pArray + 2) = 'c'` stores a `'c'` in `cArray[2]`.

To complete this association, C++ takes another shortcut by making the second, following interpretation:

```
cArray is interpreted as &cArray[0]
```

That is, an array name when it appears without a subscript is interpreted as the address of the first element of the array; thus the following:

```
cArray[n] is interpreted as *(cArray + n)
```

In fact, the C++ compiler considers the expression on the left nothing more than some human shorthand for the expression on the right.

So, if I can treat the name of an array as though it were a pointer (which it is, by the way), can I use the index operator on pointer variables? Absolutely. Thus, the following is perfectly legal:

```
char cArray[256];
char* pArray = cArray;
pArray[2] = 'c';
```

That is how I was able to write expressions like the following in Chapter 17:

```
int nTargetSize = strlen(szSrc1) + strlen(szSrc2) + 1;
char* pszTarget = new char[nTargetSize];

// first copy the first string into the target
int nT;
for(nT = 0; szSrc1[nT] != '\0'; nT++)
{
    pszTarget[nT] = szSrc1[nT];
}
```

The variable `pszTarget` is declared as `char*` (read "pointer to a char") because that's what `new char[nTargetSize]` returns. The subsequent `for` loop assigns values to elements in this array using the expression `pszTarget[nT]`, which is the same as accessing `char` elements pointed at by `pszTarget + nT`.

By the way, the `psz` prefix is the naming convention for "pointer to an ASCIIZ string." An ASCIIZ string is a character array that ends with a terminating `null` character.

Using the pointer increment operator

The following is what you might call the pointer arithmetic version of the `concatenateString()` function from the ConcatenateHeap program from Chapter 17. This version is part of the program ConcatenatePtr on the enclosed CD-ROM.

In fact, you were dealing with pointer arithmetic in Chapter 17 as well, but the pointer arithmetic was written using array indexing.

C++ programmers love their pointers. The following explicit pointer version of `concatenateString()` is much more common than the array index version in Chapter 17.

```
// concatenateString - concatenate two strings together
//                     into an array allocated off of the
//                     heap
char* concatenateString(const char* pszSrc1,
                        const char* pszSrc2)
{
    // allocate an array of sufficient length
    int nTargetSize = strlen(pszSrc1)+strlen(pszSrc2)+1;
```

```
    char* pszTarget = new char[nTargetSize];

    // first copy the first string into the target
    char* pszT = pszTarget;
    for(; *pszSrc1 != '\0'; pszT++, pszSrc1++)
    {
        *pszT = *pszSrc1;
    }

    // now copy the contents of the second string onto
    // the end of the first
    for(; *pszSrc2 != '\0'; pszT++, pszSrc2++)
    {
        *pszT = *pszSrc2;
    }

    // add the terminator to szTarget
    *pszT = '\0';

    // return the unmodified address of the array
    // to the caller
    return pszTarget;
}
```

This version of `concatenateString()` starts out exactly like the earlier ConcatenateHeap version from Chapter 17. The difference between this version and its predecessor lies in the two `for` loops. The version in Chapter 17 left the pointer to the target array, `pszTarget`, unchanged and incremented an index into that array.

The version that appears here skips the intermediate step of incrementing an index and simply increments the pointer itself. First, it checks to make sure that `pszSrc1` doesn't already point to the `null` character that indicates the end of the source character string. If not, the assignment within the `for` loop

```
*pszT = *pszSrc1;
```

says retrieve the character pointed at by `pszSrc1` and store it into the location pointed at by `pszT`. This is demonstrated graphically in Figure 18-4.

The increment clause of the `for` loop

```
pszT++, pszSrc1++
```

increments both the source pointer, `pszSrc1`, and target pointer, `pszT`, to the next character in the source and destination arrays. This is demonstrated by Figure 18-5.

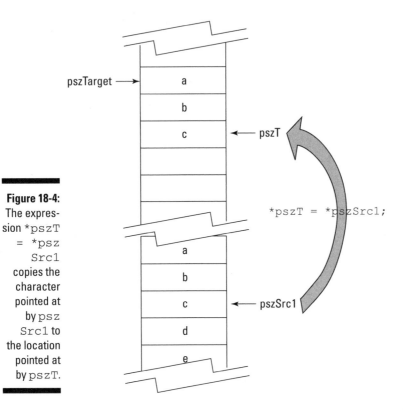

Figure 18-4:
The expression `*pszT = *pszSrc1` copies the character pointed at by `pszSrc1` to the location pointed at by `pszT`.

The remainder of the program is identical to its Chapter 17 predecessor, and the results from executing the program are identical as well:

```
This program accepts two strings
from the keyboard and outputs them
concatenated together.

Enter first string: this is a string
Enter the second string: SO IS THIS
Concatentate first string onto the second
Result: <this is a stringSO IS THIS>
Press any key to continue . . .
```

Why bother with array pointers?

The sometimes cryptic nature of pointer-based manipulation of character strings might lead the reader to wonder why. That is, what advantage does the `char*` pointer version of `concatenateString()` have over the easier-to-read index version?

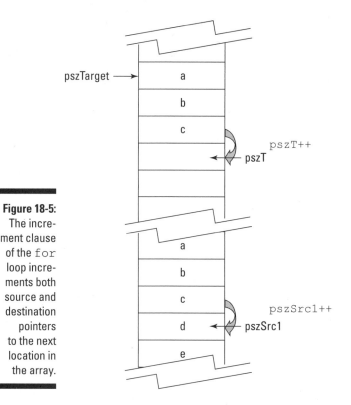

Figure 18-5:
The incre-
ment clause
of the `for`
loop incre-
ments both
source and
destination
pointers
to the next
location in
the array.

Note: "Easier-to-read" is a matter of taste. To a seasoned C++ programmer, the pointer version is just as easy to fathom as the index version.

The answer is partially historic and partially human nature. As compli-cated as it might appear to the human reader, a statement such as `*pszT = *pszSrc1` can be converted into an amazingly small number of machine instructions. Older computer processors were not very fast by today's stan-dards. When C, the progenitor of C++, was introduced to the world some 40 years ago, saving a few computer instructions was a big deal. Pointer arithmetic gave C a big advantage over other languages of the day, notably Fortran, which did not offer pointer arithmetic. This, more than any other single feature, did more to advance C and later C++ over its competitors.

In addition, programmers like to generate clever program statements to combat what can be a repetitively boring job. Once C++ programmers learn how to write compact and cryptic but efficient statements, there is no getting them back to scanning arrays with indices.

Don't fall into the trap of cramming as much as you can into a single C++ statement, thinking that a few C++ source statements will generate fewer machine instructions that will, therefore, execute faster. In the old days, when compilers were simpler, that may have worked, but today there is no obvious relationship between the number of C++ instructions and the number of machine instructions generated. For example, the expression

```
*pszT++ = '\0';
```

does not necessarily generate machine instructions that are any different from the following expression that is both easier to read and easier to debug:

```
*pszT = '\0';
pszT++;
```

Today's optimizing compilers generate minimal amounts of code.

Operations on Different Pointer Types

It's not too hard to convince yourself that `pszTarget + n` points to `pszTarget[n]` when each element in the array is 1 byte in length as is the case for `char` strings. After all, if `cArray` is located at 0x1000, then `cArray[5]` must be at 0x1005.

It is not so obvious that pointer addition works for arrays of objects other than 1-byte characters. Consider an array `nArray` of `int`s. Since an `int` occupies 4 bytes in Code::Blocks/gcc, if `nArray` is located at 0x1000, then `nArray[5]` will be located at 0x1000 + (5 * 4) or 0x1014.

Hexadecimal 0x14 is equal to 20 decimal.

Fortunately for us, in C++, `array + n` points to `array[n]` no matter how large a single element of array might be. C++ makes the necessary conversions to ensure that this relationship is true.

Constant Nags

Chapter 14 introduced the concept of `const` variables. For example, the following

```
const double PI = 3.14159;
```

declares a constant variable PI. Constant variables must be initialized when created and cannot be changed later just like numbers like 2 and 3.14159.

The concept of const-ness can be applied to pointers as well, but the question is, where does the const keyword go? Consider the following three declarations. Which of these are legal?

```
const char* pszArray1;
char const* pszArray2;
char* const pszArray3;
```

It turns out all three are legal, but one of them has a different meaning than the other two. The first two variables, pszArray1 and pszArray2, are both pointers to constant char arrays. This means that you can modify the pointers, but you cannot modify the characters that they point at. Thus, the following is legal:

```
pszArray1 = new char[128];    // this is OK
```

But the following is not:

```
(*pszArray1) = 'a';           // not legal
```

By comparison, pszArray3 is a constant pointer to a char array. In this case, you cannot change the pointer once it has been declared. Therefore, you must initialize it when declared since you won't get a chance later as in the following:

```
char* const pszArray3 = new char[128];
```

Once declared, the following is not legal:

```
pszArray3 = pszArray1;        // not legal - you
                              // can't change pszArray3
```

But you can change the characters that it points to, like this:

```
char* const pszArray3 = new char[128];
(*pszArray3) = 'a';           // legal
```

A single pointer can be both constant and point to constant characters:

```
const char* const pszMyName = "Stephen";
```

The value of this pointer cannot be changed nor can the characters that it points to.

As a beginning programmer, do you really need to worry about all these constant declarations? The answer is, "Sometimes." You will get a warning if you do the following:

```
char* pszMyName = "Stephen";
```

Because you could conceivably try to modify my name by putting *pszMyName (or the equivalent pszMyName[n]) on the left-hand side of an assignment operator. The proper declaration is

```
const char* pszMyName = "Stephen";
```

Differences Between Pointers and Arrays

With all the similarities, one might be tempted to turn the question around and ask, "What's the difference between a pointer and the address of an array?" There are basically two differences:

- ✔ An array allocates space for the objects; a pointer does not.
- ✔ A pointer allocates space for the address; an array does not.

Consider these two declarations:

```
int nArray[128];
int* pnPtr;
```

Both nArray and pnPtr are of type pointer to int, but nArray also allocates space for 128 int objects, whereas pnPtr does not. You can consider nArray to be a constant address in the same way that 3 is a constant int. You can no more put nArray on the left-hand side of an assignment than you can 3. The following is not allowed:

```
nArray = pnPtr;   // not allowed
```

Thus, pnPtr is of type int*, whereas nArray is actually of type int* const.

My main() Arguments

Now you've come far enough to learn the last secret of the program template that you've been using: What are the arguments to main()?

```
int main(int nNumberOfArgs, char* pszArgs[])
```

These point to the arguments of the program. The first argument is the number of arguments to the program, including the name of the program itself. The second argument is an array of pointers to character strings representing the arguments themselves. Arrays of pointers? What?

Arrays of pointers

If a pointer can point to an array, then it seems only fitting that the reverse should be true as well. Arrays of pointers are a type of array of particular interest.

The following declares an array of ten pointers to integers:

```
int* pInt[10];
```

Given this declaration, then pInt[0] is a pointer to an integer. The following snippet declares an array of three pointers to integers and assigns them values:

```
void fn()
{
    int n1, n2, n3;
    int* pInts[3] = {&n1, &n2, &n3};

    for(int n = 0; n < 3; n++)
    {
        // initialize the integers
        *pInts[n] = n * 10;
    }
}
```

After the declaration, pInts[0] points to the variable n1, pInts[1] points to n2, and pInts[2] points to n3. Thus, an expression like

```
*pInts[1] = 10;
```

sets the int pointed at by pInts[1] (that would be n2) to 10. The effect of the for loop in the prior snippet is to initialize n1, n2, and n3 to 0, 10, and 20, respectively. This is shown graphically in Figure 18-6.

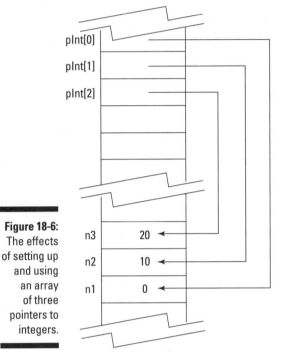

The effects of executing the following:

```
int n1, n2, n3;

int* pInt[3] = {&n1, &n2, &n3};
for(int n = 0; n < 3, n++)
{
    *pInt[n] = n * 10;
}
```

Figure 18-6:
The effects
of setting up
and using
an array
of three
pointers to
integers.

Arrays of arguments

Returning to the `main()` example, the arguments to the program are the strings that are passed to the program when it is executed. Thus, if I execute `MyProgram` as

```
MyProgram file1 file2 /w
```

the arguments to the program are `file1`, `file2`, and `/w`.

Although technically not an argument, C++ includes the name of the program as the first "argument."

Switches are not interpreted, so `/w` is passed to the program as an argument. However, the special symbols `<"`, `">` and `|` are interpreted by the command line interpreter and are not passed to the program.

The following simple PrintArgs program displays the arguments passed to it by the command line interpreter:

```
// PrintArgs - print the arguments to the program
#include <cstdio>
#include <cstdlib>
#include <iostream>
using namespace std;

int main(int nNumberofArgs, char* pszArgs[])
{
    for(int n = 0; n < nNumberofArgs; n++)
    {
        cout << "Argument " << n
             << " is <" << pszArgs[n]
             << ">" << endl;
    }

    // wait until user is ready before terminating program
    // to allow the user to see the program results
    system("PAUSE");
    return 0;
}
```

Now the trick is how to pass arguments to the program.

Passing arguments to your program through the command line

The easiest and most straightforward way is to simply type the arguments when executing the program from the command line prompt:

```
PrintArgs file1 file2 /w
```

Doing so generates the following output:

```
C:\Beginning_Programming-CPP\PrintArgs\bin\Debug>PrintArgs file1 file2 /w
Argument 0 is <printargs>
Argument 1 is <file1>
Argument 2 is <file2>
Argument 3 is </w>
Press any key to continue . . .
```

The difficulty to this approach is knowing where the executable is stored. Code::Blocks creates the executable program during the Build step in a subdirectory of the directory containing the project. Whether you used the default installation location shown in the preceding code or not, you can always find the project directory by selecting Project⇨Properties. The default Project Settings tab of the dialog box that pops up displays the path to the project file, as shown in Figure 18-7.

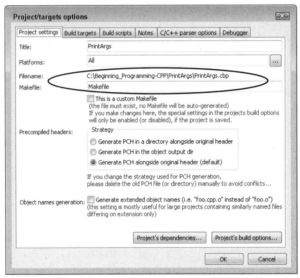

Figure 18-7:
The Code::
Blocks
Project
Settings
tab of the
Project/
Target
Options
dialog box
contains the
path to the
project file.

Select the Build Targets tab to find the path to the executable file, as shown in Figure 18-8.

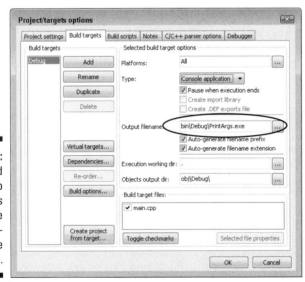

Figure 18-8:
The Build
Targets tab
indicates
the name
and loca-
tion of the
executable.

If you are using Windows, open an MS-DOS window by selecting Start➪ Programs➪Accessories➪Command Prompt (this is for Windows XP and Vista; the details differ slightly depending upon which version of Windows you are using). Navigate to the proper window using the CD command ("CD" stands for Change Directory).

Using the directory path provided in Figure 18-7, I would enter the following:

```
CD \Beginning_Programming-CPP\PrintArgs\bin\Debug
PrintArgs file1 file2 /w
```

The details for Linux and Macintosh will be slightly different but similar.

Passing arguments to your program from the Code::Blocks environment

You can pass arguments to your program from within Code::Blocks itself by selecting Project➪Set Projects' Arguments. This opens the dialog box shown in Figure 18-9. Enter the arguments into the Program Arguments entry field.

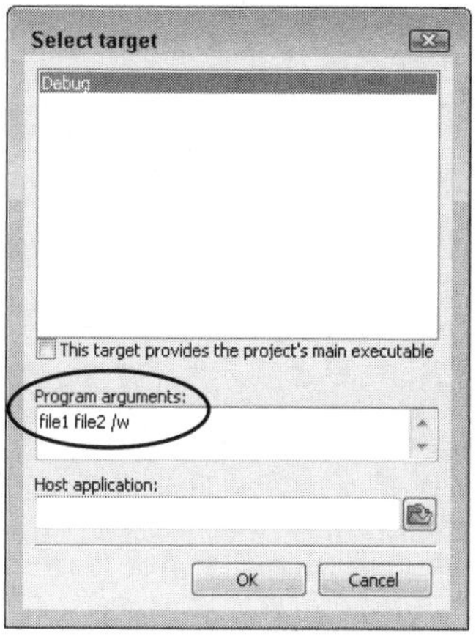

Figure 18-9:
You can set up the project to pass arguments to the program when executed from Code:: Blocks.

Executing the program from Code::Blocks opens a command line window with the following contents:

```
Argument 0 is <C:\Beginning_Programming-CPP\PrintArgs\bin\Debug\PrintArgs.exe>
Argument 1 is <file1>
Argument 2 is <file2>
Argument 3 is </w>
Press any key to continue . . .
```

This technique is a lot easier, but it works only from within the Code::Blocks environment. However, this is the only way to pass arguments to your program when using the Code::Blocks debugger. I talk about the debugger in Chapter 20.

Passing arguments to your program through Windows

In Windows, there is one final way of passing arguments to a program. Windows executes a program with no arguments if you double-click the name of the executable file. However, if you drag a set of files and drop them on the program's executable filename, Windows executes the program, passing it the name of the files as its arguments.

To demonstrate, I created a couple of dummy files in the same directory as the PrintArg.exe file called `file1.txt` and `file2.txt`, as shown in Figure 18-10.

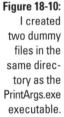

Figure 18-10: I created two dummy files in the same directory as the PrintArgs.exe executable.

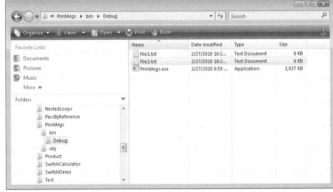

I then selected both files and dragged and dropped them onto the PrintArgs. exe filename. Figure 18-11 shows the result.

Windows does not pass the filenames to the program in any particular order. In particular, it does not necessarily pass them in the order that they appear in the directory list or the order that you selected them.

Figure 18-11:
Dropping
the two
filenames
on the
PrintArgs.
exe filename
instructs
Windows
to launch
the program
and pass the
name of the
files as argu-
ments to the
program.

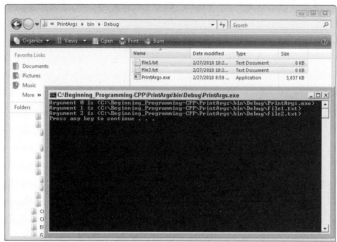

This chapter and its predecessor are not easy for a beginner. Don't despair if you are feeling a little uncertain right now. You may need to reread this section. Make sure that you understand the examples and the demonstration programs. You should find yourself growing more and more comfortable with the concept of pointer variables as you make your way through the remainder of the book.

Chapter 19

Programming with Class

. . . .

In This Chapter

▶ Grouping data using parallel arrays

▶ Grouping data in a class

▶ Declaring an object

▶ Creating arrays of objects

. . . .

*A*rrays are great at handling sequences of objects of the same type, such as ints or doubles. Arrays do not work well, however, when grouping different types of data such as when we try to combine a Social Security number with the name of a person into a single record. C++ provides a structure called the *class* (or *struct*) to handle this problem.

Grouping Data

Many of the programs in earlier chapters read a series of numbers, sometimes into an array, before processing. A simple array is great for standalone values. However, many times (if not most of the time), data comes in groups of information. For example, a program may ask the user for his first name, last name, and Social Security number. Alone, any one of these values is not sufficient — only in the aggregate do the values make any sense.

You can store associated data of different types in what are known as *parallel arrays*. For example, I might use an array of strings called pszFirstNames to hold people's first names, a second pszLastNames to hold the last names, and a third nSocialSecurities to hold the corresponding Social Security number. I would store the data such that any given index n points to the data for a given individual.

Thus, my personal data might be at offset 3. In that case, szFirstNames[3] would point to "Stephen," szLastNames[3] would point to "Davis," and nSocialSecurityNumbers[3] would contain . . . well, you get the idea. This is shown in Figure 19-1.

Figure 19-1:
Parallel
arrays are
sometimes
used to hold
collections
of related
but dissimi-
lar data in
languages
that don't
support
classes.

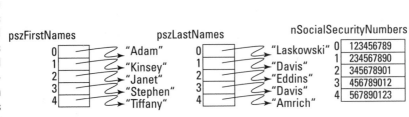

This method works, but it's prone to errors since there's nothing that directly associates the first name with the last name and the Social Security number other than an index. You could easily imagine that a missing instruction here or there, and I would become "Stephen Eddins" or any other random combination of first and last names.

Fortunately for us, C++ provides a better way.

The Class

A first name or a Social Security number doesn't make any sense except in the context of the person to whom they belong — data like that must have a context created by its association with other, related data. What we would like is to be able to create a structure, say `Person`, that contains all of the relevant properties that make up a person (in this case, first name, last name, and social security number).

C++ uses a structure known as the *class* that has the following format:

```
class Person
{
  public:
    char szFirstName[128];
    char szLastName[128];
    int  nSocialSecurityNumber;
};
```

A class definition starts with the keyword `class` followed by the name of the class and an open brace.

The naming rules for class names are the same as for variable names: The first letter must be one of the letters 'a' through 'z' or 'A' through 'Z' or underscore. Every subsequent character in the name must be one of these or the digits '0' through '9'. By convention, class names always start with an uppercase letter. Class names normally consist of multiple words jammed together, with each word starting with an uppercase letter.

The first keyword within the open brace in the early examples will always be `public`. I'll describe the alternatives to `public` in Chapter 24, but just accept it as part of the declaration for now.

You can also use the keyword `struct` instead of `class`. A `struct` is identical to a `class` in every respect except that the `public` is assumed in a `struct`. For historical reasons, the term `class` is more popular in C++, while the term `struct` is used more often in C programs.

Following the public keyword are the declarations for the entries it takes to describe the class. The `Person` class contains two arrays for the first and last names and a third entry to hold the Social Security number.

The entries within a class are known as *members* or *properties* of the class.

The Object

Declaring a class in C++ is like defining a new variable type. You can create a new instance of a class as follows:

```
Person me;
```

An instance of a class is called an *object*.

People get confused about the difference between a class and an object; sometimes people even use the terms interchangeably. Actually, the difference is easy to explain with an example. `Dog` is a class. My dog, Lollie, is an instance of a dog. My other dog, Jack, is a separate, independent instance of a dog. `Dog` is a class; `lollie` and `jack` are objects.

You can access the members of an object by including their name after the name of the object followed by a dot, as in the following:

```
Person me;
me.nSocialSecurityNumber = 456789012;
cin >> me.szLastName;
```

Here me is an object of class `Person`. The element `me.nSocialSecurity Number` is a member or property of the `me` object. The type of `me` is `Person`. The type of `me.nSocialSecurityNumber` is `int`, and its value is set to 456-78-9012. The type of `me.szLastName` is `char[]` (pronounced "array of char").

A class object can be initialized when it is created as follows:

```
Person me = {"Stephen", "Davis", 456789012};
```

Assignment is the only operation defined for user-defined classes by default. Its use is shown here:

```
Person copyOfMe;
copyOfMe = me;   // copy each member of me to copyOfMe
```

The default assignment operator copies the members of the object on the right to the members on the left. The objects on the right and left of the assignment operator must be exactly the same type.

You can define what the other operators might mean when applied to an object of a class that you define. That is considered advanced strokes, however, and is beyond the scope of this book.

Arrays of Objects

You can declare and initialize arrays of objects as follows:

```
Person people[5] = {{    "Adam", "Laskowski", 123456789},
                     { "Kinsey",      "Davis", 234567890},
                     {  "Janet",     "Eddins", 345678901},
                     {"Stephen",      "Davis", 456789012},
                     {"Tiffany",     "Amrich", 567890123}};
```

The layout of `people` in memory is shown in Figure 19-2. Compare this with the parallel array equivalent in Figure 19-1.

In this example, each one of the elements of the array `people` is an object. Thus, `people[0]` is the first object in the array. My information appears as `people[3]`. You can access the members of an individual member of an array of objects using the same "dot-member" syntax as that used for simple objects:

```
// change my social security number
people[3].nSocialSecurityNumber = 456789012;
```

class Person

szFirstName
szLastName
nSocialSecurityNumber

me

"Stephen"
"Davis"
456789012

people[0]	"Adam"
	"Laskowski"
	123456789
people[1]	"Kinsey"
	"Davis"
	234567890
people[2]	"Janet"
	"Eddins"
	345678901
people[3]	"Stephen"
	"Davis"
	456789012

Figure 19-2:
The arrange-ment in memory of an array of 5 Person objects.

The type of `people` is `Person[]`, which is read "array of `Person`" (some-times programmers use the plural of the class name as in "array of `Persons`"). The type of `people[3]` is `Person`.

Looking at an Example

I've gone far enough without an example program to demonstrate how class objects appear in a program. The following InputPerson program inputs the data for an array of people. It then sorts the array by Social Security number and outputs the sorted list.

The sorting algorithm I used is known as a *Bubble Sort*. It isn't particularly efficient, but it's very simple to code. I explain how it works in a sidebar, but don't get wrapped up in the details of the Bubble Sort. Focus instead on how the program inputs the critical elements of a `Person` into a single element of an array that it can then manipulate as a single entity.

```cpp
// InputPerson - create objects of class Person and
//               display their data
#include <cstdio>
#include <cstdlib>
#include <iostream>
using namespace std;

// Person - stores the name and social security number
class Person
{
  public:
    char szFirstName[128];
    char szLastName[128];
    int  nSocialSecurityNumber;
};

// getPerson - read a Person object from the keyboard
//             and return a copy to the caller
Person getPerson()
{
    Person person;

    cout << "\nEnter another Person\n"
         << "First name: ";
    cin  >> person.szFirstName;

    cout << "Last name: ";
    cin  >> person.szLastName;

    cout << "Social Security number: ";
    cin  >> person.nSocialSecurityNumber;

    return person;
}

// getPeople - read an array of Person objects;
//             return the number read
int getPeople(Person people[], int nMaxSize)
{
    // keep going until operator says he's done or
    // until we're out of space
    int index;
    for(index = 0; index < nMaxSize; index++)
    {
        char cAnswer;
        cout << "Enter another name? (Y or N):";
        cin  >> cAnswer;

        if (cAnswer != 'Y' && cAnswer != 'y')
        {
```

```
                break;
        }

        people[index] = getPerson();
    }
    return index;
}

// displayPerson - display a person on the default display
void displayPerson(Person person)
{
    cout << "First name: " << person.szFirstName << endl;
    cout << "Last name : " << person.szLastName  << endl;
    cout << "Social Security number : "
        << person.nSocialSecurityNumber << endl;
}

// displayPeople - display an array of Person objects
void displayPeople(Person people[], int nCount)
{
    for(int index = 0; index < nCount; index++)
    {
        displayPerson(people[index]);
    }
}

// sortPeople - sort an array of nCount Person objects
//              by Social Security Number
//              (this uses a binary sort)
void sortPeople(Person people[], int nCount)
{
    // keep going until the list is in order
    int nSwaps = 1;
    while(nSwaps != 0)
    {
        // we can tell if the list is in order by
        // the number of records we have to swap
        nSwaps = 0;

        // iterate through the list...
        for(int n = 0; n < (nCount - 1); n++)
        {
            // ...if the current entry is greater than
            // the following entry...
            if (people[n].nSocialSecurityNumber >
                people[n+1].nSocialSecurityNumber)
            {
                // ...then swap them...
                Person temp  = people[n+1];
                people[n+1] = people[n];
```

```
                people[n]    = temp;

                // ...and count it.
                nSwaps++;
            }
        }
    }
}

int main(int nNumberofArgs, char* pszArgs[])
{
    // allocate room for some names
    Person people[128];

    // prompt the user for input
    cout << "Read name/social security information\n";
    int nCount = getPeople(people, 128);

    // sort the list
    sortPeople(people, nCount);

    // now display the results
    cout << "\nHere is the list sorted by "
         << "social security number" << endl;
    displayPeople(people, nCount);

    // wait until user is ready before terminating program
    // to allow the user to see the program results
    system("PAUSE");
    return 0;
}
```

The program starts by declaring class Person with data members for the first name, last name, and Social Security number. Contrary to good programming practice, this program uses fixed-length arrays for the name strings. (If I were writing this for a commercial package, I would use variable length arrays, or I would include a test to make sure that input from the keyboard did not overflow the buffer. See Chapter 17 if you don't know what I'm talking about.)

The first function, getPerson(), prompts the user for the data necessary to describe a single Person object. It then returns a copy of that Person to the caller.

The second function, getPeople(), invokes the getPerson() function repeatedly to retrieve the data for a number of individuals. It stores the Person objects retrieved into the array people. This function accepts as an argument the maximum size of the people array and returns to the caller the actual number of elements stored there.

The displayPerson() and displayPeople() functions are the output analogs to the getPerson() and getPeople() functions. display Person() outputs the information for a single individual, whereas display People() calls that function on each element defined in the people array.

The sortPeople() function sorts the elements of the people array in order of increasing Social Security number. This function is described in the "Bubble Sort" sidebar. Don't worry too much about how this function works. You're way ahead of the game if you can follow the rest of the program.

The output from a test run of this program appears as follows:

```
Read name/social security information
Enter another name? (Y or N):y

Enter another Person
First name: Adam
Last name: Laskowski
Social Security number: 123456789
Enter another name? (Y or N):y

Enter another Person
First name: Stephen
Last name: Davis
Social Security number: 456789012
Enter another name? (Y or N):y

Enter another Person
First name: Janet
Last name: Eddins
Social Security number: 345678901
Enter another name? (Y or N):n

Here is the list sorted by social security number.
First name: Adam
Last name : Laskowski
Social Security number : 123456789
First name: Janet
Last name : Eddins
Social Security number : 345678901
First name: Stephen
Last name : Davis
Social Security number : 456789012
Press any key to continue . . .
```

You've seen most of the non–object-oriented features of C++. The next chapter introduces you to the Code::Blocks debugger, which wraps up the sections dedicated to what I call functional programming. After that, I jump into object-oriented programming in Part V.

Bubble Sort

Most of this book is dedicated to the syntax of C++. However, in addition to the details of the language, you will also need to learn common programming algorithms in order to become a proficient programmer. The Bubble Sort is one of those algorithms that every programmer should master.

There are a number of common algorithms for sorting fields. Each has its own advantages. In general, the simpler algorithms take longer to execute, whereas the really fast algorithms are more difficult to program. The Bubble Sort is very easy to program but isn't particularly fast. This is not a problem for small data sets; arrays up to several thousand entries in length can be sorted in very much less than a second on modern high-speed processors. For small to moderate amounts of data, the simplicity of the Bubble Sort far outweighs any performance penalty.

In the Bubble Sort, the program makes multiple passes through the data set. On each pass, it compares each element with the next element in the list. If element N is less than N+1, then these two are in the proper order so the Bubble Sort takes no action. However, if element N is greater than N+1, then the Bubble Sort swaps the two elements and then moves on to the next element. In practice, this looks like the following:

```cpp
// if the current entry is greater than
// the following entry...
if (people[n].nSocialSecurityNumber >
    people[n+1].nSocialSecurityNumber)
{
    // ...then swap them...
    Person temp = people[n+1];
    people[n+1] = people[n];
    people[n]   = temp;

    // ...and count it.
    nSwaps++;
}
```

At the end of the first pass through the entire array, the largest element will have moved to the end of the list, but the rest of the array will still not be in order. However, repeated passes through the array cause each element to "bubble" up to its proper place in the array. The Bubble Sort sets the number of elements that were swapped on each pass by zeroing the counter nSwaps before iterating through the list and incrementing the number of elements swapped on each pass. The algorithm doesn't really care how many swaps were executed; if any swaps were executed, then the array was not in order. However, once the Bubble Sort can make it all the way through the list without executing any swaps, then it knows that the array is in order.

The figure demonstrates how the Bubble Sort sorts an array of five integers. During the first pass through the list, two swaps are executed. On the second pass, the algorithm executes only a single swap. The resulting list is in order, but the algorithm doesn't know this until it makes its way all the way through the array without making any swaps, as shown in the third pass. At this point, the Bubble Sort is finished.

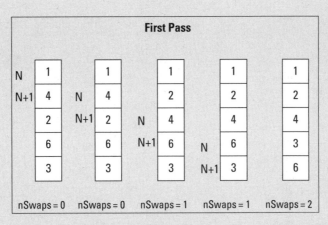

First Pass

N 1	1	1	1	1
N+1 4	N 4	2	2	2
2	N+1 2	N 4	4	4
6	6	N+1 6	N 6	3
3	3	3	N+1 3	6
nSwaps = 0	nSwaps = 0	nSwaps = 1	nSwaps = 1	nSwaps = 2

Second Pass

N 1	1	1	1	1
N+1 2	N 2	2	2	2
4	N+1 4	N 4	3	3
3	3	N+1 3	N 4	4
6	6	6	N+1 6	6
nSwaps = 0	nSwaps = 0	nSwaps = 1	nSwaps = 1	nSwaps = 1

Third Pass

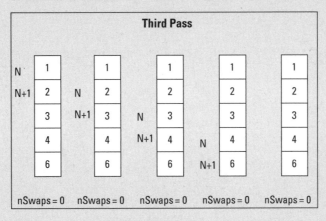

N 1	1	1	1	1
N+1 2	N 2	2	2	2
3	N+1 3	N 3	3	3
4	4	N+1 4	N 4	4
6	6	6	N+1 6	6
nSwaps = 0	nSwaps = 0	nSwaps = 0	nSwaps = 0	nSwaps = 0

Chapter 20

Debugging Your Programs, Part 3

· ·

In This Chapter

▶ Debugging using the built-in debugger

▶ Building your application with debugger information

▶ Setting a breakpoint

▶ Single-stepping your program

▶ Fixing a sample problem

· ·

*I*ntroduced a few techniques for finding errors at the end of Parts II (Chapter 8) and III (Chapter 13). Now that you are nearing the end of Part IV, I want to touch on debugging techniques one final time.

In this chapter, I introduce you to the debugging tools built into the Code::Blocks development environment (similar tools exist for most other environments). Learning to use the debugger will give you clear insight into what your program is doing (and what it's not doing, at times).

A New Approach to Debugging

Chapters 8 and 13 demonstrated how to find problems by adding output statements in key positions. Outputting key variables lets you see what intermediate values your program is calculating and what path it's taking through your C++ code.

However, the output technique has several distinct disadvantages. The first is that it's difficult to know what to display. In a small program, such as most of the programs in this book, you can display almost everything — there just aren't that many variables to slug through. However, in a major league program, there may be many hundreds of variables, especially if you include all of the elements in the arrays. Knowing which variables to display can be problematic.

A second problem is the time it takes to rebuild the program. Once again, this isn't a problem with small programs. Code::Blocks can rebuild a small program in just a few seconds. In these cases, adding or changing output statements doesn't take more than a few minutes. However, I have been on projects where rebuilding the entire program took many hours. In a big program, adding new output statements as you zero in on a bug can take a long time.

Finally, it's very difficult to debug a pointer problem using the output approach. If a pointer is invalid, any attempt to use it will cause the program to abort, and knowing a valid pointer from an invalid one simply by displaying its value on cout is almost impossible.

The solution

What you need is a way to stop the program in the middle of its execution and query the value of key variables. That's exactly what the debugger does.

The debugger is actually a utility built into the Code::Blocks environment. Every environment has some type of debugger, and they all offer the same basic features though the specific commands may be different. The debugger allows the programmer to control the execution of her program. She can execute one step in the program at a time, she can stop the program at any point, and she can examine the value of variables.

Unlike the C++ language, which is standardized, every debugger has its own command set. Fortunately, once you've learned how to use the Code::Blocks debugger, you won't have any trouble learning to use the debugger that comes with your favorite C++ environment.

The programmer controls the debugger through commands entered from the keyboard within the Code::Blocks environment exactly as she would use the edit commands to modify the C++ source code or build commands to create the executable program. The debug commands are available from both menu items and hot keys.

The best way to learn how to use the Code::Blocks debugger is to use it to find a couple of nasty problems in a buggy version of one of the programs you've already seen.

Entomology for Dummies

The following version of the Concatenate program (which you'll find on the enclosed CD-ROM as ConcatenateError1) represents my first attempt at the ConcatenateHeap program from Chapter 18.

This version has at least two serious bugs, both of which are in the
concatenateString() function.

```cpp
//
//   ConcatenateError1 - similar to ConcatenatePtr except
//                       this version has several bugs in it
//                       that can be easily found with the
//                       debugger
//
#include <cstdio>
#include <cstdlib>
#include <iostream>
#include <cstring>
using namespace std;


// concatenateString - concatenate two strings together
//                       into an array allocated off of the
//                       heap
char* concatenateString(const char* pszSrc1,
                        const char* pszSrc2)
{
    // allocate an array of sufficient length
    int nTargetSize = strlen(pszSrc1)+strlen(pszSrc2)+1;
    char* pszTarget = new char[nTargetSize];

    // first copy the first string into the target
    while(*pszSrc1 != '\0')
    {
        *pszTarget++ = *pszSrc1++;
    }

    // now copy the contents of the second string onto
    // the end of the first
    while(*pszSrc2 != '\0')
    {
        *pszTarget++ = *pszSrc2++;
    }

    // return the resulting string to the caller
    return pszTarget;
}

int main(int nNumberofArgs, char* pszArgs[])
{
    // Prompt user
    cout << "This program accepts two strings\n"
         << "from the keyboard and outputs them\n"
         << "concatenated together.\n" << endl;

    // input two strings
```

```
    cout << "Enter first string: ";
    char szString1[256];
    cin.getline(szString1, 256);

    cout << "Enter the second string: ";
    char szString2[256];
    cin.getline(szString2, 256);

    // now concatenate one onto the end of the other
    cout << "Concatentate first string onto the second"
        << endl;
    char* pszT = concatenateString(szString1, szString2);

    // and display the result
    cout << "Result: <"
        << pszT
        << ">" << endl;

    // return the memory to the heap
    delete pszT;
    pszT = NULL;

    // wait until user is ready before terminating program
    // to allow the user to see the program results
    system("PAUSE");
    return 0;
}
```

The following shows the results of executing the program:

```
This program accepts two strings
from the keyboard and outputs them
concatenated together.

Enter first string: this is a string
Enter the second string: THIS IS ALSO A STRING
Concatentate first string onto the second
Result: <OF_fdT D>
Press any key to continue . . .
```

Clearly, the result is not correct, so something must be wrong. Rather than start inserting output statements, I will use the debugger to find the problems this time.

I suggest that you follow along with me and take the same steps I do in the following section. You can start with the ConcatenateError1 program from the CD-ROM.

Starting the debugger

I can tell the debugger that I want to execute the program up to a certain line or view a particular variable. In order to do that, however, the debugger has to know exactly where each C++ line of code is stored and where each variable is kept. It does this by attaching extra information onto the executable — actually, quite a bit of extra information. Because this information can get really lengthy and because I don't need it for the release version that I ship to the public, including debug information is optional.

I decided whether to include debug information in the executable when I created the project. Figure 20-1 shows the next to last dialog box presented by the Project Wizard, the Console Application dialog box. The default is to generate debug information as shown here. The Release configuration is the version of the executable without the extra debug information. I cannot use the debugger if I do not create a Debug configuration version.

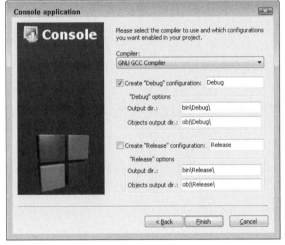

Figure 20-1:
The Console
Application
dialog box of
the Project
Wizard
allows you
to select
whether
to build a
debug ver-
sion of the
executable
or not.

I can turn debugger information on at any time by selecting Settings➪Compiler and Debugger and then making sure that the Produce Debugging Symbols [-g] check box is checked in the Compiler Flags subwindow of the Compiler Settings window. I have to rebuild the executable by selecting Build➪Rebuild for the change to have any effect.

So assume that I did tell Code::Blocks to include debug information in the executable.

I am reasonably certain that the problem is in the `concatenateString()` function itself. So I decide that I want to stop executing the program at the call to `concatenateString()`. To do this, I need to do what's called *setting a breakpoint*.

A *breakpoint* is a command to the debugger that says stop execution of the program if you get to this spot. There are at least four ways to set a breakpoint, all of which are equivalent:

- Click with the cursor just to the right of the line number on line 60 (see Figure 20-2).

- Right-click on line 60 and select Toggle Breakpoint from the menu that appears (it's the first option).

- Put the cursor on line 60 and select F5 (Toggle Breakpoint).

- Put the cursor on line 60 and select Debug➪Toggle Breakpoint.

Multiple methods exist for entering almost every other debugger command that I describe in this chapter, but in the interest of brevity, I describe only one. You can experiment to find the others.

A small stop sign appears just to the right of the line number, as shown in Figure 20-2.

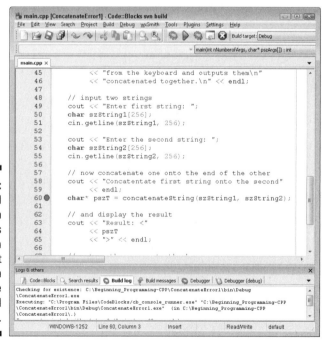

Figure 20-2:
A small, red stop sign indicates that a breakpoint has been set at the specified location.

To start the program, I select Debug⇨Start. At first the program seems to execute like normal. It first prompts me for the first string. It follows that by prompting me for a second string. As soon as I enter that string, however, the program appears to stop, and a small, yellow arrow appears inside the stop sign on the source code display. This is shown in Figure 20-3. This little, yellow arrow is the *current location indicator*. This points to the next C++ line to be executed.

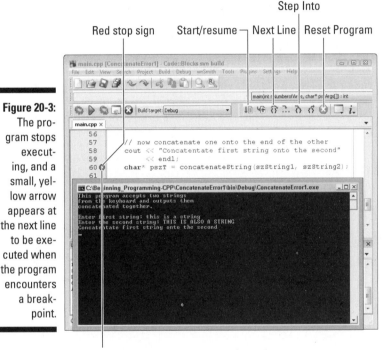

Figure 20-3:
The program stops executing, and a small, yellow arrow appears at the next line to be executed when the program encounters a breakpoint.

Yellow arrow indicating current location pointer.

You will also notice from Figure 20-3 that another toolbar appears. The Debugger toolbar includes the most common debug commands, including most of the commands that I demonstrate in this chapter. (I have added callouts for the commands I will describe later in this chapter.)

Navigating through a program with the debugger

Okay, so I've managed to stop the execution of my program in the middle with the debugger. What can I do now?

I'll start by executing the `concatenateString()` function one statement at a time. I could set a new breakpoint at the first instruction in the function, but setting a new breakpoint on every line is tedious. Fortunately, the Code::Blocks debugger offers a more convenient choice: the *Step Into* command.

On the Debug toolbar, this is the fifth command from the left. However, if you get confused, this menu has Tool Tips — just point at the command in the toolbar and leave the arrow motionless. After a few seconds, the name of the command will pop up. Or you can select Debug⇨Step Into from the main menu.

The Step Into command executes a single C++ statement; in this case, the command steps into the function call. Execution stops immediately before the first executable statement in `concatenateString()`. Next, I select Debug⇨Debugging Windows⇨Watches to display the window shown in Figure 20-4. From this window, I can see that the two arguments to the function, `pszSrc1` and `pszSrc2`, appear to be correct.

The values of `nTargetSize` and `pszTarget` have no meaning at this point since they have yet to be initialized.

Figure 20-4:
The Watches window shows both the arguments to the functions and any locally defined variables.

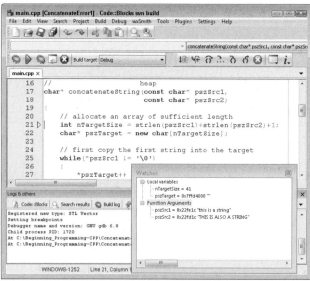

I could select Step Into again to move forward, but this will step me into the `strlen()` functions. Since these are C++ library routines, I'm willing to accept that these are working fine.

The other option is known as Next Line. Next Line steps to the next line of C++ code in the current function, treating function calls just like any other C++ command.

Together, Step Into and Next Line are known as *single-step* commands. For commands other than function calls, the two commands are equivalent. Many debuggers use the term Step Over rather than Next Line to highlight the distinction from Step Into.

I select Next Line from the Debug toolbar. Notice how the Current location pointer moves from line 21 to line 22, as shown in Figure 20-5. In addition, the nTargetSize variable is highlighted red in the Watch window to indicate that its value has changed. The value of nTargetSize is now 38, the correct length of the sum of the two strings.

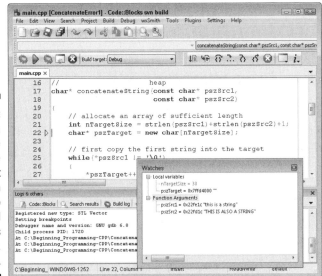

Figure 20-5:
Selecting Next Line moves the current location pointer to line 22 and initializes nTarget Size.

You need to be absolutely clear about what just happened. All you see is that the screen blinks and the current location pointer moves down one line. What actually happened is that the debugger set a temporary breakpoint at line 22 and then restarted the program at line 21. The program executed the two calls to strlen() and then performed the addition, storing the results in nTarget Size. You may have seen only the one line of code get executed, but in fact many lines of C++ code were executed within the strlen() functions (executed twice, actually).

So far, so good, so I select Next Line a few more times until I enter the `while` loop.

TIP

This `while` loop is structured a little differently than what you've seen before. Here, I increment the pointer as part of the assignment itself, rather than in the increment clause of a `for` loop, as follows:

```
while(*pszSrc1 != '\0')
{
    *pszTarget++ = *pszSrc1++; // Line 27
}
```

Line 27 of the program says, "store the value of the `char` pointed at by `pszSrc1` into the `char` location pointed at by `pszTarget` and then increment `pszSrc1` and `pszTarget`."

Figure 20-6 shows the debug display after I execute the loop a few times. Notice after each execution that, since their value is modified, both `pszSrc1` and `pszTarget` are highlighted in the Watches window.

Figure 20-6:
The `while` loop increments `pszSrc1` and `psz Target` on each pass.

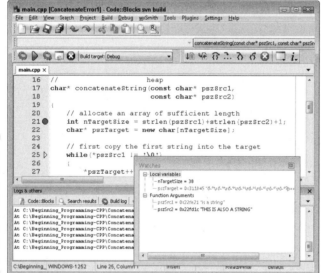

Also notice that the string pointed at by `pszSrc1` seems to be shrinking. This is because as `pszSrc1` is incremented, it is effectively moving down the string until eventually it will point to nothing more than the terminating `null`. That's when control will leave the `while` loop and continue on to the next loop.

But wait! The string pointed at by `pszTarget` is not growing. Remember that the intent is to copy the contents of `pszSrc1` into `pszTarget`. What's happening?

After a moment's reflection, the answer is obvious: I'm also changing the value of `pszTarget` and leaving the characters I've copied behind. That's what was wrong with my function in the first place. I need to keep a copy of the original pointer unmodified to return to the caller!

Now that I know the problem (or, at least, a problem — there may be more) I stop the debugger by clicking Stop Debugger on the Debug tool-bar. The Console Application dialog box disappears immediately, and the Code::Blocks display returns to that used for editing.

Fixing the (first) bug

To solve the problem that I noted, I only need to save the value returned by `new` and return it rather than the modified `pszTarget` pointer from the function. I include only the modified `concatenateString()` function here (the rest of the program is unchanged — the entire program is included on the enclosed CD-ROM as ConcatenateError2):

```
char* concatenateString(const char* pszSrc1,
                        const char* pszSrc2)
{
    // allocate an array of sufficient length
    int nTargetSize = strlen(pszSrc1)+strlen(pszSrc2)+1;
    char* pszTarget = new char[nTargetSize];
    char* pszT = pszTarget;  // save a pointer to return

    // first copy the first string into the target
    while(*pszSrc1 != '\0')
    {
        *pszTarget++ = *pszSrc1++;
    }

    // now copy the contents of the second string onto
    // the end of the first
    while(*pszSrc2 != '\0')
    {
        *pszTarget++ = *pszSrc2++;
    }

    // return the original pointer to the caller
    return pszT;
}
```

Here, I save the pointer returned by new into both `pszTarget`, which I intend to increment, and `pszT`, which will stay unmodified. The function returns the latter, unmodified pointer to the caller.

I rebuild the application, and then I repeat my earlier steps to single-step through the first loop within `concatenateString()`. Figure 20-7 shows the display after executing the loop seven times.

Figure 20-7:
The Watches window of the updated concatenate String() function shows the string being built in the array pointed at by `pszT`.

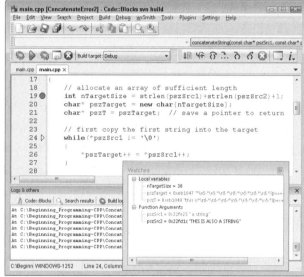

Notice how `pszT` points to an array containing the first seven characters of the source string `this is`. Also notice that the value of `pszTarget` is 7 larger than `pszT`.

But also notice all the garbage characters in the `pszT` string that appear after `this is`. Code::Blocks displays extra garbage because the target string has no terminating null. It doesn't need one yet, since I haven't completed constructing it.

Finding and fixing the second bug

The two source strings aren't all that long, so I use the Next Line command to single-step through the entire loop. Figure 20-8 shows the Debug window after executing the second loop for the last time. Here, `pszT` points to the completed target string with both source strings concatenated together. Without a terminating `null`, however, the string still displays garbage after the final character.

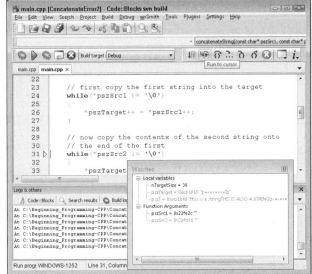

Figure 20-8:
The Debug
window
after exe-
cuting the
second loop
for the last
time.

Because I'm now done with the function, I select Debug➪Continue from the
Code::Blocks menu. This causes the debugger to resume the program where
it left off and to continue to the next breakpoint or to the end of the program,
whichever comes first.

Sure enough, the displayed concatenated array includes the same garbage
that I saw in the debugger:

```
This program accepts two strings
from the keyboard and outputs them
concatenated together.

Enter first string: this is a string
Enter the second string: THIS IS ALSO A STRING
Concatentate first string onto the second
Result: <this is a stringTHIS IS ALSO A STRING          >
Press any key to continue . . .
```

If I didn't include a terminating `null`, then what caused the string returned
by `concatenateString()` to terminate at all? Why didn't the string continue on for pages? The short answer is, "Nothing." It could be that C++ had
to display many thousands of characters before eventually hitting a character
containing a `null`. In practice, this rarely happens, however. Zero is by far
the most common value in memory. You generally don't have to look too far
before you find a byte containing a zero that terminates the string.

All I need to do to fix this problem is add a terminating `null` after the final `while` loop:

```cpp
char* concatenateString(const char* pszSrc1,
                        const char* pszSrc2)
{
    // allocate an array of sufficient length
    int nTargetSize = strlen(pszSrc1)+strlen(pszSrc2)+1;
    char* pszTarget = new char[nTargetSize];
    char* pszT = pszTarget;   // save a pointer to return

    // first copy the first string into the target
    while(*pszSrc1 != '\0')
    {
        *pszTarget++ = *pszSrc1++;
    }

    // now copy the contents of the second string onto
    // the end of the first
    while(*pszSrc2 != '\0')
    {
        *pszTarget++ = *pszSrc2++;
    }

    // add a terminating NULL
    *pszTarget = '\0';

    // return the unmodified pointer to the caller
    return pszT;
}
```

Executing this version in the debugger creates the display shown in Figure 20-9. Notice that once the terminating `null` has been added, the string pointed at by `pszT` magically "cleans up," losing all the garbage that strings on after the data that I put there.

Let me be clear: Those garbage characters are still there. It's just that the terminating `null` causes C++ to not display them. The output from the program is the predictable string that you've come to love and admire:

```
This program accepts two strings
from the keyboard and outputs them
concatenated together.

Enter first string: this is a string
Enter the second string: THIS IS ALSO A STRING
Concatentate first string onto the second
Result: <this is a stringTHIS IS ALSO A STRING>
Press any key to continue . . .
```

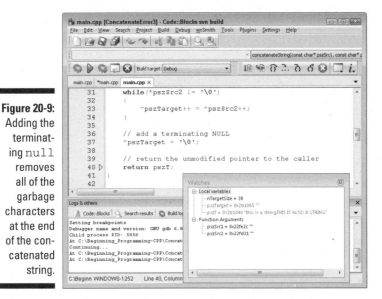

Figure 20-9:
Adding the
terminat-
ing null
removes
all of the
garbage
characters
at the end
of the con-
catenated
string.

It's possible to find problems in small programs by adding output statements at key locations. However, the debugger is a much more elegant and power-ful tool for finding problems. Single-stepping your way through a program in the debugger gives you a real feel for what the computer is doing with your source code. You develop an understanding for how the computer works that I don't think you can get any other way. The debugger that comes with Code::Blocks is about as easy to use as any that I've seen. I recommend that you use it early and often.

Part V
Object-Oriented Programming

The 5th Wave
By Rich Tennant

"Yes, I know how to query information from the program, but what if I just want to leak it instead?"

In this part . . .

Parts I through IV describe C++ as just another functional language, not very different from its predecessor, C. This part introduces you to the concepts behind object-oriented programming. These concepts revolutionized the programming world when they became widely adopted in the late 1980s. This is the part that describes what makes C++ the truly powerful language that it is.

Chapter 21

What Is Object-Oriented Programming?

*E*xamples of objects abound in everyday life. Right in front of me is a chair, a table, a computer, and a red Starbucks mug. I have no trouble grouping these objects into taxonomies based upon their properties. For example, the mug is a container, it's also a thermal insulator, so I can use it to hold hot or cold things, and it has mass, so that I can use it as a paperweight or to throw at the dog. Object-oriented programming applies this view of the world to that of programming. To explain what I mean, let me start with a story.

Abstraction and Microwave Ovens

Sometimes when my son and I are watching football, I whip up a batch of nachos. Nothing fancy, mind you — I dump some chips on a plate, throw on refried beans, cheese, and a batch of jalapenos, and nuke the lot in the microwave oven for five minutes. To use the oven, I open the door, place the nachos inside, punch some buttons on the front, and hit start. After a few minutes, the bell rings to tell me they're done. If I do something wrong, the oven beeps at me and doesn't start. Sometimes it displays an error message on the little display.

This doesn't sound very profound, and it isn't really until you consider all the things that I don't do to use my microwave oven:

✔ I limit myself to the front panel of the microwave. I don't look inside the case. I don't look at the listings of the code that tells the processor unit what to do. I don't study the wiring diagram that's pasted on the inside wall of the case.

✔ I don't rewrite or change anything inside the microwave to get it to work. The microwave oven that I use to make nachos is the exact same microwave that I used earlier to heat up chili dogs (nothing but health food at my house). And it will be the same microwave I use to heat up my Malt-O-Meal tomorrow (assuming it doesn't break).

✔ I don't think about what might be going on inside my microwave oven in order to use it. Even if I designed microwaves for a living, I'm not likely to think about how it works when I make nachos before the big game.

These are not profound observations. Humans can think about only so much at any one time. We tend to reduce the number of things that we have to deal with by abstracting away all the little details. This allows us to work at the level of detail appropriate to the problem we're trying to solve.

Note: In object-oriented (OO) terms, this level of detail is known as the *level of abstraction*.

When I'm working on nachos, I view my microwave oven as a black box. I don't concern myself with what's going on inside that box unless, of course, it breaks. Then I might take the top off and see if I can figure out what's wrong with it; then I am working at a different level of abstraction. I still don't take the tops off the chips on the circuit board or try to take apart the individual components. (I'm not *that* crazy.)

As long as the microwave is heating food, I limit myself to the interface that it exposes to the outside world: the keypad and LCD display. It is very important that from this interface there is nothing that I can do that will cause the microwave to:

✔ Enter an inconsistent state and crash (causing me to have to reboot my microwave)

✔ Worse, turn my nachos into a blackened, flaming mass

✔ Worse yet, catch on fire and burn down the house

Functional nachos

Suppose I were to ask my son to write an algorithm for making nachos using the same basic approach used for changing tires in Chapter 1. He would probably write something like, "Open a can of beans, grate some cheese, cut the jalapenos," and so on. For the part about heating the nachos, he would write something similar to, "Cook in the oven until cheese is melted."

That description is straightforward and complete, but it's not how a functional programmer would code a program to make nachos. Functional programmers live in a world devoid of objects such as microwave ovens. They tend to worry about flowcharts with their myriad functional paths. In a functional solution, the flow of control would pass from my finger through the microwave's front panel and on into the interior of the thing. Soon, the flow would be wiggling through complex logic paths concerned with how long to charge up some capacitor and whether it's time to sound the "come and get it" tone.

In a world like this, it's hard to think in terms of levels of abstraction. There are no objects, no abstractions behind which to hide inherent complexity.

Object-oriented nachos

In an object-oriented approach to making nachos, I would start by identifying the types of objects in the problem: chips, beans, cheese, and an oven. These are the nouns that I have to work with. That done, I would identify the verbs relevant to each object. Next, I would solve the problem using nothing but the nouns and verbs identified before. Finally, then, and only then, I would implement each of these objects in software.

I identified the nouns and verbs relevant to tire changing for you in Chapter 1. You were left with the job of implementing the solution using the nouns and verbs I gave you.

While I am writing object-level code, I am said to be working (and thinking) at the level of abstraction of the basic objects. I need to think about making a useful oven, but I don't have to think about the process of making nachos yet. After all, the designers of my microwave didn't think about the specific problem of my making a snack. Rather, they set about the problem of designing and building a useful microwave oven.

After I have successfully coded and tested the objects I need, I can ratchet up to the next level of abstraction. I can start thinking at the nacho-making level, rather than at the microwave-making level. At this point, I can pretty much translate my son's instructions directly into C++ code.

Classification and Microwave Ovens

Critical to the concept of abstraction is that of classification. If I were to ask my son, "What's a microwave oven?" he would probably say, "It's an oven that. . . ." If I then ask, "What's an oven?" he might reply, "It's a kitchen appliance that. . . ." I could keep asking this question, ratcheting myself up the abstraction ladder until I ended up with, "It's a thing," which is another way of saying, "It's an object."

My son understands that our particular microwave is an instance of the type of things called microwave ovens. In addition, he sees microwave ovens as just a special kind of oven, which is, in turn, a special type of kitchen appliance, and so on.

The technical way of saying this is that our oven is an *instance* of the class *microwave*. The class *microwave* is a *subclass* of the class *oven,* and the class *oven* is a *superclass* of the class *microwave*.

Humans classify. Everything about our world is ordered into taxonomies. We do this to reduce the number of things that we have to remember. Consider, for example, the first time that you saw a hybrid car. The advertisement called it a "revolutionary automobile, unlike any car you've ever seen," but you and I know that this just isn't so. Sure, its propulsion system is different from conventional cars, but it's still a car and as such does the same things that all cars do: convey you and your kin from one place to another. It has a steering wheel, seats, a motor, brakes, and so on. I bet I could even drive one without help.

I don't have to clutter my limited storage with all the things that a hybrid card has in common with other cars. All I have to remember is that "a hybrid car is a car that. . . ." and tack on those few things that are unique to a hybrid. Cars are a subclass of wheeled vehicles, of which there are other members, such as trucks and pickups. Maybe wheeled vehicles are a subclass of vehicles, which includes boats and planes. And on and on and on.

Why Build Objects This Way?

It may seem easier to design and build a microwave oven specifically for this one problem, rather than to build a separate, more generic oven object. Suppose, for example, that I were to build a microwave to cook nachos and nachos only. I wouldn't need to put a front panel on it, other than a START button. I always cook nachos the same amount of time. I could dispense with all that DEFROST and TEMP COOK nonsense. The microwave could be tiny. It would need to hold only one fat, little plate. The cubic feet of space would be completely wasted on nachos.

For that matter, suppose I just dispense with the concept of "microwave oven" altogether. All I really need is the guts of the oven. Then in the recipe, I can put the instructions to make it work: "Put nachos in the box. Connect the red wire to the black wire. Notice a slight hum. Don't stand too close if you intend to have children." Stuff like that.

Nevertheless, the functional approach does have some problems:

- **Too complex.** You don't want the details of oven building mixed in with the details of nacho building. If you can't define the objects and pull them out of the morass of details to deal with separately, you must deal with all the complexities of the problem at the same time.

- **Not flexible.** If you need to replace the microwave oven with some other type of oven, you should be able to do so as long as the interface to the new oven is about the same as the old one. Without a simple and clearly delineated interface, it becomes impossible to cleanly remove an object type and replace it with another.

- **Not reusable.** Ovens are used to make many different dishes. You don't want to create a new oven each time you encounter a new recipe. Having solved a problem once, it would be nice to reuse the solution in future programs.

It does cost more to write a generic object. It would be cheaper to build a microwave made specifically for nachos. You could dispense with expensive timers, buttons, and the like that aren't needed to make nachos. After you have used a generic object in more than one application, however, the costs of a slightly more expensive class more than outweigh the repeated costs of building cheaper, less flexible classes for every new application.

Self-Contained Classes

Now, it's time to reflect on what you've learned. In an object-oriented approach to programming:

- The programmer identifies the classes necessary to solve the problem. (I knew right off that I was going to need an oven to make decent nachos.)

- The programmer creates self-contained classes that fit the requirements of the problem and doesn't worry about the details of the overall application.

- The programmer writes the application using the classes just created without thinking about how they work internally.

An integral part of this programming model is that each class is responsible for itself. A class should be in a defined state at all times. It should not be possible to crash the program by calling a class with illegal data or with an illegal sequence of correct data.

Many of the features of C++ that are shown in subsequent chapters deal with giving the class the capability to protect itself from errant programs just waiting to trip it up.

Chapter 22

Structured Play: Making Classes Do Things

Classes were introduced to the C language as a convenient way to group unalike but related data elements — for example, the Social Security number and name of the same person. That's the way I introduce them in Chapter 19. C++ expanded the concept of classes to give them the ability to mimic objects in the real world. That's the essence of the difference between C and C++.

In the previous chapter, I review at a high level the concept of object-oriented programming. In this chapter, I make it more concrete by examining the active features of a class that allow them to better mimic the object-oriented world we live in.

Activating Our Objects

C++ uses classes to simulate real-world objects. However, the classes in Chapter 19 are lacking in that regard because classes do things. (The classes in Chapter 19 don't have any verbs associated with them — they don't do anything.) Consider for example, a savings account. It is necessary for a `Savings` class to save the owner's name, probably her Social Security number, certainly her account number and balance. But this isn't sufficient.

Objects in the real world do things. Ovens cook. Savings accounts accumulate interest. CDs charge a substantial penalty for early withdrawal. Stuff like that.

Consider the problem of handling deposits in a `Savings` account class. Functional programs do things via functions. Thus, a function program might create a separate function that takes as its argument a pointer to a `Savings` account object that it wants to update followed by the amount to deposit.

Never mind for now exactly how to pass a pointer to a `Savings` account object. You'll see more about that in the next chapter.

But that's not the way that savings accounts work in the real world. When I drive up to the bank window and tell them I want to make a deposit to my savings account, the teller doesn't hand me a ledger into which I note the deposit and write the new balance. She doesn't do it herself either. Instead, she types in the amount of the deposit at some terminal and then places that amount in the till. The machine spits out a deposit slip with the new balance on it that she hands me, and it's all done. Neither of us touches the bank's books directly.

This may seem like a silly exercise but consider why the bank doesn't do things "the functional way." Ignore for a minute the temptation I might have to add a few extra zeros to the end of my deposit before adding it up. The bank doesn't do things this way for the same reason that I don't energize my microwave oven by connecting and disconnecting wires inside the box — the bank wants to maintain tight controls on what happens to its balances.

If something screws up and my savings account balance gets incremented by a million dollars or so ("My gosh, how did that happen?"), the bank has a vested interest in being able to figure out exactly what happened and make sure that it doesn't happen again. A simple arithmetic error made by me or the teller is not sufficient justification for a mistake like that. The bank has a legal and fiduciary responsibility for maintaining its accounts in good order. It can't do that if every person who sallies up to the teller window has direct access to the books.

This care extends to programmers as well. You can rest easy at night knowing that not every programmer gets direct access to the bank balances either. Only the most trusted of programmers get to write the code that increments and decrements bank balances.

I use the term "trusted" here in two senses. First, the bank trusts these individuals not to intentionally steal. However, the bank also trusts these programmers to take all of the necessary process steps to fully vet and test the `deposit()` and `withdraw()` functions to make sure that they are bug-free and implement the bank's rules accurately.

To make the `Savings` class mimic a real-world savings account, it needs active properties of its own, like `deposit()` and `withdrawal()` (and `chargePenalty()` for who knows why, in my case). Only in this way can a `Savings` class be held responsible for its state.

Creating a Member Function

A function that is part of a class definition is known as a *member function*. The data within the class is known as *data members*. Member functions are the verbs of the class, whereas data members are the nouns.

Member functions are also known as *methods* because that's what they were called in the original object-oriented language, Smalltalk. The term methods had meaning to Smalltalk, but it has no special meaning in C++, except that it's easier to say and sounds more impressive in a conversation. I'll try not to bore you with this trivia, but you will hear the term method bandied about at object-oriented parties, so you might as well get used to it. I'll try to stick with the term member functions, but even I slip into technical jargon from time to time.

Note: Functions that you have seen so far that are not members of a class don't have a special name. I refer to them as *non-member functions* when I need to differentiate them from their member cousins.

There are three aspects to adding a member function to a class: defining the function, naming the function, and calling the function. Sounds pretty obvious when you say it that way.

Defining a member function

The following class demonstrates how to define two key member functions, `deposit()` and `withdraw()`, in a class `Savings` account:

```
// Savings - a simple savings account class
class Savings
{
  public:
    int     nAccountNumber;
    double dBalance;

    // deposit - deposit an amount to the balance;
    //           deposits must be positive number; return
    //           the resulting balance or zero on error
    double deposit(double dAmount)
```

```
    {
        // no negative deposits - that's a withdrawal
        if (dAmount < 0)
        {
            return 0.0;
        }

        // okay - add to the balance and return the total
        dBalance += dAmount;
        return dBalance;
    }

    // withdraw - execute a withdrawal if sufficient funds
    //            are available
    double withdraw(double dAmount)
    {
        if (dBalance < dAmount)
        {
            return 0.0;
        }

        dBalance -= dAmount;
        return dBalance;
    }
};
```

A real savings account class would have a lot of other information like the customer's name. Adding that extra stuff doesn't help explain the concepts, however, so I've left it off to keep the listings as short as possible.

You can see that the definition of the `deposit()` and `withdraw()` member functions look just like those of any other function except that they appear within the definition of the class itself. There are some other subtle differences that I address later in this chapter.

It is possible to define a member function outside of the class, as you will see a little later in this chapter.

Naming class members

A member function is a lot like a member of a family. The full name of the deposit function is `Savings::deposit(double)` just like my name is Stephen Davis. My mother doesn't call me that unless I'm in trouble. Normally, members of my family just call me by my first name, Stephen.

Similarly, from within the `Savings` class, the deposit function is known simply as `deposit(double)`.

The class name at the beginning indicates that this is a reference to the `deposit()` function that is a member of the class `Savings`. The `::` is simply a separator between the class name and the member name. The name of the class is part of the extended name of the member function just like Stephen Davis is my extended name. (See Chapter 11 if you don't remember about extended names.)

Classes are normally named using nouns that describe concepts like `Savings` or `SavingsAccount`. Member functions are normally named with the associated verbs like `deposit()` or `withdraw()`. Other than that, member functions follow the same naming convention as other functions. Data members are normally named using nouns that describe specific properties like `szName` or `nSocialSecurityNumber`.

You can define a different `deposit()` function that has nothing to do with the `Savings` class — there are Stephens out there who have nothing to do with my family. (I mean this literally: I know several Stephens who want *nothing* to do with my family.) For example, `Checking::deposit(double)` or `River::deposit()` are easily distinguishable from `Savings::deposit(double)`.

A non-member function can appear with a null class name. For example, if there were a deposit function that was not a member of any class, its name would be `::deposit()` or simply `deposit()`.

Calling a member function

Before I show you how to invoke a member function, let me quickly refresh you on how to access a data member of an object. Given the earlier definition of the `Savings` class, you could write the following:

```
void fn()
{
    Savings s;

    s.nAccountNumber = 0;
    s.dBalance = 0.0;
}
```

The function `fn()` creates a `Savings` object `s` and then zeros the data members `nAccountNumber` and `dBalance` of that object.

Notice that the following does not make sense:

```
void fn()
{
    Savings s1, s2;

    nAccountNumber = 0;   // doesn't work
    dBalance = 0.0;
}
```

Which nAccountNumber and dBalance are you talking about? The account number and balance of s1 or s2. Or some other object entirely? A reference to a data member makes sense only in the context of an object.

Invoking a member function is the same. You must first create an object and then you can invoke the member function on that object:

```
void fn()
{
    // create and initialize an object s
    Savings s = {0, 0.0};

    // now make a deposit of $100
    s.deposit(100.0);

    // or a withdrawal
    s.withdraw(50.0);
}
```

The syntax for calling a member function looks like a cross between the syntax for accessing a data member and that used for calling functions. The right side of the dot looks like a conventional function call, but an object appears on the left side of the dot.

This syntax makes sense when you think about it. In the call s.deposit(), s is the savings object to which the deposit() is to be made. You can't make a deposit without knowing to which account. Calling a member function without an object makes no more sense than referencing a data member without an object.

Accessing other members from within a member function

I can see it now: You repeat to yourself, "You can't access a member without reference to an object. You can't access a member without reference to an object. You can't. . . ." And then, wham, it hits you. Savings::deposit() appears to do exactly that:

```
double deposit(double dAmount)
{
    // no negative deposits - that's a withdrawal
    if (dAmount < 0)
    {
        return 0.0;
    }

    // okay - add to the balance and return the total
    dBalance += dAmount;
    return dBalance;
}
```

The `Savings::deposit()` function references `dBalance` without an explicit reference to any object. It's like that TV show: "How Do They Do It?"

So, okay, which is it? Can you or can you not reference a member without an object? Believe me, the answer is no. When you reference one member from within another member of the same class without explicitly referring to an object, the reference is implicitly against the "current object."

What is the current object? Go back and look at the example in greater detail. I am pulling out just the key elements of the example here for brevity's sake:

```
class Savings
{
  public:
    int     nAccountNumber;
    double dBalance;

    double deposit(double dAmount)
    {
        dBalance += dAmount;
        return dBalance;
    }
};

void fn()
{
    // create and initialize two objects
    Savings s1 = {0, 0.0};
    Savings s2 = {1, 0.0};

    // now make a deposit of $100 to one account
    s1.deposit(100.0);

    // and then the other
    s2.deposit(50.0);
}
```

When deposit() is invoked with s1, the unqualified reference to dBalance refers to s1.dBalance. At that moment in time, s1 is the "current object." During the call to s2.deposit(50.0), s2 becomes the current object. During this call, the unqualified reference to dBalance refers to s2.dBalance.

The "current object" has a name. It's called this as in "this object." Clever, no? Its type is "pointer to an object of the current class." I say more about this in Chapter 23 when I talk about pointers to objects.

Keeping a Member Function after Class

One of the things that I don't like about C++ is that it provides multiple ways of doing most things. Keeping with that penchant for flexibility, C++ allows you to define member functions outside the class as long as they are declared within the class.

The following is an example of the withdraw() function written outside the class declaration (once again, I've left out the error checking to make the example as short as possible):

```
// this part normally goes in the Savings.h include file
class Savings
{
  public:
    int     nAccountNumber;
    double dBalance;

    double deposit(double dAmount);
};

// this part appears in a separate Savings.cpp file
double Savings::deposit(double dAmount)
{
    dBalance += dAmount;
    return dBalance;
}
```

Now the definition of Savings contains nothing more than the prototype declaration of the member function deposit(). The actual definition of the function appears later. Notice, however, that when it does appear, it appears with its full extended name, including the class name — there is no default class name outside of the class definition.

This form is ideal for larger member functions. In these cases, the number of lines of code within the member functions can get so large that it obscures the definition of the class itself. In addition, this form is useful when defining classes in their own C++ source modules. The definition of the class can appear in an include file, `Savings.h`, while the definition of the function appears in a separately compiled `Savings.cpp`.

Overloading Member Functions

You can overload member functions just like you overload any other functions. Remember, however, that the class name is part of the extended name. That means that the following is completely legal:

```
class Student
{
  public:
    double grade();  // return Student's grade
    double grade(double dNewGPA); // set Student's grade
};

class Hill
{
  public:
    double grade(double dSlope); // set the slope
};
    void grade(double);

void fn()
{
    Student s;
    Hill h;

    // set the student's grade
    s.grade(3.0);

    // now query the grade
    double dGPA = s.grade();

    // now grade a hill to 3 degrees slope
    h.grade(3.0);

    // call the non-member function
    grade(3.0);
}
```

When calling a member function, the type of the object is just as important as the number and type of the arguments. The first call to grade() invokes the function Student::grade(double) to set the student's grade point average. The second call is to Student::grade(), which returns the student's grade point average without changing it.

The third call is to a completely unrelated function, Hill::grade(double), that sets the slope on the side of the hill. And the final call is to the non-member function ::grade(double).

Chapter 23

Pointers to Objects

Chapters 17 and 18 focus on various aspects of the care and feeding of pointers. Surely, you think, nothing more can be said on the subject. But I hadn't introduced the concept classes before those chapters. In this chapter, I describe the intersection of pointer variables and object-oriented programming. This chapter deals with the concept of pointers to class objects. I'll describe how to create one, how to use it, and how to delete it once you're finished with it.

Pointers to Objects

A pointer to a programmer-defined type such as a class works essentially the same as a pointer to an intrinsic type:

```
int nInt;
int* pInt = &nInt;

class Savings
{
  public:
    int nAccountNumber;
    double dBalance;
};
Savings s;
Savings* pS = &s;
```

The first pair of declarations defines an integer, nInt, and a pointer to an integer, pInt. The pointer pInt is initialized to point to the integer nInt.

Similarly, the second pair of declarations creates a Savings object s. It then declares a pointer to a Savings object, pS, and initializes it to the address of s.

The type of pS is "pointer to Savings" which is written Savings*.

I feel like the late Billy Mays when I say, "But wait! There's more!" The similarities continue. The following statement assigns the value 1 to the int pointed at by pInt:

```
*pInt = 1;
```

Similarly, the following assigns values to the account number and balance of the Savings object pointed at by pS.

```
(*pS).nAccountNumber = 1234;
(*pS).dBalance = 0.0;
```

The parentheses are required because the precedence of . is higher than *. Without the parentheses, *pS.nAccountNumber = 1234 would be interpreted as *(pS.nAccountNumber) = 1234, which means "store 1234 at the location pointed at by pS.nAccountNumber." This generates a compiler error because nAccountNumber isn't a pointer (nor is pS a Savings).

Arrow syntax

The only thing that I can figure is that the authors of the C language couldn't type very well. They wasted no efforts in finding shorthand ways of saying things. Here is another case where they made up a shorthand to save keystrokes, inventing a new operator -> to stand for *():

```
pS->dBalance = 0.0; // same as (*pS).dBalance = 0.0
```

Even though the two are equivalent, the arrow operator is used almost exclusively because it's easier to read (and type). Don't lose sight of the fact, however, that the two forms are completely equivalent.

Calling all member functions

The syntax for invoking a member function with a pointer is similar to accessing a data member:

```
class Savings
{
  public:
    int nAccountNumber;
    double dBalance;

    double withdraw(double dAmount);
    double deposit(double dAmount);
};

void fn()
{
    Savings s = {1234, 0.0};
    Savings* pS = &s;

    // deposit money into the account pointed at by pS
    pS->deposit(100.0);
}
```

The last statement in this snippet says "invoke the deposit() member function on the object pointed at by pS."

Passing Objects to Functions

Passing pointers to functions is just one of the many ways to entertain yourself with pointers.

Calling a function with an object value

As you know, C++ passes arguments to functions by value by default. If you don't know that, refer to Chapter 11. Complex, user-defined objects are passed by value as well:

```
class Savings
{
  public:
    int nAccountNumber;
    double dBalance;

    double withdraw(double dAmount);
    double deposit(double dAmount);
```

```
};

void someOtherFunction(Savings s)
{
    s.deposit(100.0);
}

void someFunction()
{
    Savings s = {1234, 0.0};

    someOtherFunction(s);
}
```

Here the function someFunction() creates and initializes a Savings object s. It then passes a copy of that object to someOtherFunction(). The fact that it's a copy is important for two reasons:

✔ Making copies of large objects can be very inefficient, causing your program to run slower.

✔ Changes made to copies don't have any effect on the original object in the calling function.

In this case, the second problem is much worse than the former. I can stand a little bit of inefficiency since a Savings object isn't very big anyway, but the deposit made in someOtherFunction() got booked against a copy of the original account. My Savings account back in someFunction() still has a balance of zero. This is shown graphically in Figure 23-1.

Calling a function with an object pointer

The programmer can pass the address of an object rather than the object itself as demonstrated in the following example:

```
class Savings
{
  public:
    int nAccountNumber;
    double dBalance;

    double withdraw(double dAmount);
    double deposit(double dAmount);
```

```
};

void someOtherFunction(Savings* pS)
{
    pS->deposit(100.0);
}

void someFunction()
{
    Savings s = {1234, 0.0};

    someOtherFunction(&s);
}
```

The type of the argument to someOtherFunction() is "pointer to Savings." This is reflected in the way that someFunction() performs the call, passing not the object s but the address of the object, &s. This is shown graphically in Figure 23-2.

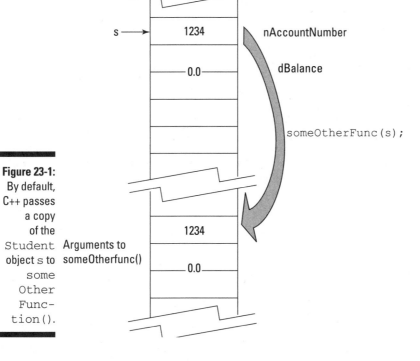

Figure 23-1:
By default,
C++ passes
a copy
of the
Student
object s to
some
Other
Func-
tion().

s ⟶ 1234   nAccountNumber

0.0   dBalance

someOtherFunc(s);

Arguments to someOtherfunc()

1234

0.0

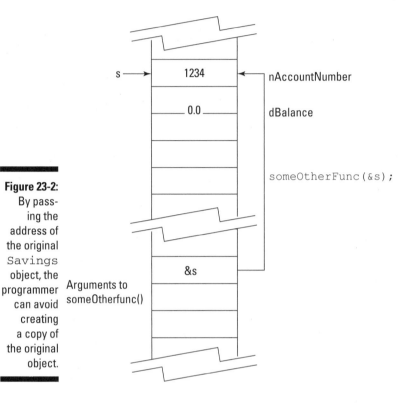

Figure 23-2:
By passing the address of the original `Savings` object, the programmer can avoid creating a copy of the original object.

This addresses both of the problems with passing a copy:

✔ No matter how large and complicated the object might be, the call passes only a single address.

✔ Changes made in `someOtherFunction()` are permanent because they refer to the original object and not a copy.

Looking at an example

The following program demonstrates the difference between passing an object by value versus passing the address of an object:

```
//
//   PassObjects - this program demonstrates passing an
//                 object by value versus passing the
//                 address of the object
//
#include <cstdio>
```

```cpp
#include <cstdlib>
#include <iostream>
#include <cstring>
using namespace std;


// Savings - a simple savings account class
class Savings
{
  public:
    int    nAccountNumber;
    double dBalance;

    // deposit - deposit an amount to the balance;
    //           deposits must be positive number; return
    //           the resulting balance or zero on error
    double deposit(double dAmount)
    {
        // no negative deposits - that's a withdrawal
        if (dAmount < 0)
        {
            return 0.0;
        }

        // okay - add to the balance and return the total
        dBalance += dAmount;
        return dBalance;
    }

    // withdraw - execute a withdrawal if sufficient funds
    //            are available
    double withdraw(double dAmount)
    {
        if (dBalance < dAmount)
        {
            return 0.0;
        }

        dBalance -= dAmount;
        return dBalance;
    }

    // balance - return the balance of the current object
    double balance()
    {
        return dBalance;
    }
};

// someFunction(Savings) - accept object by value
```

```
void someFunction(Savings s)
{
    cout << "In someFunction(Savings)" << endl;

    cout << "Depositing $100" << endl;
    s.deposit(100.0);

    cout << "Balance in someFunction(Savings) is "
        << s.balance() << endl;
}

// someFunction(Savings*) - accept address of object
void someFunction(Savings* pS)
{
    cout << "In someFunction(Savings*)" << endl;

    cout << "Depositing $100" << endl;
    pS->deposit(100.0);

    cout << "Balance in someFunction(Savings) is "
        << pS->balance() << endl;
}

int main(int nNumberofArgs, char* pszArgs[])
{
    Savings s = {0, 0.0};

    // first, pass by value
    someFunction(s);
    cout << "Balance back in main() is "
        << s.balance() << endl;

    // now pass the address
    someFunction(&s);
    cout << "Balance back in main() is "
        << s.balance() << endl;

    // wait until user is ready before terminating program
    // to allow the user to see the program results
    system("PAUSE");
    return 0;
}
```

This program starts by defining a conventional `Savings` class with `deposit()`, `withdrawal()`, and `balance()` member functions (the last one just returns the current balance).

The program then defines two overloaded functions `someFunction()`, one of which accepts as its argument an object of type `Savings` and the second a pointer to an object of type `Savings` (written `Savings*`). Both functions do the same things, first outputting a "Here I am" message and then depositing $100 to the account.

Passing by reference

In an attempt to make things simpler, C++ added a level of complexity by allowing the programmer to declare a function that accepts its argument by reference as follows:

```
// pass by reference
void someFunction(Savings& refS)
{
    refS.deposit(100.0);   // this deposits back into the original
                           // object in fn() even though it looks
                           // copy semantics
}
void fn()
{
    Savings s;
    someFunction(s);       // this passes a reference, not a copy
}
```

This causes C++ to pass the address of s to the function someFunction(Savings). Within the function, C++ automatically dereferences the address for you. The effect is exactly the same as if you had passed the address yourself except that C++ handles the pointer grammar. You might think that this makes things simpler. (I suspect the authors of C++ thought it would.) In practice, however, it makes things more complicated since it becomes difficult to tell a value from a reference.

I mention pass by reference not to encourage its use, but because you are likely to see others that aren't as comfortable as you with pointer manipulation using it. I would encourage you to avoid use of references until you are really comfortable with pointers.

The main() program creates a Savings object s, which it first passes to someFunction(Savings). It then passes the address of the s object to someFunction(Savings*).

The output from this program appears as follows:

```
In someFunction(Savings)
Depositing $100
Balance in someFunction(Savings) is 100
Balance back in main() is 0
In someFunction(Savings*)
Depositing $100
Balance in someFunction(Savings) is 100
Balance back in main() is 100
Press any key to continue . . .
```

Notice how both functions deposit $100 into a Savings account object. However, since someFunction(Savings) makes the deposit into a copy, the original s object back in main() is left unchanged as demonstrated by the zero balance.

By passing the address of s to someFunction(Savings*), the program allows that function to modify the original object so the value "stays modified" in main() as demonstrated by the fact that the balance is $100 after control returns.

Allocating Objects off the Heap

You can allocate objects off of the heap using the new keyword as shown in the following example:

```
Savings* newSavings(int nAccountNum)
{
    Savings* pS = new Savings;
    pS->nAccountNumber = nAccountNum;
    pS->dBalance = 0.0;
    return pS;
}
```

The function allocates a new object of class Savings and then initializes it with the account number passed as an argument and a zero balance.

This is useful when you don't know how many objects you are going to need, like in the case of dynamically sized character arrays in Chapter 18. Then, I first counted how many characters I needed room for and then allocated an array of the appropriate size off of the heap.

In this case, I can determine how many Savings accounts I need in memory at one time and allocate them dynamically off of the heap.

Of course, there is the little matter of how do you store an unknown quantity of objects. C++ provides several variable-sized data structures in addition to the fixed-sized array as part of the Standard Template Library. A general discussion of the STL is beyond the scope of a beginner book

You must return every object that you allocate off of the heap by passing the unmodified address of that object to the keyword delete. Otherwise, your program will slowly run out of memory and die a horrible death.

What is `this` anyway?

In Chapter 22, I mention that an otherwise unqualified reference to a member made from within a member function always refers to the "current object." I even mention that the current object has a name: `this`. You can reference `this` explicitly. I could have written the `Savings` class as follows:

```
class Savings
{
  public:
    int nAccountNumber;
    double dBalance;

    double withdraw(double dAmount)
    {
        this->dBalance -= dAmount;
        return this->dBalance;
    }
    double deposit(double dAmount)
    {
        this->dBalance += dAmount;
        return this->dBalance;
    }
    double balance()
    {
        return this->dBalance;
    }
}
```

In fact, even without explicitly referring to it, you use `this` all the time. If you don't specify an object within a member function, C++ assumes a reference to `this`. Thus, the preceding is what C++ actually "sees" even if you don't mention `this`.

Chapter 24

Do Not Disturb: Protected Members

My goal with this part of the book, starting with Chapter 21, has been to model real-world objects in C++ using the class structure. In Chapter 22, I introduce the concept of member functions in order to assign classes' active properties. Returning to the microwave oven example in Chapter 21, assigning active properties allows me to give my Oven class properties like `cook()` and `defrost()`.

However, that's only part of the story. I still haven't put a box around the insides of my classes. I can't very well hold someone responsible if the microwave catches on fire as long as the insides are exposed to anyone who wants to mess with them.

This chapter "puts a box" around the classes by declaring certain members off limits to user functions.

Protecting Members

Members of a class can be flagged as inaccessible from outside the class with the keyword `protected`. This is in direct opposition to the `public` keyword, which designates those members that are accessible to all functions. The public members of a class form the interface to the class (think of the keypad on the front of the microwave oven) while the protected members form the inner workings.

There is a third category called `private`. The only difference between private and protected members is the way they react to inheritance, which I don't present until Chapter 28.

Why you need protected members

Declaring a member `protected` allows a class to put a protective box around the class. This makes the class responsible for its own internal state. If something in the class gets screwed up, the class, rather the author of the class, has nowhere to look except herself. It's not fair, however, to ask the programmer to take responsibility for the state of the class if any ol' function can reach in and muck with it.

In addition, limiting the interface to a class makes the class easier to learn for programmers that use that interface in their programs. In general, I don't really care how my microwave works inside as long as I know how to use the controls. In a similar fashion, I don't generally worry about the inner workings of library classes as long as I understand the arguments to the public member functions.

Finally, limiting the class interface to just some choice public functions reduces the level of coupling between the class and the application code.

Note: *Coupling* refers to how much knowledge the application has of how the class works internally and vice versa. A tightly coupled class has intimate knowledge of the surrounding application and uses that knowledge. A loosely coupled class works only through a simple, generic public interface. A loosely coupled class knows little about its surroundings and hides most of its own internal details as well. Loosely coupled classes are easier to test and debug and easier to replace when the application changes.

I know what you functional types out there are saying: "You don't need some fancy feature to do all that. Just make a rule that says certain members are publicly accessible and others are not." This is true in theory, and I've even been on projects that employed such rules, but in practice it doesn't work. People start out with good intentions, but as long as the language doesn't at least discourage direct access of protected members, these good intentions get crushed under the pressure to get the product out the door.

Making members protected

Adding the keyword `public:` to a class makes subsequent members publicly accessible. Adding the keyword `protected:` makes subsequent members protected, which means they are accessible only to other members of the same class or functions that are specifically declared *friends* (more on that later in this chapter). They act as toggles — one overrides the other. You can switch back and forth between protected and public as often as you like.

Take, for example, a class Student that describes the salient features of a college student. This class has the following public member functions:

✔ addGrade(int nHours, double dGrade) — add a grade to the student.

✔ grade() — return the student's grade point average (GPA).

✔ hours() — return the number of semester hours toward graduation.

The remaining members of Student should be declared protected to keep prying expressions out of his business.

The following SimpleStudent program defines such a Student class and includes a simple main() that exercises the functions:

```
//
//   SimpleStudent - this program demonstrates how the
//                   protected keyword is used to protect
//                   key internal members
//
#include <cstdio>
#include <cstdlib>
#include <iostream>
using namespace std;

class Student
{
  protected:
    double dGrade;            // the student's GPA
    int    nSemesterHours;

  public:
    // init() - initialize the student to a legal state
    void init()
    {
        dGrade = 0.0;
        nSemesterHours = 0;
    }

    // getGrade() - return the current grade
    double getGrade()
    {
        return dGrade;
```

```
    }

    // getHours() - get the class hours towards graduation
    int getHours()
    {
        return nSemesterHours;
    }

    // addGrade - add a grade to the GPA and total hours
    double addGrade(double dNewGrade, int nHours)
    {
        double dWtdHrs = dGrade * nSemesterHours;
        dWtdHrs += dNewGrade * nHours;
        nSemesterHours += nHours;
        dGrade = dWtdHrs / nSemesterHours;
        return dGrade;
    }
};

int main(int nNumberofArgs, char* pszArgs[])
{
    // create a student and initialize it
    Student s;
    s.init();

    // add the grades for three classes
    s.addGrade(3.0, 3);   // a B
    s.addGrade(4.0, 3);   // an A
    s.addGrade(2.0, 3);   // a C (average should be a B)

    // now print the results
    cout << "Total # hours = " << s.getHours()
         << ", GPA = " << s.getGrade()
         << endl;

    // wait until user is ready before terminating program
    // to allow the user to see the program results
    system("PAUSE");
    return 0;
}
```

This `Student` protects its members `dGrade` and `nSemesterHours`. Outside functions can't surreptitiously set their own GPA high by slipping in the following:

```
void MyFunction(Student* pS)
{
    // set my grade to A+
    pS->dGrade = 3.9;   // generates a compiler error
}
```

This assignment generates a compiler error.

You can start with either the protected or public members; it doesn't matter. In fact, you can switch back and forth as often as you like.

Any function can read a student's GPA through the function `getGrade()`. This is known as an *access* function. However, though external functions can read a value, they cannot change the value via this access function.

An access function is also known as a *getter function* (as in "get the value"). A function that sets the value is also known as a *setter function*.

The `main()` function in this program creates a `Student` object `s`. It cannot initialize `s` to some legal state since the data members are protected. Fortunately, the `Student` class has provided an `init()` function for `main()` to call that initializes the data members to their proper starting state.

After initializing `s`, `main()` calls `addGrade()` to add three different courses and prints out the results using the access member functions. The results appear as follows:

```
Total # hours = 9, GPA = 3
Press any key to continue . . .
```

So what?

So what's the big deal? "Okay," you say, "I see the point about not letting other functions set the GPA to some arbitrary value, but is that it?" No. A finer point lies behind this loose coupling. I chose to implement the algorithms for calculating the GPA as simply as I possibly could. With no more than five minutes' thought, I can imagine at least three different ways I could have chosen to store the grades and semester hours internally, each with their own advantages and disadvantages.

For example, I could save off each grade along with the number of semester hours in an internal array. This would allow the student to review the grades that are going into his GPA.

The point is that the application programmer shouldn't care. As long as the member functions `getGrade()` and `getHours()` calculate the GPA and total number of semester hours accurately, no application is going to care.

Now suppose the school changes the rules for how to calculate the GPA. Suppose, for example, that it declares certain classes to be Pass/Fail, meaning that you get credit toward graduation but the grade in the class doesn't go into the GPA calculation. This may require a total rewrite of the `Student` class. That, in turn, would require modification to any functions that rely upon the way that the information is stored internally — that is, any functions that have access to the protected members. However, functions that limit themselves to the public members are unaffected by the change.

That is the true advantage of loose coupling: tolerance to change.

Who Needs Friends Anyway?

Occasionally, you need to give a non-member function access to the protected members of a class. You can do this by declaring the function to be a *friend*. Declaring a function to be a friend means you don't have to expose the protected member to everyone by declaring it public.

It's like giving your neighbor a key to check on your house during your vacation. Giving non–family members keys to the house is not normally a good idea, but it beats the alternative of leaving the house unlocked.

The friend declaration appears in the class that contains the protected member. The friend declaration consists of the keyword `friend` followed by a prototype declaration. In the following example, the `initialize()` function is declared as a non-member. However, `initialize()` clearly needs access to all the data members of the class, protected or not:

```
class Student
{
    friend void initialize(Student*);
  protected:
    double dGrade;          // the student's GPA
    int     nSemesterHours;

  public:
    double grade();
    int hours();
    double addGrade(double dNewGrade, int nHours);
};

void initialize(Student* pS)
{
    pS->dGrade = 0.0;
    pS->nSemesterHours = 0;
}
```

A single function can be declared to be a friend of two different classes at the same time. Although this may seem convenient, it tends to bind the two classes together. However, sometimes the classes are bound together by their very nature, as in the following teacher-student example:

```
class Student;    // forward declaration
class Teacher
{
    friend void registration(Teacher*, Student*);
  protected:
    int noStudents;
    Student *pList[128];

  public:
    void assignGrades();
};

class Student
{
    friend void registration(Teacher*, Student*);
  protected:
    Teacher *pTeacher;
    int nSemesterHours;
    double dGrade;
};
```

In this example, the `registration()` function can reach into both the Student object to set the pTeacher pointer and into the Teacher object to add to the teacher's list of students.

Notice how the class Student first appears by itself with no body. This is called a *forward declaration* and declares the intention of the programmer to define a class Student somewhere within the module. This is a little bit like the prototype declaration for a function. This is generally necessary only when two or more classes reference each other; in this case, Teacher contains a reference to Student and Student to Teacher.

Without the forward declaration to Student, the declaration within Teacher of Student *pList[100] generates a compiler error because the compiler doesn't yet know what a Student is. Swap the order of the definitions, and the declaration Teacher *pTeacher within Student generates a compiler error because Teacher has not been defined yet.

The forward declaration solves the problem by informing the compiler to be patient — a definition for this new class is coming very soon.

A member of one class can be declared a friend of another class:

```
class Student;

class Teacher
{
    // ...other members...
  public:
    void assignGrade(Student*, int nHours, double dGrade);
};

class Student
{
    friend void Teacher::assignGrade(Student*,
                                     int, double);
    // ...other members...
};
```

An entire class can be declared a friend of another class. This has the effect of making every member function of the class a friend. For example:

```
class Student;

class Teacher
{
  protected:
    int noStudents;
    Student* pList[128];

  public:
    void assignGrade(Student*, int nHours, double dGrade);
};

class Student
{
    friend class Teacher;

    // ...other members...
};
```

Now every member of Teacher can access the protected members of Student (but not the other way around). Declaring one class to be a friend of another binds the classes together inseparably.

Chapter 25

Getting Objects Off to a Good Start

*N*ormally an object is initialized when it is created as in the following:

```
double PI = 3.14159;
```

This is true of class objects as well:

```
class Student
{
  public:
    int nHours;
    double dGrade;
};

Student s = {0, 0.0};
```

However, this is no longer possible when the data elements are declared protected if the function that's creating the objects is not a friend or member of the class (which, in most cases it would not be).

Some other mechanism is required to initialize objects when they are created, and that's where the constructor comes in.

The Constructor

One approach to initializing objects with protected members would be to create an init() member function that the application could call when the object is created. This `init()` function would initialize the object to some legal starting point. In fact, that's exactly what I do in Chapter 24.

This approach would work, but it doesn't exactly fit the "microwave oven" rules of object-oriented programming because it's akin to building a microwave oven that requires you to hit the Reset button before you could do anything with it. It's as if the manufacturer put some big disclaimer in the manual: "DO NOT start any sequence of commands without FIRST depressing the RESET button. Failure to do so may cause the oven to explode and kill everyone in the vicinity or WORSE." (What could be worse than that?)

Now I'm no lawyer, but even I know that putting a disclaimer like that in your manual is not going to save your butt when you end up in court because someone got cut with shrapnel from an exploding microwave, even though you say very clearly to hit reset first.

Fortunately, C++ takes the responsibility for calling the initialization function away from the applications programmer and calls the function automatically whenever an object is created.

You could call this initialization function anything you want as long as there is a rule for everyone to follow. (I'm kind of partial to `init()` myself, but I didn't get a vote.) The rule is that this initialization function is called a *constructor,* and it has the same name as the name of the class.

Outfitted with a constructor, the `Student` class appears as follows:

```
class Student
{
  protected:
    int nSemesterHours;
    double dGrade;

  public:
    Student()
    {
        nSemesterHours = 0;
        dGrade = 0.0;
    }

    // ...other public member functions...
};
void fn()
{
    Student s;  // create an object and invoke the
                // constructor on it
}
```

At the point of the declaration of s, C++ embeds a call to
`Student::Student()`.

Notice that the constructor is called once for every object created. Thus, the
following declaration calls the constructor five times in a row:

```
void fn()
{
    Student s[5];
}
```

It first calls the constructor for `s[0]`, then for `s[1]`, and so forth.

Limitations on constructors

The constructor can only be invoked automatically by C++. You cannot call a
constructor like a normal member function. That is, you cannot do something
like the following:

```
void fn()
{
    Student s;

    // ...do stuff...

    // now reinitialize s back to its initial state
    s.Student();    // this doesn't work
}
```

The constructor is not just any ol' function.

In addition, the constructor has no return type, not even `void`. The default
constructor has no arguments either.

The next chapter shows you how to declare and use a constructor with
arguments.

Finally, the constructor must be declared public, or else you will be able to
create objects only from within other member functions.

The constructor can call other functions. Thus, your constructor could
invoke a publicly available `init()` function that could then be used by
anyone to reset the object to its initial state.

Can I see an example?

The following StudentConstructor program looks a lot like the SimpleStudent program from Chapter 24, except that this version includes a constructor that outputs every time it's creating an object. The interesting part to this program is seeing the cases during which the constructor is invoked.

I highly encourage you to single-step this program in the debugger using the Step-Into debugger command from Chapter 20. Use the Step Into debugger command near the declaration of the Student objects to step into the constructor automatically.

```cpp
//
//  StudentConstructor - this program demonstrates the use
//                of a default constructor to initialize
//                objects when they are created
//
#include <cstdio>
#include <cstdlib>
#include <iostream>
using namespace std;

class Student
{
  protected:
    double dGrade;          // the student's GPA
    int    nSemesterHours;

  public:
    // constructor - init the student to a legal state
    Student()
    {
        cout << "Constructing a Student object" << endl;
        dGrade = 0.0;
        nSemesterHours = 0;
    }

    // getGrade() - return the current grade
    double getGrade()
    {
        return dGrade;
    }

    // getHours() - get the class hours towards graduation
    int getHours()
    {
        return nSemesterHours;
    }

    // addGrade - add a grade to the GPA and total hours
    double addGrade(double dNewGrade, int nHours)
    {
```

```
            double dWtdHrs = dGrade * nSemesterHours;
            dWtdHrs += dNewGrade * nHours;
            nSemesterHours += nHours;
            dGrade = dWtdHrs / nSemesterHours;
            return dGrade;
        }
};

int main(int nNumberofArgs, char* pszArgs[])
{
    // create a student and initialize it
    cout << "Creating the Student s" << endl;
    Student s;

    // add the grades for three classes
    s.addGrade(3.0, 3);   // a B
    s.addGrade(4.0, 3);   // an A
    s.addGrade(2.0, 3);   // a C (average should be a B)

    // now print the results
    cout << "Total # hours = " << s.getHours()
         << ", GPA = " << s.getGrade()
         << endl;

    // create an array of Students
    cout << "Create an array of 5 Students" << endl;
    Student sArray[5];

    // now allocate one off of the heap
    cout << "Allocating a Student from the heap" << endl;
    Student *pS = new Student;

    // wait until user is ready before terminating program
    // to allow the user to see the program results
    system("PAUSE");
    return 0;
}
```

The output from this program appears as follows:

```
Creating the Student s
Constructing a Student object
Total # hours = 9, GPA = 3
Create an array of 5 Students
Constructing a Student object
Constructing a Student object
Constructing a Student object
Constructing a Student object
Constructing a Student object
Allocating a Student from the heap
Constructing a Student object
Press any key to continue . . .
```

The Student class has been outfitted with a constructor that not only initializes the number of semester hours and grade point average to zero but also outputs a message to the console to announce that a Student object is being created.

The main() program then simply creates Student objects in various ways:

- ✔ The first declaration creates a single Student object s resulting in C++ invoking the constructor.

- ✔ The second declaration creates an array of five Student objects. C++ calls the constructor five times, once for each object in the array.

- ✔ The program allocates a Student object from the heap. C++ invokes the constructor again to initialize the object.

Constructing data members

The data members of a class are created at the same time as the object itself. Consider the following simple class TutorPair consisting of a Student and a Teacher:

```
class TutorPair
{
  protected:
    Student s;
    Teacher t;

    int nNumberOfMeetings;

  public:
    TutorPair()
    {
        nNumberOfMeetings = 0;
    }

    // ...other stuff...
};
```

It's not the responsibility of the TutorPair class to initialize the member Student or the member Teacher; these objects should be initialized by constructors in their respective classes. The constructor for TutorPair is responsible only for initializing the non-class members of the class.

Thus, when a TutorPair is created, C++ does the following (in the order shown):

✔ It invokes the constructor for the Student s.

✔ It invokes the constructor for the Teacher t.

✔ It enters the constructor for TutorPair itself.

The constructors for the data members are invoked in the order that they appear in the class.

The following TutorPairConstructor program demonstrates:

```
//
//   TutorPairConstructor - this program demonstrates
//              how data members are constructed automatically
//
#include <cstdio>
#include <cstdlib>
#include <iostream>
using namespace std;

class Student
{
  protected:
    double dGrade;          // the student's GPA
    int    nSemesterHours;

  public:
    // constructor - init the student to a legal state
    Student()
    {
        cout << "Constructing a Student object" << endl;
        dGrade = 0.0;
        nSemesterHours = 0;
    }
};

class Teacher
{
  public:
    // constructor - init the student to a legal state
    Teacher()
    {
        cout << "Constructing a Teacher object" << endl;
    }
};

class TutorPair
{
  protected:
    Student s;
```

```
    Teacher t;

    int nNumberOfMeetings;

  public:
    TutorPair()
    {
        cout << "Constructing the TutorPair members"
             << endl;
        nNumberOfMeetings = 0;
    }
};

int main(int nNumberofArgs, char* pszArgs[])
{
    // create a TutorPair and initialize it
    cout << "Creating the TutorPair tp" << endl;
    TutorPair tp;

    // wait until user is ready before terminating program
    // to allow the user to see the program results
    system("PAUSE");
    return 0;
}
```

The `main()` program does nothing more than output a message and then creates an object `tp` of class `TutorPair`. This causes C++ to invoke the constructor for `TutorPair`. However, before the first line of that function is executed, C++ goes through the data members and constructs any objects that it finds there.

The first object C++ sees is the `Student` object `s`. This constructor outputs the first message that you see on the output. The second object that C++ finds is the `Teacher` member `t`. This constructor generates the next line of output.

With all the data members out of the way, C++ passes control to the body of the `TutorPair` constructor that outputs the final line of output:

```
Creating the TutorPair tp
Constructing a Student object
Constructing a Teacher object
Constructing the TutorPair members
Press any key to continue . . .
```

Destructors

Just as objects are created, so they are destroyed. (I think there's a Biblical passage to that effect.) If a class can have a constructor to set things up, it should also have a special member function to take the object apart and put back any resources that the constructor may have allocated. This function is known as the *destructor*.

A destructor has the name of the class preceded by a tilde (~). Like a constructor, the destructor has no return type (not even `void`), and it cannot be invoked like a normal function.

Technically, you can call the destructor explicitly: `s.~Student()`. However, this is rarely done, and it's needed only in advanced programming techniques, such as allocating an object on a predetermined memory address.

In logic, the tilde is sometimes used to mean "NOT" so the destructor is the "NOT constructor." Get it? Cute.

C++ automatically invokes the destructor in the following three cases:

- ✔ A local object is passed to the destructor when it goes out of scope.
- ✔ An object allocated off the heap is passed to the destructor when it is passed to delete.
- ✔ A global object is passed to the destructor when the program terminates.

Looking at an example

The following StudentDestructor program features a Student class that allocates memory off of the heap in the constructor. Therefore, this class needs a destructor to return that memory to the heap.

Any class whose constructor allocates resources, in particular, a class that allocates memory off of the heap, requires a destructor to put that memory back.

The program creates a few objects within a function `fn()` and then allows those objects to go out of scope and get destructed when the function returns. The function returns a pointer to an object that `fn()` allocates off of the heap. This object is returned to the heap back in `main()`.

```
//
//   StudentDestructor - this program demonstrates the use
//                of the destructor to return resources
//                allocated by the constructor
//
#include <cstdio>
#include <cstdlib>
#include <iostream>
using namespace std;

class Student
{
  protected:
    double* pdGrades;
    int*    pnHours;

  public:
    // constructor - init the student to a legal state
    Student()
    {
        cout << "Constructing a Student object" << endl;
        pdGrades = new double[128];
        pnHours  = new int[128];
    }
    ~Student()
    {
        cout << "Destructing a Student object" << endl;
        delete[] pdGrades;
        pdGrades = 0;

        delete[] pnHours;
        pnHours = 0;
    }
};

Student* fn()
{
    cout << "Entering fn()" << endl;

    // create a student and initialize it
    cout << "Creating the Student s" << endl;
    Student s;

    // create an array of Students
    cout << "Create an array of 5 Students" << endl;
    Student sArray[5];

    // now allocate one off of the heap
    cout << "Allocating a Student from the heap" << endl;
```

```
        Student *pS = new Student;

        cout << "Returning from fn()" << endl;
        return pS;
}

int main(int nNumberofArgs, char* pszArgs[])
{
        // now allocate one off of the heap
        Student *pS = fn();

        // delete the pointer returned by fn()
        cout << "Deleting the pointer returned by fn()"
             << endl;
        delete pS;
        pS = 0;

        // wait until user is ready before terminating program
        // to allow the user to see the program results
        system("PAUSE");
        return 0;
}
```

The output from the program appears as follows:

```
Entering fn()
Creating the Student s
Constructing a Student object
Create an array of 5 Students
Constructing a Student object
Constructing a Student object
Constructing a Student object
Constructing a Student object
Constructing a Student object
Allocating a Student from the heap
Constructing a Student object
Returning from fn()
Destructing a Student object
Destructing a Student object
Destructing a Student object
Destructing a Student object
Destructing a Student object
Destructing a Student object
Deleting the pointer returned by fn()
Destructing a Student object
Press any key to continue . . .
```

The first message is from `fn()` itself as it displays an opening banner to let us know that control has entered the function. The `fn()` function then creates an object s that causes the constructor to output a message. It then creates an array of five Student objects, which causes five more messages from the Student constructor. And finally fn() allocates one more Student object from the heap using the new keyword.

The last thing fn() does before returning is output an exit banner message. C++ automatically calls the destructor six times: five times for the elements of the array and once for the s object created at the beginning of the function.

You can't tell from the output, but the objects are destructed in the reverse order that they are constructed.

The destructor is not invoked for the object allocated off of the heap until main() deletes the pointer returned by fn().

A memory block allocated off of the heap does not go out of scope when the pointer to it goes out of scope. It is the programmer's responsibility to make sure that the object is returned to the heap using the delete command.

Return a pointer to a non-array with delete. Return an array using delete[].

Destructing data members

Data members are also destructed automatically. Destruction occurs in the reverse order to the order of construction: The body of the destructor is invoked first, and then the destructor for each data member in the reverse order that the data members were constructed.

To demonstrate this, I added a destructor to the TutorPairConstructor program. The entire listing is a bit lengthy to include here, but it is contained on the enclosed CD-ROM as TutorPairDestructor. I include just the TutorPair class here:

```
class TutorPair
{
  protected:
    Student s;
    Teacher t;

    int nNumberOfMeetings;

  public:
```

```
    TutorPair()
    {
        cout << "Constructing the TutorPair members"
             << endl;
        nNumberOfMeetings = 0;
    }
  ~TutorPair()
    {
        cout << "Destructing the TutorPair object"
             << endl;
    }
};

void fn()
{
    // create a TutorPair and initialize it
    cout << "Creating the TutorPair tp" << endl;
    TutorPair tp;

    cout << "Returning from fn()" << endl;
}
```

The output from this program appears as follows:

```
Creating the TutorPair tp
Constructing a Student object
Constructing a Teacher object
Constructing the TutorPair members
Returning from fn()
Destructing the TutorPair object
Destructing a Teacher object
Destructing a Student object
Press any key to continue . . .
```

This program creates the TutorPair object within the function fn(). The messages from the constructors are identical to the TutorPairConstructor program. The messages from the TutorPair destructor appear as control is returning to main, and they appear in the exact reverse of the order of messages from the constructors, coming first from ~TutorPair itself, then from ~Teacher, and finally from ~Student.

Static data members

A special type of data member that deserves separate mention is known as a class member or static member because it is flagged with the keyword `static`:

```
class Student
{
  protected:
    static int nNumberOfStudents;
    int nSemesterHours;
    double dGrade;

  public:
    Student()
    {
        nSemesterHours = 0;
        dGrade = 0.0;

        // count how many Students
        nNumberOfStudents++;
    }
    ~Student()
    {
        nNumberOfStudents--;
    }
};

// allocate space for the static member; be sure to
// initialize it here (when the program starts) because
// the class constructor will not initialize it
int Student::nNumberOfStudents = 0;
```

Static members are a property of the class and not of each object. In this example, a single variable `Student::nNumberOfStudents` is shared by all `Student` objects. This example demonstrates exactly what such members are good for: In this case, nNumberOf Students keeps a running count of the number of `Student` objects that currently exist.

Static members are initialized when the program starts. You can manipulate them from the constructor for each object — in this case, I increment the counter in the `Student` constructor and decrement it in the destructor. In general, you do not want to initialize a static member in the class constructor since it will get reinitialized every time an object is created.

Chapter 26

Making Constructive Arguments

· ·

In This Chapter

▶ Creating and invoking a constructor with arguments

▶ Overloading the constructor

▶ Constructing data members with arguments

▶ Looking forward to a new format of constructor in the 2009 standard

· ·

*T*he Student class in Chapter 25 was extremely simple — almost unreasonably so. After all, a student has a name and a student ID as well as a grade point average and other miscellaneous data. I chose GPA as the data to model in Chapter 25 because I knew how to initialize it without someone telling me — I could just zero out this field. But I can't just zero out the name and ID fields; a no-named student with a null ID probably does not represent a valid student. Somehow I need to pass arguments to the constructor to tell it how to initialize fields that start out with a value that's not otherwise predictable.

Constructors with Arguments

C++ allows the program to define a constructor with arguments as shown here:

```cpp
class Student
{
  public:
    Student(const char* pszNewName, int nNewID)
    {
        int nLength = strlen(pszNewName) + 1;
        pszName = new char[nLength];
        strcpy(pszName, pszNewName);
        nID = nNewID;
    }
```

```
    ~Student()
    {
        delete[] pszName;
        pszName = 0;
    }

  protected:
    char* pszName;
    int   nID;
};
```

Here the arguments to the constructor are a pointer to an ASCIIZ string that contains the name of the new student and the student's ID. The constructor first allocates space for the student's name. It then copies the new name into the pszName data member. Finally, it copies over the student ID.

A destructor is required to return the memory to the heap once the object is destroyed. Any class that allocates a resource like memory in the constructor must return that memory in the destructor.

Remember, you can't call a constructor like you call a function, so you have to somehow associate the arguments to the constructor with the object when it is declared. The following code snippets show how this is done:

```
void fn()
{
    // put arguments next to object normally
    Student s1("Stephen Davis", 1234);

    // or next to the class name when allocating
    // an object from the heap
    Student* pS2 = new Student("Kinsey Davis", 5678);
}
```

The arguments appear next to the object normally and next to the class name when allocating an object off of the heap.

Looking at an example

The following NamedStudent program uses a constructor similar to the one shown in the snippets to create a Student object and display my, I mean his, name:

```
//
//  NamedStudent - this program demonstrates the use
//               of a constructors with arguments
//
```

```cpp
#include <cstdio>
#include <cstdlib>
#include <iostream>
#include <cstring>
using namespace std;

class Student
{
  protected:
    char*   pszName;
    int     nID;

  public:
    Student(const char* pszNewName, int nNewID)
    {
        cout << "Constructing " << pszNewName << endl;
        int nLength = strlen(pszNewName) + 1;
        pszName = new char[nLength];
        strcpy(pszName, pszNewName);
        nID = nNewID;
    }
    ~Student()
    {
        cout << "Destructing " << pszName << endl;
        delete[] pszName;
        pszName = 0;
    }

    // getName() - return the student's name
    const char* getName()
    {
        return pszName;
    }

    // getID() - get the student's ID
    int getID()
    {
        return nID;
    }
};

Student* fn()
{
    // create a student and initialize it
    cout << "Constructing a local student in fn()" <<endl;
    Student student("Stephen Davis", 1234);

    // display the student's name
    cout << "The student's name is "
         << student.getName() << endl;

    // now allocate one off of the heap
```

```
        cout << "Allocating a Student from the heap" << endl;
        Student *pS = new Student("Kinsey Davis", 5678);

        // display this student's name
        cout << "The second student's name is "
             << pS->getName() << endl;

        cout << "Returning from fn()" << endl;
        return pS;
}

int main(int nNumberofArgs, char* pszArgs[])
{
    // call the function that creates student objects
    cout << "Calling fn()" << endl;
    Student* pS = fn();
    cout << "Back in main()" << endl;

    // delete the object returned by fn()
    delete pS;
    pS = 0;

    // wait until user is ready before terminating program
    // to allow the user to see the program results
    system("PAUSE");
    return 0;
}
```

The `main()` program starts by outputting a message and then calling the function `fn()`. This function creates a student with the unlikely name "Stephen Davis" and an ID of 1234. The function then asks the object for its name just to prove that the name was accurately noted in the object. The function goes on to create another `Student` object, this time off of the heap, and similarly asks it to display its name.

The `fn()` function then returns control to `main()`; this causes the `student` object to go out of scope, which causes C++ to invoke the destructor. `main()` restores the memory returned from `fn()` to the heap using the keyword `delete`. This invokes the destructor for that object.

The constructor for class `Student` accepts a pointer to an ASCIIZ string and an `int` student ID. The constructor allocates a new character array from the heap and then copies the string passed it into that array. It then copies the value of the student ID.

Refer to Chapter 16 if you don't remember what an ASCIIZ string is or what `strlen()` does.

The destructor for class `Student` simply restores the memory allocated by the constructor to the heap by passing the address in `pszName` to delete[].

Use `delete[]` when restoring an array to the heap and `delete` when restoring a single object.

The `getName()` and `getID()` member functions are access functions for the name and ID. Declaring the return type of `getName()` as `const char*` (read "pointer to constant `char`") — as opposed to simply `char*` — means that the caller cannot change the name using the address returned by `getName()`.

Refer to Chapter 18 if you don't remember the difference between a `const char*` and a `char * const` (or if you have no idea what I'm talking about).

The output from this program appears as follows:

```
Calling fn()
Constructing a local student in fn()
Constructing Stephen Davis
The student's name is Stephen Davis
Allocating a Student from the heap
Constructing Kinsey Davis
The second student's name is Kinsey Davis
Returning from fn()
Destructing Stephen Davis
Back in main()
Destructing Kinsey Davis
Press any key to continue . . .
```

I've said it before (and you probably ignored me), but I really must insist this time: You need to invoke the preceding constructor in the debugger to get a feel for what C++ is doing with your declaration.

But what if you need both a named constructor and a default constructor? Keep reading.

Overloading the Constructor

You can have two or more constructors as long as they can be differentiated by the number and types of their arguments. This is called *overloading the constructor*.

Overloading a function means to define two or more functions with the same short name but with different arguments. Refer to Chapter 11 for a discussion of function overloading.

Thus, the following Student class from the OverloadedStudent program has
three constructors:

```
//
//   OverloadedStudent - this program overloads the Student
//                       constructor with 3 different choices
//                       that vary by number of arguments
//
#include <cstdio>
#include <cstdlib>
#include <iostream>
#include <cstring>
using namespace std;

class Student
{
  protected:
    char*  pszName;
    int    nID;
    double dGrade;          // the student's GPA
    int    nSemesterHours;


  public:
    Student(const char* pszNewName, int nNewID,
            double dXferGrade, int nXferHours)
    {
        cout << "Constructing " << pszNewName
             << " as a transfer student." << endl;
        int nLength = strlen(pszNewName) + 1;
        pszName = new char[nLength];
        strcpy(pszName, pszNewName);
        nID = nNewID;
        dGrade = dXferGrade;
        nSemesterHours = nXferHours;
    }
    Student(const char* pszNewName, int nNewID)
    {
        cout << "Constructing " << pszNewName
             << " as a new student." << endl;
        int nLength = strlen(pszNewName) + 1;
        pszName = new char[nLength];
        strcpy(pszName, pszNewName);
        nID = nNewID;
        dGrade = 0.0;
        nSemesterHours = 0;
    }
    Student()
    {
        pszName = 0;
```

```
            nID = 0;
            dGrade = 0.0;
            nSemesterHours = 0;
        }
    ~Student()
    {
        cout << "Destructing " << pszName << endl;
        delete[] pszName;
        pszName = 0;
    }

    // access functions
    const char* getName()
    {
        return pszName;
    }
    int getID()
    {
        return nID;
    }
    double getGrade()
    {
        return dGrade;
    }
    int getHours()
    {
        return nSemesterHours;
    }

    // addGrade - add a grade to the GPA and total hours
    double addGrade(double dNewGrade, int nHours)
    {
        double dWtdHrs = dGrade * nSemesterHours;
        dWtdHrs += dNewGrade * nHours;
        nSemesterHours += nHours;
        dGrade = dWtdHrs / nSemesterHours;
        return dGrade;
    }
};

int main(int nNumberofArgs, char* pszArgs[])
{
    // create a student and initialize it
    Student student("Stephen Davis", 1234);

    // now create a transfer student with an initial grade
    Student xfer("Kinsey Davis", 5678, 3.5, 12);

    // give both students a B in the current class
    student.addGrade(3.0, 3);
```

```
        xfer.addGrade(3.0, 3);

        // display the student's name and grades
        cout << "Student "
            << student.getName()
            << " has a grade of "
            << student.getGrade()
            << endl;

        cout << "Student "
            << xfer.getName()
            << " has a grade of "
            << xfer.getGrade()
            << endl;

        // wait until user is ready before terminating program
        // to allow the user to see the program results
        system("PAUSE");
        return 0;
}
```

Starting with the Student class, you can see that the first constructor within Student accepts a name, a student ID, and transfer credit in the form of an initial grade point average (GPA) and number of semester hours. The second constructor accepts only a name and ID; this constructor is intended for new students as it initializes the GPA and hours to zero. It's unclear what the third constructor is for — this default constructor initializes everything to zero.

The main() function creates a new student using the second constructor with the name "Stephen Davis"; then it creates a transfer student with the name "Kinsey Davis" using the second constructor. The program adds three hours of credit to both (just to show that this still works) and displays the resulting GPA.

The output from this program appears as follows:

```
Constructing Stephen Davis as a new student.
Constructing Kinsey Davis as a transfer student.
Student Stephen Davis has a grade of 3
Student Kinsey Davis has a grade of 3.4
Press any key to continue . . .
```

Notice how similar the first two Student constructors are. This is not uncommon. This case is one in which you can create an init() function that both constructors call (only the constructors are shown in this example for brevity's sake):

```
class Student
{
  protected:
    void init(const char* pszNewName, int nNewID,
              double dXferGrade, int nXferHours)
    {
        cout << "Constructing " << pszNewName
             << " as a transfer student." << endl;
        int nLength = strlen(pszNewName) + 1;
        pszName = new char[nLength];
        strcpy(pszName, pszNewName);
        nID = nNewID;
        dGrade = dXferGrade;
        nSemesterHours = nXferHours;
    }
  public:
    Student(const char* pszNewName, int nNewID,
            double dXferGrade, int nXferHours)
    {
        init(pszNewName, nNewID, dXferGrade, nXferHours);
    }
    Student(const char* pszNewName, int nNewID)
    {
        init(pszNewName, nNewID, 0.0, 0);
    }

    // ...class continues as before...
};
```

In general, the init() function will look like the most complicated constructor. All simpler constructors call init() passing default values for some of
the arguments, such as a 0 for transfer grade and credit for new students.

You can also default the arguments to the constructor (or any function for
that matter) as follows:

```
class Student
{
  public:
    Student(const char* pszNewName, int nNewID,
            double dXferGrade = 0.0, int nXferHours = 0);

    // ...and so it goes...
};
```

C++ will supply the defaulted arguments if they are not provided in the declaration. However, default arguments can generate strange error messages and
are beyond the scope of this book.

You can also invoke one constructor from another starting with the C++ 2009 standard. However, as of this writing, no compiler that I know of supports this feature.

The Default default Constructor

As far as C++ is concerned, every class must have a constructor; otherwise, you can't create any objects of that class. If you don't provide a constructor for your class, C++ should probably just generate an error, but it doesn't. To provide compatibility with existing C code, which knows nothing about constructors, C++ automatically provides an implicitly defined default constructor (sort of a *default* default constructor) that invokes the default constructor for any data members. Sometimes I call this a Miranda constructor. You know, "If you cannot afford a constructor, a constructor will be provided for you."

If your class already has a constructor, however, C++ doesn't provide the automatic default constructor. (Having tipped your hand that this isn't a C program, C++ doesn't feel obliged to do any extra work to ensure compatibility.)

The result is: If you define a constructor for your class but you also want a default constructor, you must define it yourself.

The following code snippets help demonstrate this principle. The following is legal:

```
class Student
{
    // ...all the same stuff but no constructors...
};

void fn()
{
    Student s; // create Student using default constructor
}
```

Here, the object s is built using the default constructor. Because the programmer has not provided a constructor, C++ provides a default constructor that doesn't really do anything in this case.

However, the following snippet does not compile properly:

```
class Student
{
  public:
    Student(const char* pszName);

    // ...all the same stuff...
};

void fn()
{
    Student s; // doesn't compile
}
```

The seemingly innocuous addition of the `Student(const char*)` construc-tor precludes C++ from automatically providing a `Student()` constructor with which to build the s object. Now the compiler complains that it can no longer find `Student::Student()` with which to build s. Adding a default constructor solves the problem:

```
class Student
{
  public:
    Student(const char* pszName);
    Student();

    // ...all the same stuff...
};

void fn()
{
    Student s; // this does compile
}
```

It's just this type of illogic that explains why C++ programmers make the really big bucks.

Constructing Data Members

In the preceding examples, all of the data members have been simple types, like `int` and `double` and arrays of `char`. With these simple types it's suf-ficient to just assign the variable a value within the constructor. But what if the class contains data members of a user-defined class? There are two cases to consider here.

Initializing data members with the default constructor

Consider the following example:

```cpp
class StudentID
{
  protected:
    static int nBaseValue;
    int        nValue;

  public:
    StudentID()
    {
        nValue = nBaseValue++;
    }

    int getID()
    {
        return nValue;
    }
};

// allocate space for the class property
int StudentID::nBaseValue = 1000;

class Student
{
  protected:
    char*       pszName;
    StudentID   sID;

  public:
    Student(const char* pszNewName)
    {
        int nLength = strlen(pszNewName) + 1;
        pszName = new char[nLength];
        strcpy(pszName, pszNewName);
    }
    ~Student()
    {
        delete pszName;
        pszName = 0;
    }

    // getName() - return the student's name
    const char* getName()
    {
```

```
            return pszName;
    }

    // getID() - get the student's ID
    int getID()
    {
            return sID.getID();
    }
};
```

The class `StudentID` is designed to allocate student IDs sequentially. The class retains the "next value" in a static variable `StudentID::nBaseValue`.

Static data members, also known as class members, are shared among all objects.

Each time a `StudentID` is created, the constructor assigns `nValue` the "next value" from `nBaseValue` and then increments `nBaseValue` in preparation for the next time the constructor is called.

The `Student` class has been updated so that the `sID` field is now of type `StudentID`. The constructor now accepts the name of the student but relies on `StudentID` to assign the next sequential ID each time a new `Student` object is created.

The constructor for each data member, including `StudentID`, is invoked before control is passed to the body of the `Student` constructor.

All the `Student` constructor has to do is make a copy of the student's name — the `sID` field takes care of itself.

Initializing data members with a different constructor

So now the boss comes in and wants an addition to the program. Now she wants to update the program so that it can assign a new student ID instead of always accepting the default value handed over by the `StudentID` class.

Accordingly, I make the following changes:

```
class StudentID
{
  protected:
    static int nBaseValue;
    int        nValue;
```

```cpp
  public:
    StudentID(int nNewID)
    {
        nValue = nNewID;
    }
    StudentID()
    {
        nValue = nBaseValue++;
    }

    int getID()
    {
        return nValue;
    }
};

// allocate space for the class property
int StudentID::nBaseValue = 1000;

class Student
{
  protected:
    char*       pszName;
    StudentID   sID;

    void initName(const char* pszNewName)
    {
        int nLength = strlen(pszNewName) + 1;
        pszName = new char[nLength];
        strcpy(pszName, pszNewName);
    }

  public:
    Student(const char* pszNewName, int nNewID)
    {
        initName(pszNewName);
        StudentID sID(nNewID);
    }
    Student(const char* pszNewName)
    {
        initName(pszNewName);
    }
    ~Student()
    {
        delete[] pszName;
        pszName = 0;
    }

    // getName() - return the student's name
    const char* getName()
    {
        return pszName;
    }
```

```
        // getID() - get the student's ID
        int getID()
        {
            return sID.getID();
        }
};
```

I added a constructor to StudentID to allow the caller to pass a value to use for the student ID rather than accept the default. Now, if the program doesn't provide an ID, the student is assigned the next sequential ID. If the program does provide an ID, however, then it is used instead, and the static counter is left untouched.

I also added a constructor to Student to allow the program to provide a studentID when the student is created. This Student(const char*, int) constructor first initializes the student's name and then invokes the StudentID(int) constructor on sID.

When I execute the program, however, I am disappointed to find that this seems to have made no apparent difference. Students are still assigned sequential student IDs whether or not they are passed a value to use instead.

The problem, I quickly realize, is that the Student(const char*, int) constructor is not invoking the new StudentID(int) constructor on the data member sID. Instead, it is creating a new local object called sID within the constructor, which it then immediately discards without any effect on the data member of the same name.

Remember that the constructor for the data members is called before control is passed to the body of the constructor. Rather than create a new value locally, I need some way to tell C++ to use a constructor other than the default constructor when creating the data member sID. C++ uses the following syntax to initialize a data member with a specific constructor:

```
class Student
{
  public:
    Student(const char* pszName,
            int nNewID) : sID(nNewID)
    {
        initName(pszName);
    }

    // ...remainder of class unchanged...
};
```

The data member appears to the right of a colon used to separate such declarations from the arguments to the function but before the open brace of the function itself. This causes the StudentID(int) constructor to be invoked, passing the nNewID value to be used as the new student ID.

Looking at an example

The following CompoundStudent program creates one Student object with the default, sequential student ID, while assigning a specific student ID to a second Student object:

```
//
//   CompoundStudent - this version of the Student class
//                     includes a data member that's also
//                     of a user defined type
//
#include <cstdio>
#include <cstdlib>
#include <iostream>
#include <cstring>
using namespace std;

class StudentID
{
  protected:
    static int nBaseValue;
    int        nValue;

  public:
    StudentID()
    {
        nValue = nBaseValue++;
    }

    StudentID(int nNewValue)
    {
        nValue = nNewValue;
    }

    int getID()
    {
        return nValue;
    }
};

// allocate space for the class property
int StudentID::nBaseValue = 1000;
```

```cpp
class Student
{
  protected:
    char*        pszName;
    StudentID    sID;

    void initName(const char* pszNewName)
    {
        int nLength = strlen(pszNewName) + 1;
        pszName = new char[nLength];
        strcpy(pszName, pszNewName);
    }

  public:
    Student(const char* pszNewName,
                    int nNewID) : sID(nNewID)
    {
        initName(pszNewName);
    }
    Student(const char* pszNewName)
    {
        initName(pszNewName);
    }
   ~Student()
    {
        delete[] pszName;
        pszName = 0;
    }

    // getName() - return the student's name
    const char* getName()
    {
        return pszName;
    }

    // getID() - get the student's ID
    int getID()
    {
        return sID.getID();
    }
};


int main(int nNumberofArgs, char* pszArgs[])
{
    // create a student and initialize it
    Student student1("Stephen Davis");
```

```
    // display the student's name and ID
    cout << "The first student's name is "
         << student1.getName()
         << ", ID is "
         << student1.getID()
         << endl;

    // do the same for a second student
    Student student2("Janet Eddins");
    cout << "The second student's name is "
         << student2.getName()
         << ", ID is "
         << student2.getID()
         << endl;

    // now create a transfer student with a unique ID
    Student student3("Tiffany Amrich", 1234);
    cout << "The third student's name is "
         << student3.getName()
         << ", ID is "
         << student3.getID()
         << endl;

    // wait until user is ready before terminating program
    // to allow the user to see the program results
    system("PAUSE");
    return 0;
}
```

The `Student` and `StudentID` classes are similar to those shown earlier. The `main()` function creates three students, the first two using the
`Student(const char*)` constructor that allocates the default student
ID. The third student is created using the `Student(const char*, int)`
constructor and passed an ID of 1234. The resulting display confirms that the
default IDs are being allocated sequentially and that the third student has a
unique ID.

```
The first student's name is Stephen Davis, ID is 1000
The second student's name is Janet Eddins, ID is 1001
The third student's name is Tiffany Amrich, ID is 1234
Press any key to continue . . .
```

The `:` syntax here can also be used to initialize simple variables if you prefer:

```
class SomeClass
{
  protected:
    int nValue;
    const double PI;

  public:
    SomeClass(int n) : nValue(n), PI(3.14159) {}
};
```

Here, the data member nValue is initialized to n, and the constant double is initialized to 3.14159.

In fact, this is the only way to initialize a data member flagged as const. You can't put a const variable on the left-hand side of an assignment operator.

Notice that the body of the constructor is now empty since all the work is done in the header; however, the empty body is still required (otherwise, the definition would look like a prototype declaration).

New with C++ 2009

Starting with the 2009 standard, you can initialize data members to a constant value in the declaration itself, as in the following:

```
class SomeClass
{
  protected:
    int nValue;
    const double PI = 3.14159;
    char* pSomeString = new char[128];

  public:
    SomeClass(int n) : nValue(n) {}
};
```

The effect is the same as if you had written the constructor as follows:

```
class SomeClass
{
  protected:
    int nValue;
    const double PI;
    char* pSomeString;

  public:
    SomeClass(int n)
      : nValue(n), PI(3.14159), pSomeString(new char[128])
    {}
};
```

The earlier assignment format is easier to read and just seems more natural (it is accepted by other C++–like programming languages such as Java and C#). However, as of this writing, this format is not yet accepted by any C++ compiler, including the one enclosed in this book.

Chapter 27

Coping with the Copy Constructor

· ·

In This Chapter

▶ Letting C++ make copies of an object

▶ Creating your own copy constructor

▶ Making copies of data members

▶ Avoiding making copies completely

· ·

*T*he constructor is a special function that C++ invokes when an object is created in order to allow the class to initialize the object to a legal state. Chapter 25 introduces the concept of the constructor. Chapter 26 demonstrates how to create constructors that take arguments. This chapter concludes the discussion of constructors by examining a particular constructor known as the copy constructor.

Copying an Object

A *copy constructor* is the constructor that C++ uses to make copies of objects. It carries the name `X::X(const X&)`, where `X` is the name of the class. That is, it's the constructor of class `X` that takes as its argument a reference to an object of class `X`. I know that sounds pretty useless, but let me explain why you need a constructor like that on your team.

A reference argument type like `fn(X&)` says, "pass a reference to the object" rather than "pass a copy of the object." I discuss reference arguments in Chapter 23.

Think for a minute about the following function call:

```
void fn(Student s)
{
    // ...whatever fn() does...
}

void someOtherFn()
{
    Student s;
    fn(s);
};
```

Here the function `someOtherFn()` creates a `Student` object and passes a copy of that object to `fn()`.

By default, C++ passes objects by value, meaning that it must make a copy of the object to pass to the functions it calls (refer to Chapter 23 for more).

Consider that creating a copy of an object means creating a new object and, by definition, means invoking a constructor. But what would the arguments to that constructor be? Why, a reference to the original object. That, by definition, is the copy constructor.

The default copy constructor

C++ provides a default copy constructor that works most of the time. This copy constructor does a member-by-member copy of the source object to the destination object.

A member-by-member copy is also known as a *shallow copy* for reasons that soon will become clear.

There are times when copying one member at a time is not a good thing, however. Consider the `Student` class from Chapter 26:

```
class Student
{
  protected:
    char* pszName;
    int   nID;

  // ...other stuff...
};
```

Copying the `int` data member `nID` from one object to another is no problem. However, copying the pointer `pszName` from the source to the destination object could cause problems.

For example, what if pszName points to heap memory (which it almost surely does)? Now you have two objects that both point to the same block of memory on the heap. This is shown in Figure 27-1.

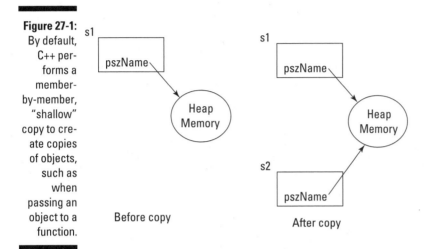

When the copy of the Student object goes out of scope, the destructor for that class will likely delete the pszName pointer, thereby returning the block of memory to the heap, even though the original object is still using that memory. When the original object deletes the same pointer again, the heap gets messed up, and the program is sure to crash with a bizarre and largely misleading error message.

Looking at an example

The following ShallowStudent program demonstrates how making a shallow copy can cause serious problems:

```
//
//   ShallowStudent - this program demonstrates why the
//                    default shallow copy constructor
//                    isn't always the right choice.
//
#include <cstdio>
#include <cstdlib>
#include <iostream>
#include <cstring>
using namespace std;
```

```cpp
class Student
{
  protected:
    char*  pszName;
    int    nID;

  public:
    Student(const char* pszNewName, int nNewID)
    {
        cout << "Constructing " << pszNewName << endl;
        int nLength = strlen(pszNewName) + 1;
        pszName = new char[nLength];
        strcpy(pszName, pszNewName);
        nID = nNewID;
    }
    ~Student()
    {
        cout << "Destructing " << pszName << endl;
        delete[] pszName;
        pszName = 0;
    }

    // access functions
    const char* getName()
    {
        return pszName;
    }
    int getID()
    {
        return nID;
    }
};

void someOtherFn(Student s)
{
    // we don't need to do anything here
}

void someFn()
{
    Student student("Adam Laskowski", 1234);
    someOtherFn(student);

    cout << "The student's name is now "
         << student.getName() << endl;
}

int main(int nNumberofArgs, char* pszArgs[])
{
    someFn();
```

```
        // wait until user is ready before terminating program
        // to allow the user to see the program results
        system("PAUSE");
        return 0;
}
```

This deceptively simple program contains a serious problem. The function `main()` does nothing more than call the function `someFn()`. This function creates a local `student` object and passes it by value to the function `some OtherFn()`. This second function does nothing except return to the caller. The `someFn()` function then displays the name of the `student` and returns to `main()`.

The output from the program shows some interesting results:

```
Constructing Adam Laskowski
Destructing Adam Laskowski
The student's name is now X$±
Destructing X$±
Press any key to continue . . .
```

The first message comes from the `Student` constructor as the `student` object is created at the beginning of `someFn()`. No message is generated by the default copy constructor that's called to create the copy of `Student` for `someOtherFn()`. The destructor message is invoked at the end of `some OtherFn()` when the local object s goes out of scope.

The output message in `someFn()` shows that the object is now messed up as the memory allocated by the `Student` constructor to hold the student's name has been returned to the heap. The subsequent destructor that's invoked at the end of `someFn()` verifies that things are amiss.

This type of error is normally fatal (to the program, not the programmer). The only reason this program didn't crash is that it was about to stop anyway.

Creating a Copy Constructor

Classes that allocate resources in their constructor should normally include a copy constructor to create copies of these resources. For example, the `Student` copy constructor should allocate another block of memory off the heap for the name and copy the original object's name into this new block. This is shown in Figure 27-2.

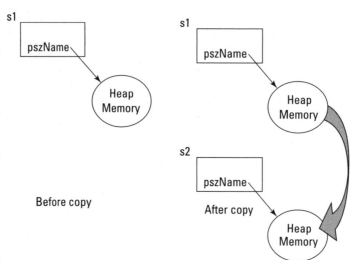

Figure 27-2:
A class that allocates resources in the constructor requires a copy constructor that performs a so-called deep copy of the source object.

Allocating a new block of memory and copying the contents of the original into this new block is known as creating a *deep copy* (as opposed to the default shallow copy).

The following DeepStudent program includes a copy constructor that performs a deep copy of the student object:

```cpp
//
//   DeepStudent - this program demonstrates how a copy
//                 constructor that performs a deep copy
//                 can be used to solve copy problems
//
#include <cstdio>
#include <cstdlib>
#include <iostream>
#include <cstring>
using namespace std;

class Student
{
  protected:
    char*  pszName;
    int    nID;

  public:
    Student(const char* pszNewName, int nNewID)
    {
        cout << "Constructing " << pszNewName << endl;
        int nLength = strlen(pszNewName) + 1;
        pszName = new char[nLength];
        strcpy(pszName, pszNewName);
        nID = nNewID;
    }
```

```
    Student(const Student& s)
    {
        cout<<"Constructing copy of "<< s.pszName << endl;

        int nLength = strlen(s.pszName) + 25;
        this->pszName = new char[nLength];
        strcpy(this->pszName, "Copy of ");
        strcat(this->pszName, s.pszName);
        this->nID = s.nID;
    }

    ~Student()
    {
        cout << "Destructing " << pszName << endl;
        delete[] pszName;
        pszName = 0;
    }

    // access functions
    const char* getName()
    {
        return pszName;
    }
    int getID()
    {
        return nID;
    }
};

void someOtherFn(Student s)
{
    // we don't need to do anything here
}

void someFn()
{
    Student student("Adam Laskowski", 1234);
    someOtherFn(student);

    cout << "The student's name is now "
        << student.getName() << endl;
}

int main(int nNumberofArgs, char* pszArgs[])
{
    someFn();

    // wait until user is ready before terminating program
    // to allow the user to see the program results
    system("PAUSE");
    return 0;
}
```

This program is identical to its ShallowStudent cousin except for the addition of the copy constructor Student(const Student&), but what a difference it makes in the output from the program:

```
Constructing Adam Laskowski
Constructing copy of Adam Laskowski
Destructing Copy of Adam Laskowski
The student's name is now Adam Laskowski
Destructing Adam Laskowski
Press any key to continue . . .
```

The first message is output by the Student(const char*, int) constructor that's invoked when the student object is created at the beginning of someFn(). The second message comes from the copy constructor Student(const Student&) that's invoked to create the copy of student as part of the call to SomeOtherFn().

This constructor first allocates a new block of heap memory for the pszName of the copy. It then copies the string Copy of into this field before concatenating the student's name in the next line.

You would normally make a true copy of the name and not tack Copy of onto the front; I do so for instructional reasons.

The destructor that's invoked as s goes out of scope at the end of some OtherFn() is now clearly returning the copy of the name to the heap and not the original string. This is verified back in someFn() when the student's name is intact (as you would expect). Finally, the destructor at the end of someFn() returns the original string to the heap.

Avoiding Copies

Passing arguments by value is just one of several reasons that C++ invokes a copy constructor to create temporary copies of your object. You may be wondering, "Doesn't all this creating and deleting copies of objects take time?" The obvious answer is, "You bet!" Is there some way to avoid creating copies?

One way is not to pass objects by value but to pass the address of the object. There wouldn't be a problem if someOtherFn() were declared as follows:

```
// the following does not cause a copy to be created
void someOtherFn(const Student *pS)
{
    // ...whatever goes here...
}
void someFn()
{
    Student student("Adam Laskowski", 1234);
    someOtherFn(&student);
}
```

This is faster because a single address is smaller than an entire Student
object, but it also avoids the need to allocate memory off the heap for holding copies of the student's name.

You can get the same effect using reference arguments as in the following:

```
// the following function doesn't create a copy either
void someOtherFn(const Student& s)
{
    // ...whatever you want to do...
}

void someFn()
{
    Student student("Adam Laskowski", 1234);
    someOtherFn(student);
}
```

See Chapter 23 if you don't remember about referential arguments.

Part VI
Advanced Strokes

The 5th Wave
By Rich Tennant

"Why, of course. I'd be very interested in seeing this new milestone in the project."

In this part . . .

Here you pick up a few loose ends that are nevertheless important to any C++ programmer: You'll learn to overload the assignment operator, you'll learn how to perform file I/O, and you'll discover how to throw error exceptions.

Chapter 28

Inheriting a Class

· ·

· ·

*1*nheritance occurs all around us every day. I am a human. I inherit certain properties from the class Human, such as my ability to converse intelligently (more or less) and my dependence on air, water, and carbohydrate-based nourishment like Twinkies. These latter properties are not unique to humans. The class Human inherits these from class Mammal (along with something about bearing live young), which inherited them from class Animal, and so on.

The capability to pass down properties is a powerful one. It enables you to describe things in an economical way. For example, if my son asks me, "What's a duck?" I might say, "It's a bird that floats and goes quack." Despite your first reaction, that answer actually conveys a significant amount of knowledge. My son knows what a bird is. He knows that birds have wings, that birds can fly (he doesn't know about ostriches yet), and that birds lay eggs. Now, he knows all those same things about a duck *plus* the facts that ducks can float and make a quacking sound. (This might be a good time to refer to Chapter 21 for a discussion about Microwave ovens and their relationship to ovens and kitchen appliances.)

Object-oriented languages express this relationship by allowing one class to inherit from another. Thus, in C++ the class Duck might well inherit from Bird, and that class might also inherit from Animal. Exactly how C++ does this is the topic of this chapter.

Advantages of Inheritance

Inheritance was added to C++ for several reasons. Of course, the major reason is the capability to express the inheritance relationship: that `MicrowaveOven` is an `Oven` is a `KitchenAppliance` thing. More on the IS_A relationship a little later in this and the next chapter.

A minor reason is to reduce the amount of typing and the number of lines of code that you and I have to write. You may have noticed that the commands in C++ may be short, but you need a lot of them to do anything. C++ programs tend to get pretty lengthy, so anything that reduces typing is a good thing.

To see how inheritance can reduce typing, consider the `Duck` example. I don't have to document all the properties about `Duck` that have to do with flying and landing and eating and laying eggs. It inherits all that stuff from `Bird`. I just need to add `Duck`'s quackness property and its ability to float. That's a considerable savings.

A more important and related issue is the major buzzword, *reuse*. Software scientists realized some time ago that starting from scratch with each new project and rebuilding the same software components doesn't make much sense.

Compare the situation in the software industry to that in other industries. How many car manufacturers start from scratch each time they want to design a new car? None. Practitioners in other industries have found it makes more sense to start from screws, bolts, nuts, and even larger existing off-the-shelf components such as motors and transmissions when designing a car.

Unfortunately, except for very small functions like those found in the Standard C++ Library, it's rare to find much reuse of software components. One problem is that it's virtually impossible to find a component from an earlier program that does exactly what you want. Generally, these components require "tweaking." Inheritance allows you to adopt the major functionality of an existing class and tweak the smaller features to adapt an existing class to a new application.

This carries with it another benefit that's more subtle but just as important: *adaptability*. It never fails that as soon as users see your most recent program, they like it but want just one more fix or addition. Consider checking accounts for a moment. How long after I finish the program that handles checking accounts for a bank will it be before the bank comes out with a new "special" checking account that earns interest on the balance?

Not everyone gets this checking account, of course (that would be too easy) — only certain customers get `InterestChecking` accounts. With inheritance, however, I don't need to go through the entire program and recode all the checking account functions. All I need to do is create a new subclass `InterestChecking` that inherits from `Checking` but has the one additional property of `accumulatesInterest()` and, *voilà*, the feature is implemented. (It isn't quite that easy, of course, but it's not much more difficult than that. I actually show you how to do this in Chapter 29.)

Learning the lingo

You need to get some terms straight before going much further. The class `Dog` inherits properties from class `Mammal`. This is called *inheritance*. We also say that `Dog` is a *subclass* of `Mammal`. Turning that sentence around, we say that `Mammal` is a *base class* of `Dog`. We can also say that `Dog` IS_A `Mammal`. (I use all caps as a way of expressing this unique relationship.) C++ shares this terminology with other object-oriented languages.

The term is adopted from other languages, but you will also find C++ programmers saying things like, "the class `Dog` *extends* `Mammal` with its barkiness and tail wagging properties." Well, maybe not in those exact words, but a subclass extends a base class by adding properties.

Notice that although `Dog` IS_A `Mammal`, the reverse is not true. A `Mammal` is not a `Dog`. (A statement like this always refers to the general case. It could be that a particular mammal is, in fact, a dog, but in general a mammal is not a dog.) This is because a `Dog` shares all the properties of other `Mammals`, but a `Mammal` does not have all the properties of a `Dog`. Not all `Mammals` can bark, for example, or wag their tails.

Implementing Inheritance in C++

The following is an outline of how to inherit one class from another:

```
class Student
{
    // ...whatever goes here...
};

class GraduateStudent : public Student
{
    // ...graduate student unique stuff goes here...
};
```

The class `Student` is declared the usual way. The class appears with the name followed by a colon, the keyword `public`, and the name of the base class, `Student`.

The keyword `public` implies that there's probably something called protected inheritance. It's true, there is; but protected inheritance is very uncommon, and I don't discuss it in this book.

Now, I can say that a `GraduateStudent` IS_A `Student`. More to the point, I
can use a `GraduateStudent` object anywhere that a `Student` is required,
including as arguments to functions. That is, the following is allowed:

```
void fn(Student* pS);
void someOtherFn()
{
    GraduateStudent gs;
    fn(&gs);
}
```

This is allowed because a `gs` object has all the properties of `Student`. Why?
Because a `GraduateStudent` IS_A `Student`!

Looking at an example

The following GSInherit program makes this more concrete by creating a
`Student` class and a `GraduateStudent` class and invoking functions of
each:

```
//
//  GSInherit - demonstrate inheritance by creating
//              a class GraduateStudent that inherits
//              from Student.
//
#include <cstdio>
#include <cstdlib>
#include <iostream>
#include <cstring>
using namespace std;

class Student
{
  protected:
    char*  pszName;
    int    nID;
    double dGrade;              // the student's GPA
    int    nSemesterHours;

  public:
    Student(const char* pszNewName, int nNewID)
    {
        cout << "Constructing student "
```

```
                    << pszNewName << endl;
        pszName = new char[strlen(pszNewName) + 1];
        strcpy(pszName, pszNewName);
        nID = nNewID;
        dGrade = 0.0;
        nSemesterHours = 0;
    }
  ~Student()
    {
        cout << "Destructing " << pszName << endl;
        delete[] pszName;
        pszName = 0;
    }

    // access functions
    const char* getName()
    {
        return pszName;
    }
    int getID()
    {
        return nID;
    }
    double getGrade()
    {
        return dGrade;
    }
    int getHours()
    {
        return nSemesterHours;
    }

    // addGrade - add a grade to the GPA and total hours
    double addGrade(double dNewGrade, int nHours)
    {
        double dWtdHrs = dGrade * nSemesterHours;
        dWtdHrs += dNewGrade * nHours;
        nSemesterHours += nHours;
        dGrade = dWtdHrs / nSemesterHours;
        return dGrade;
    }
};

class Advisor
{
  public:
    Advisor() { cout << "Advisor constructed" << endl;}
};

class GraduateStudent : public Student
```

```
{
  protected:
    double dQualifierGrade;
    Advisor advisor;

  public:
    GraduateStudent(const char* pszName, int nID) :
      Student(pszName, nID)
    {
        cout << "Constructing GraduateStudent" << endl;
        dQualifierGrade = 0.0;
    }
};

void someOtherFn(Student* pS)
{
    cout << "Passed student " << pS->getName() << endl;
}

void someFn()
{
    Student student("Lo Lee Undergrad", 1234);
    someOtherFn(&student);

    GraduateStudent gs("Upp R. Class", 5678);
    someOtherFn(&gs);
}

int main(int nNumberofArgs, char* pszArgs[])
{
    someFn();

    // wait until user is ready before terminating program
    // to allow the user to see the program results
    system("PAUSE");
    return 0;
}
```

This example appears lengthy at first blush. Fortunately, however, the
Student class is identical to its predecessors in earlier chapters.

The fact that the Student class hasn't changed is an important point: You
don't have to modify a class in order to inherit from it. I did not have to make
any changes to Student in order to create the subclass GraduateStudent.

The GraduateStudent class extends Student by adding the data
member dQualifierGrade. In addition, I provided GraduateStudent
with a constructor that accepts the student name and ID. Of course,
GraduateStudent doesn't need to manipulate the student's name and ID on
its own — it calls the perfectly serviceable Student constructor to do that
instead, as the following small excerpt demonstrates:

```
GraduateStudent(const char* pszName, int nID) :
    Student(pszName, nID)
{
    cout << "Constructing GraduateStudent" << endl;
    dQualifierGrade = 0.0;
}
```

The constructor for the base class is invoked before any part of the current class is constructed. Next to be invoked are the constructors for any data members — this accounts for the message from `Advisor`. Control passes into the body of the `GraduateStudent` constructor last.

The output from this program appears as follows:

```
Constructing student Lo Lee Undergrad
Passed student Lo Lee Undergrad
Constructing student Upp R. Class
Advisor constructed
Constructing GraduateStudent
Passed student Upp R. Class
Destructing Upp R. Class
Destructing Lo Lee Undergrad
Press any key to continue . . .
```

You can follow the chain of events by starting with `main()`. The `main()` function does nothing more than call `someFn()`. The `someFn()` function first creates a `Student` object `Lo Lee Undergrad`. The constructor for `Student` generates the first line of output.

`someFn()` then passes the address of "Lo Lee" to `someOtherFn(Student*)`. `someOtherFn()` does nothing more than display the student's name, which accounts for the second line of output.

The `someFn()` function then creates a `GraduateStudent` "Upp R. Class." Returning to the output for a minute, you can see that this invokes the `Student(const char*, int)` constructor first with the name `Upp R. Class`. Once that constructor has completed building the `Student` foundation, the `GraduateStudent` constructor gets a chance to output its message and build on the graduate student floor.

The `someFn()` function then does something rather curious: It passes the address of the `GraduateStudent` object to `someOtherFn(Student*)`. This apparent mismatch of object types is easily explained by the fact that (here it comes) a `GraduateStudent` IS_A `Student` and can be used anywhere a `Student` is required. (Similarly a `GraduateStudent*` can be used in place of a `Student*`.)

The remainder of the output is generated when both `student` and `gs` go out of scope at the return from `someFn()`. The objects are destructed in the reverse order of their construction, so gs goes first and then student. In addition, the destructor for GraduateStudent is called before the destructor for Student().

The destructor for the subclass should destruct only those fields that are unique to the subclass. Leave the destructing of the base class data members to the subclass's destructor.

Having a HAS_A Relationship

Notice that the class GraduateStudent includes the members of class Student and Advisor but in a different way. By defining a data member of class Advisor, a GraduateStudent contains all the members of Advisor within it. However, you can't say that a GraduateStudent IS_AN Advisor. Rather, a GraduateStudent HAS_AN Advisor.

The analogy is like a car with a motor. Logically, you can say that car is a subclass of vehicle, so it inherits the properties of all vehicles. At the same time, a car has a motor. If you buy a car, you can logically assume that you are buying a motor as well (unless you go to the used car lot where I got my last junk heap).

If some friends ask you to show up at a rally on Saturday with your vehicle of choice, and you arrive in your car, they can't complain and kick you out. But if you were to appear on foot carrying a motor, your friends would have reason to laugh you off the premises, because a motor is not a vehicle.

These assertions appear as follows when written in C++:

```
class Vehicle {};
class Motor {};
class Car : public Vehicle
{
  public:
    Motor motor;
};

void vehicleFn(Vehicle* pV);
void motorFn(Motor* pM);

void someFn()
{
    Car c;

    vehicleFn(&c);      // this is allowed
    motorFn(&c.motor);  // so is this

    motorFn(&c);        // this is not allowed
}
```

Chapter 29

Are Virtual Functions for Real?

In This Chapter

▶ Overriding between functions that are members of a class

▶ Introducing virtual member functions

▶ Some special considerations for virtual functions

▶ Declaring your destructor virtual — when to and when not to do it

*I*nheritance gives users the ability to describe one class in terms of another. Just as important, it highlights the relationship between classes. I describe a duck as "a bird that . . .", and that description points out the relationship between duck and bird. From a C++ standpoint, however, a piece of the puzzle is still missing.

You have probably noticed this, but a microwave oven looks nothing like a conventional oven and nor does it work the same internally. Nevertheless, when I say "cook," I don't want to worry about the details of how each oven works internally. This chapter describes this problem in C++ terms and then goes on to describe the solution as well.

Overriding Member Functions

It has always been possible to overload a member function with another member function in the same class as long as the arguments differ:

```
class Student
{
  public:
    double grade();       // return the student's gpa
    double grade(double); // set the student's gpa

    // ...other stuff...
};
```

You see this in spades in Chapters 26 and 27 where I overload the constructor with a number of different types of constructors. It is also possible to overload a function in one class with a function in another class even if the arguments are the same, because the class is not the same:

```
class Student
{
  public:
    double grade(double); // set the student's gpa
};

class Hill
{
  public:
    double grade(double); // set the slope of the hill
};
```

Inheritance offers another way to confuse things: A member function in a subclass can overload a member function in the base class.

Overloading a base class member function is called *overriding*.

Early binding

Overriding is fairly straightforward. Consider, for example, the following EarlyBinding demonstration program:

```
//
//  EarlyBinding - demonstrates early binding in
//                 overriding one member function with
//                 another in a subclass.
//
#include <cstdio>
#include <cstdlib>
#include <iostream>
using namespace std;

class Student
{
  public:
    double calcTuition() { return 0.0; }
};

class GraduateStudent : public Student
{
  public:
    double calcTuition() { return 1.0; }
```

```
};

int main(int nNumberofArgs, char* pszArgs[])
{
    // the following calls Student::calcTuition()
    Student s;
    cout << "The value of s.calcTuition() is "
         << s.calcTuition()
         << endl;

    // the following calls GraduateStudent::calcTuition()
    GraduateStudent gs;
    cout << "The value of gs.calcTuition() is "
         << gs.calcTuition()
         << endl;

    // wait until user is ready before terminating program
    // to allow the user to see the program results
    system("PAUSE");
    return 0;
}
```

Here both the `Student` and `GraduateStudent` classes include a
`calcTuition()` member function (and nothing else, just to keep the
listings short). Presumably, the university calculates tuition for graduate and undergraduate students differently, but for this demonstration, determining which function is being called is the only important
thing. Therefore, `Student::calcTuition()` returns a `0`, while
`GraduateStudent::calcTuition()` returns a `1` — can't get much simpler
than that!

The `main()` function first creates a `Student` object `s` and then
invokes `s.calcTuition()`. Not surprisingly, this call is passed to
`Student::calcTuition()` as is clear from the output of the program as quoted here. The `main()` function then does the same for
`GraduateStudent` with predictable results:

```
The value of s.calcTuition() is 0
The value of gs.calcTuition() is 1
Press any key to continue . . .
```

In this program, the C++ compiler is able to decide at compile time which
member function to call based upon the declared type of `s` and `gs`.

Resolving calls to overridden member functions based on the declared type of
the object is called *compile-time* or *early binding*.

This simple example is not too surprising so far, but let me put a wrinkle in this simple fabric.

Ambiguous case

The following AmbiguousBinding program is virtually identical to the earlier EarlyBinding program. The only difference is that instead of invoking `calcTuition()` directly, this version of the program calls the function through a pointer passed to a function:

```
//
//   AmbiguousBindng - demonstrates a case where it's not
//                     clear what should happen. In this
//                     case, C++ goes with early binding
//                     while languages like Java and C#
//                     use late binding.
//
#include <cstdio>
#include <cstdlib>
#include <iostream>
using namespace std;

class Student
{
  public:
    double calcTuition() { return 0.0; }
};

class GraduateStudent : public Student
{
  public:
    double calcTuition() { return 1.0; }
};

double someFn(Student* pS)
{
    return pS->calcTuition();
}

int main(int nNumberofArgs, char* pszArgs[])
{
    // the following calls Student::calcTuition()
    Student s;
    cout << "The value of someFn(&s) is "
         << someFn(&s)
         << endl;

    // the following calls GraduateStudent::calcTuition()
```

```
    GraduateStudent gs;
    cout << "The value of someFn(&gs) is "
        << someFn(&gs)
        << endl;

    // wait until user is ready before terminating program
    // to allow the user to see the program results
    system("PAUSE");
    return 0;
}
```

Just as in the EarlyBinding example, this program starts by creating a `Student` object `s`. Rather than invoke `s.calcTuition()` directly, however, this version passes the address of the `s` to `someFn()` and that function does the honors. The program repeats the process with a `GraduateStudent` object `gs`.

Now without looking ahead, I have a question: Which `calcTuition()` will `pS->calcTuition()` call when `main()` passes the address of a `GraduateStudent` to `someFn()`? You could argue that it will call `Student::calcTuition()` because the declared type of `pS` is `Student*`. On the other hand, you could argue that the same call will invoke `GraduateStudent::calcTuition()` because the "real type" is `GraduateStudent*`.

The "real type" of an object is known as the *run-time type* (as opposed to the *declared type*). These are also known as *dynamic type* and *static type*, respectively.

The output from this program appears as follows:

```
The value of someFn(&s) is 0
The value of someFn(&gs) is 0
Press any key to continue . . .
```

You can see that, by default, C++ bases its decision on the declared type of the object. Therefore, `someFn()` calls `Student::calcTuition()` because that's the way the object is declared irrespective of the run-time type of the object provided in the call.

The alternative to early binding is to decide which member function to call based on the run-time type of the object. This is known as *late binding*.

Thus, we say that C++ prefers early binding.

Enter late binding

Early binding does not capture the essence of object-oriented programming. Let's return to how I made nachos in Chapter 21. In a sense, I acted as the late binder. The recipe said, "Heat the nachos in the oven." It didn't say, "If the type of oven is microwave, do this; if the type is convection oven, do this; if the type is conventional oven, do this; if using a campfire, do this." The recipe (the code) relied on me (the late binder) to decide what the action (member function) heat means when applied to the oven (the particular instance of class Oven) or any of its variations (subclasses), such as a microwave (MicrowaveOven). People think this way, and designing a language along these lines enables the software model to more accurately describe a real-world solution a person might think up.

There are also mundane reasons of maintainability and reusability to justify late binding. Suppose I write a great program around the class Student. This program, cool as it is, does lots of things, and one of the things it does is calculate the student's tuition for the upcoming year. After months of design, coding, and testing, I release the program to great acclaim and accolades from my peers.

Time passes and my boss asks me to change the rules for calculating the tuition on graduate students. I'm to leave the rules for students untouched, but I'm to give graduate students some type of break on their tuition so that the university can attract more and better postgraduate candidates. Deep within the program, someFunction() calls the calcTuition() member function as follows:

```cpp
void someFunction(Student* pS)
{
    pS->calcTuition();

    // ...function continues on...
}
```

This should look familiar. If not, refer to the beginning of this chapter.

If C++ did not support late binding, I would need to edit someFunction() to do something similar to the following:

```cpp
void someFunction(Student* pS)
{
    if (pS->type() == STUDENT)
    {
        pS->Student::calcTuition();
    }
```

```
    if (pS->type() == GRADUATESTUDENT)
    {
        pS->GraduateStudent::calcTuition();
    }

    // ...function continues on...
}
```

Using the extended name of the function, including the class name, forces the compiler to use the specific version of `calcTuition()`.

I would add a `member type()` to the class that would return some constant. I could establish the value of this constant in the constructor.

This change doesn't seem so bad until you consider that `calcTuition()` isn't called in just one place; it's called throughout the program. The chances are not good that I will find all the places that it's called.

And even if I do find them all, I'm editing (read "breaking") previously debugged, tested, checked in, and certified code. Edits can be time-consuming and boring, and they introduce opportunities for error. Any one of my edits could be wrong. At the very least, I will have to retest and recertify every path involving `calcTuition()`.

What happens when my boss wants another change? (My boss, like all bosses, is like that.) I get to repeat the entire process.

What I really want is for C++ to keep track of the real-time type of the object and to perform the call using late binding.

The ability to perform late binding is called *polymorphism* ("poly" meaning "varied" and "morph" meaning "form"). Thus, a single object may take varied actions based upon its run-time type.

All I need to do is add the keyword `virtual` to the declaration of the member function in the base class as demonstrated in the following LateBinding example program:

```
//
//  LateBinding - addition of the keyword 'virtual'
//                changes C++ from early binding to late
//                binding.
//
#include <cstdio>
#include <cstdlib>
#include <iostream>
```

```
using namespace std;

class Student
{
  public:
    virtual double calcTuition() { return 0.0; }
};

class GraduateStudent : public Student
{
  public:
    virtual double calcTuition() { return 1.0; }
};

double someFn(Student* pS)
{
    return pS->calcTuition();
}

int main(int nNumberofArgs, char* pszArgs[])
{
    // the following calls Student::calcTuition()
    Student s;
    cout << "The value of someFn(&s) is "
         << someFn(&s)
         << endl;

    // the following calls GraduateStudent::calcTuition()
    GraduateStudent gs;
    cout << "The value of someFn(&gs) is "
         << someFn(&gs)
         << endl;

    // wait until user is ready before terminating program
    // to allow the user to see the program results
    system("PAUSE");
    return 0;
}
```

It's not necessary to add the `virtual` keyword to the subclass as well, but doing so is common practice. A member function that is bound late is known as a *virtual member function*.

Other than the `virtual` keyword, there is no other difference between the LateBinding program and its AmbiguousBinding predecessor, but the results are strikingly different:

```
The value of someFn(&s) is 0
The value of someFn(&gs) is 1
Press any key to continue . . .
```

This is exactly what I want: C++ is now deciding which version of calcTuition() to call, not based upon its declared type but based upon its run-time type.

It may seem surprising that the default for C++ is early binding, but the reason is simple. Late binding adds a small amount of overhead to every call to virtual member functions. The inventors of C++ did not want to give critics any reasons to reject the language, so, by default, C++ does not include the overhead of late binding with functions that are not virtual.

When Is Virtual Not?

Just because you think a particular function call is bound late doesn't mean that it is. C++ generates no indication at compile time which calls it thinks are bound early and which are bound late.

The most critical thing to watch for is that all of the member functions in question are declared identically, including the return type. If they aren't declared with the same arguments in the subclass, the member functions aren't overridden; without overriding, there can't be late binding. Consider the following code snippet:

```
class Base
{
  public:
    virtual void fn(int x);
};

class Subclass : public Base
{
  public:
    virtual void fn(double x);
};
void test(Base* pB)
{
    pB->fn(1);

    pB->fn(2.0);
};
```

The function fn() is not bound late because the arguments don't match. Not surprisingly, the first call to fn() within test() goes to Base::fn(int) even if test() is passed to an object of class Subclass. Somewhat surprisingly, the second call goes to Base::fn(int) as well after converting the double to an int. Again, no overriding, no late binding.

The only exception to this rule is best explained by the following example:

```
class Base
{
  public:
    virtual Base* fn();
};

class Subclass : public Base
{
  public:
    virtual Subclass* fn();
};
```

Here, the function `fn()` is bound late, even though the return type doesn't match exactly. In practice, this is quite natural. If a function is dealing with `Subclass` objects, it seems natural that it should return a `Subclass` object as well.

Virtual Considerations

Specifying the class name in the call forces the call to find out early whether the function is declared virtual or not. For example, the following call is to `Base::fn()` because that's what the programmer indicated that she intended:

```
void test(Base* pB)
{
    pB->Base::fn();  // this call is not bound late
}
```

Constructors cannot be declared virtual because there is no completed object at the time the constructor is invoked to use as the basis for late binding.

On the other hand, destructors should almost always be declared virtual. If not, you run the risk of not completely destructing the object, as demonstrated in the following snippet:

```
class Base
{
  public:
    ~Base() {}  // this should be declared virtual
};

class Subclass
```

```
{
  protected:
    MyObject* pMO;

  public:
    Subclass()
    {
        pMO = new MyObject;
    }
    ~Subclass()
    {
        delete pMO;
        pMO = 0;
    }
};

Base* someOtherFn()
{
    return new Subclass;
}

void someFn()
{
    Base* pB = someOtherFn();
    delete pB;
}
```

The program has a subtle but devastating bug. When someFn() is called, it immediately calls someOtherFn(), which creates an object of class Subclass. The constructor for Subclass allocates an object of class MyObject off the heap. Ostensibly, all is well because the destructor for Subclass returns MyObject to the heap when the Subclass object is destructed.

However, when someFn() calls delete, it passes a pointer of type Base*. If this call is allowed to bind early, it will invoke the destructor for Base, which knows nothing about MyObject. The memory will not be returned to the heap.

I realize that technically delete is a keyword and not a function call, but the semantics are the same.

Declaring the destructor for Base virtual solves the problem. Now the call to delete is bound late — realizing that the pointer passed to delete actually points to a Subclass object, delete invokes the Subclass destructor, and the memory is returned, as it's supposed to be.

So is there a case in which you don't want to declare the destructor virtual? Only one. Earlier I said that virtual functions introduce a "little" overhead. Let me be more specific. One thing they add is an additional hidden pointer to every object — not one pointer per virtual function, just one pointer, period. A class with no virtual functions does not have this pointer.

Now, one pointer doesn't sound like much, and it isn't, unless the following two conditions are true:

- ✔ The class doesn't have many data members (so that one pointer is a lot compared with what's there already).
- ✔ You create a lot of objects of this class (otherwise, the overhead doesn't matter).

If either of these two conditions is not true, always declare your destructors virtual.

Chapter 30

Overloading Assignment Operators

In This Chapter

▶ Overloading operators — in general, a bad idea

▶ Overloading the assignment operator — why that one is critical

▶ What to do when you just can't be bothered with writing an assignment operator

The little symbols like +, -, =, and so on are called *operators*. These operators are already defined for the intrinsic types like `int` and `double`. However, C++ allows you to define the existing operators for classes that you create. This is called *operator overloading*.

Operator overloading sounds like a great idea. The examples that are commonly named are classes like `Complex` that represent a complex number. (Don't worry if you don't know what a complex number is. Just know that C++ doesn't handle them intrinsically.) Having defined the class `Complex`, you can then define the addition, multiplication, subtraction, and division operators (all of these operations are defined for complex numbers). Then you write cool stuff like:

```
Complex c1(1, 0), c2(0, 1);
Complex c3 = c1 + c2;
```

Overloading operators turns out to be much more difficult in practice than in theory. So much so that I consider operator overloading beyond the scope of this book with two exceptions, one of which is the subject of this chapter: overloading the assignment operator. The second operator worth overloading is the subject of the next chapter.

Overloading an Operator

C++ considers an operator as a special case of a function call. It considers the + operator to be shorthand for the function `operator+()`. In fact, for any operator %, the function version is known as operator%(). So to define what addition means when applied to a Complex object, for example, you need merely to define the following function:

```
Complex& operator+(Complex& c1, Complex& c2);
```

You can define what existing operators mean when applied to objects of your making, but there are a lot of things you *can't* do when overloading operators. Here are just a few:

- ✔ You can't define a new operator, only redefine what an existing operator means when applied to your user-defined class.
- ✔ You can't overload the intrinsic operators like operator+(int, int).
- ✔ You can't affect the precedence of the operators.

In addition, the assignment operator must be a member function — it cannot be a non-member function like the addition operator just defined.

Overloading the Assignment Operator Is Critical

The C++ language does provide a default assignment operator. That's why you can write things like the following:

```
Student s1("Stephen Davis", 1234);
Student s2;
s2 = s1;      // use the default assignment operator
```

The default assignment operator does a member-by-member copy of each data member from the object on the right into the object on the left. This is completely analogous to the default copy constructor. Remember that this member-by-member copy is called a *shallow copy*. (Refer to Chapter 27 for more on copy constructors and shallow copies.)

The problems inherent in the default assignment operator are similar to the copy constructor, only worse. Consider the following example snippet:

```
class Student
{
  protected:
    char*  pszName;
    int    nID;

  public:
```

```
    Student(const char* pszNewName, int nNewID)
    {
        cout << "Constructing " << pszNewName << endl;
        int nLength = strlen(pszNewName) + 1;
        pszName = new char[nLength];
        strcpy(pszName, pszNewName);
        nID = nNewID;
    }
    ~Student()
    {
        cout << "Destructing " << pszName << endl;
        delete[] pszName;
        pszName = 0;
    }

    // ...other members...
};

void someFn()
{
    Student s1("Stephen Davis", 1234);
    Student s2("Cayden Amrich", 5678);

    s2 = s1;   // this is legal but very bad
}
```

The function `someFn()` first creates an object s1. The `Student(const char*, int)` constructor for `Student` allocates memory from the heap to use to store the student's name. The process is repeated for s2.

The function then assigns s1 to s2. This does two things, both of which are bad:

- ✔ Copies the `s1.pszName` pointer into `s2.pszName` so that both objects now point to the same block of heap memory.

- ✔ Wipes out the previous value of `s2.pszName` so that the block of memory used to store the student name `Cayden Amrich` is lost.

Here's what the assignment operator for `Student` needs to do:

- ✔ Delete the memory block pointed at by `s2.pszName` (like a destructor).

- ✔ Perform a deep copy of the string from `s1.pszName` into a newly allocated array in `s2.pszName` (like a copy constructor). (Again, see Chapter 27 for a description of deep copying.)

In fact, you can make this general statement: An assignment operator acts like a destructor to wipe out the current values in the object followed by a copy constructor that copies new values into the object.

Looking at an Example

The following StudentAssignment program contains a `Student` class that has a constructor and a destructor along with a copy constructor and an assignment operator — everything a self-respecting class needs!

```
//
//   StudentAssignment - this program demonstrates how to
//                  create an assignment operator that
//                  performs the same deep copy as the copy
//                  constructor
//
#include <cstdio>
#include <cstdlib>
#include <iostream>
#include <cstring>
using namespace std;

class Student
{
  protected:
    char*  pszName;
    int    nID;

    void init(const char* pszNewName, int nNewID)
    {
        int nLength = strlen(pszNewName) + 1;
        pszName = new char[nLength];
        strcpy(pszName, pszNewName);
        nID = nNewID;
    }

    void destruct()
    {
        delete[] pszName;
        pszName = 0;
    }

  public:
    Student(const char* pszNewName, int nNewID)
    {
        cout << "Constructing " << pszNewName << endl;
        init(pszNewName, nNewID);
```

```
    }
    Student(Student& s)
    {
        cout<<"Constructing copy of "<< s.pszName << endl;
        init(s.pszName, s.nID);
    }

    virtual ~Student()
    {
        cout << "Destructing " << pszName << endl;
        destruct();
    }

    // overload the assignment operator
    Student& operator=(Student& source)
    {
        // don't do anything if we are assigned to
        // ourselves
        if (this != &source)
        {
            cout << "Assigning " << source.pszName
                 << " to "        << pszName << endl;

            // first destruct the existing object
            destruct();

            // now copy the source object
            init(source.pszName, source.nID);
        }

        return *this;
    }


    // access functions
    const char* getName()
    {
        return pszName;
    }
    int getID()
    {
        return nID;
    }
};

void someFn()
{
    Student s1("Adam Laskowski", 1234);
    Student s2("Vanessa Barbossa", 5678);
```

```
    s2 = s1;
}

int main(int nNumberofArgs, char* pszArgs[])
{
    someFn();

    // wait until user is ready before terminating program
    // to allow the user to see the program results
    system("PAUSE");
    return 0;
}
```

The data members of this Student class are the same as the versions from earlier chapters. The constructor and copy constructor are the same as well, except that the actual work is performed in an init() function that is invoked from both constructors. The assignment operator can reuse the same init() function as well to perform its construction function.

The code that implements the destruct sequence has also been transferred from ~Student() to a protected destruct() member function.

Following the destructor is the assignment operator operator=(). This function first tests to see if the address of the object passed is the same as the current object. This is to detect the following case:

```
s1 = s1;
```

In this case, the assignment operator does nothing. If the source and current objects are not the same, the function first destructs the current object and then copies the contents of the source object into the current object. Finally, it returns a reference to the current object.

The someFn() function shows how this works in practice. After first declaring two Student objects s1 and s2, someFn() executes the assignment

```
s2 = s1;
```

which is interpreted as if it had been written as

```
s2.operator=(s1);
```

That is, the assignment operator destructs s2 and then copies the contents of s1 into s2.

The destructor invoked at the end of `someFn()` demonstrates that the two objects, s1 and s2, don't both refer to the same piece of heap memory. The output from the program appears as follows:

```
Constructing Adam Laskowski
Constructing Vanessa Barbossa
Assigning Adam Laskowski to Vanessa Barbossa
Destructing Adam Laskowski
Destructing Adam Laskowski
Press any key to continue . . .
```

The reason that the assignment operator returns a reference to the current object is to allow the following:

```
s3 = s1 = s2;
```

Writing Your Own (or Not)

I don't expect you to learn all the ins and outs of overloading operators; however, you can't go too wrong if you follow the pattern set out by the Student example:

1. Check to make sure that the left-hand and right-hand objects aren't the same — if so, return without taking any action.

2. Destruct the left-hand object (the current object which is the same object referred to by `this`).

3. Copy construct the left-hand object using the right-hand object as the source.

4. Return a reference to the left-hand object (that is, `return *this;`).

If this is too much, you can always do the following:

```
class Student
{
  protected:
    Student& operator=(Student&)
    {
        return *this;
    }

    // ...whatever else...
};
```

This assignment operator doesn't do anything, but by being declared protected, it precludes any application software from trying to use the default assignment operator. Now

```
s1 = s2;
```

will generate a compiler error.

Chapter 31

Performing Streaming I/O

. . . .

In This Chapter

▶ Using stream I/O — an overview

▶ Opening an object for file input and output

▶ Detecting errors when performing file I/O

▶ Formatting output to a file

▶ Using the stream classes on internal buffers for easy string formatting

. . . .

I gave you a template to follow when generating new programs in Chapter 2. Since you were just starting the journey to C++, I asked you to take a lot of what was in that template on faith; then throughout subsequent chapters, I explained each of the features of the template. There's just one item remaining: stream input/output (commonly shortened to just I/O).

I must warn you that stream I/O can't be covered completely in a single chapter — entire books are devoted to this one topic. Fortunately, however, you don't need to know too much about stream I/O in order to write the vast majority of programs.

How Stream I/O Works

Stream I/O is based on overloaded versions of operator>>() and operator<<() (known as the right-shift and left-shift operators, respectively)

Note: I don't cover the << (left-shift) and >> (right-shift) operators in my discussion of arithmetic operators in Chapter 4, as these perform bit operations that are beyond the scope of a beginning programmer.

The prototype declarations for the stream operators are found in the include file iostream. The code for these functions is part of the Standard C++ Library that your programs link with by default. That's why the standard template starts out with #include <iostream> — without it, you can't perform stream I/O. The following excerpt shows just a few of the prototype declarations that appear in iostream:

```
//for input we have:
istream& operator>>(istream& source, int    &dest);
istream& operator>>(istream& source, double &dest);
istream& operator>>(istream& source, char   *pDest);
//...and so forth...

//for output we have:
ostream& operator<<(ostream& dest, const char *pSource);
ostream& operator<<(ostream& dest, int         source);
ostream& operator<<(ostream& dest, double      source);
//...and so it goes...
```

When overloaded to perform stream input, operator<<() is called the *extractor*. The class istream is the basic class for performing input from a file. C++ creates an istream object cin and associates it with the keyboard when your program first starts and before main() is executed.

The first prototype in the earlier extract from the iostream include file refers to the function that is invoked when you enter the following C++ code:

```
int i;
cin >> i;
```

As you've seen, extracting from cin is the standard way of performing keyboard input.

When overloaded to perform stream output, operator<<() is called the *inserter*. C++ uses the ostream class for performing formatted output from a file. C++ creates an ostream object cout at program start and associates it with the console display.

The first prototype among the output functions is called when you enter the following:

```
cout << "C++ programming is fn()";
```

Inserting to cout is the standard means for displaying stuff to the operator.

Both cin and cout are declared in the iostream include file. That's how your program knows what they are.

C++ opens a second ostream object at program startup. This object, cerr, is also associated with the display by default, but it is used as a standard error output. If you've used Linux, Unix, or the Windows console window much, you know that you can redirect standard input and output. For example, the command

```
myprogram <file1.txt >file2.txt
```

says, "Execute `myprogram.exe`, but read from `file1.txt` rather than the keyboard, and output to `file2.txt` rather than the display." That is, `cin` is associated with `file1.txt` and `cout` with `file2.txt`. In this case, if you send error messages to `cout`, the operator will never see them because they will be sent to the file. However, messages sent to `cerr` will continue to go to the display since it is not redirected with `cout`.

Always send error messages to `cerr` rather than `cout` just in case `cout` has been redirected.

Stream Input/Output

C++ provides separate classes for performing input and output to files. These classes, `ifstream` and `ofstream`, are defined in the include file `fstream`.

Collectively both `ifstream` and `ofstream` are known as `fstream` classes.

Creating an input object

The class `ifstream` provides a constructor used to open a file for input:

```
ifstream(const char* pszFileName,
                ios_base::openmode mode);
```

This constructor opens a file, creates an object of class `ifstream`, and associates that object with the opened file to be used for input. The first argument to the constructor is a pointer to the name of the file to open. You can provide a full pathname or just the filename.

If you provide the filename without a path, C++ will look in the current directory for the file to read. When executing from your program from within Code::Blocks, the current directory is the directory that contains the project file.

Don't forget that a Windows/DOS backslash is written "`\\`" in C++. Refer to Chapter 5 for details.

The second argument directs some details about how the file is to be opened when the object is created. The type `openmode` is a user-defined type within the class `ios_base`. The legal values of `mode` are defined in Table 31-1. If `mode` is not provided, the default value is `ios_base::in`, which means open the file for input. (Pretty logical for a file called `ifstream`.)

The following example code snippet opens the text file `MyData.txt` and reads a few integers from it:

```
void someFn()
{
    // open the file MyData.txt in the current directory
    ifstream input("MyData.txt");

    int a, b, c;

    input >> a >> b >> c;
    cout <<    "a = " << a
        << ", b = " << b
        << ", c = " << c << endl;
}
```

To specify the full path, I could write something like the following:

```
ifstream input("C:\\\\MyFolder\\MyData.txt");
```

This opens the "C:\\MyFolder\MyData.txt" file.

The destructor for class `ifstream` closes the file. In the preceding snippet, the file "MyData.txt" is closed when control exits `someFn()` and the `input` object goes out of scope.

Table 31-1	Constants That Control How Files Are Opened for Input
Flag	*Meaning*
`ios_ base::binary`	Open file in binary mode (alternative is text mode)
`ios_base::in`	Open file for input (implied for `istream`)

Creating an output object

The class `ofstream` is the output counterpart to `ifstream`. The constructor for this class opens a file for output using the inserter operator:

```
ofstream(const char* pszFileName,
         ios_base::openmode mode);
```

This constructor opens a file for output. Here again, pszFileName points to the name of the file, whereas mode controls some aspects about how the file is to be opened. Table 31-2 lists the possible values for mode. If you don't provide a mode, the default value is out + trunc, which means "open the file for output and truncate whatever is already in the file" (the alternative is to append whatever you output to the end of the existing file).

The following example code snippet opens the text file MyData.txt and writes some absolutely true information into it:

```
void someFn()
{
    // open the file MyData.txt in the current directory
    ofstream output("MyData.txt");

    output <<   "Stephen is suave and handsome\n"
            << "and definitely not balding prematurely"
            << endl;
}
```

The destructor for class ofstream flushes any buffers to disk and closes the file before destructing the object and returning any local memory buffers to the heap when the output object goes out of scope at the end of someFn().

Table 31-2	Constants That Control How Files Are Opened for Output
Flag	*Meaning*
ios_base::app	Seek to End of File before each write
ios_base::ate	Seek to End of File immediately after opening the file
ios_base::binary	Open file in binary mode (alternative is text mode)
ios_base::out	Open file for output (implied for ostream)
ios_base::trunc	Truncate file, if it exists (default for ostream)

Open modes

Tables 31-1 and 31-2 show the different modes that are possible when opening a file. To set these values properly, you need to answer the following three questions:

✔ Do you want to read from the file or write to the file? Use `ifstream` to read and `ofstream` to write. If you intend to both read and write to the same file, then use the class `fstream` and set the mode to `in | out`, which opens the file for both input and output. Good luck, however, because getting this to work properly is difficult. It's much better to write to a file with one object and read from the file with another object.

✔ If you are writing to the file and it already exists, do you want to add to the existing contents (in which case, open with mode set to `out | ate`) or delete the contents and start over (in which case, open with mode set to `out | trunc`)?

✔ Are you reading or writing text or binary data? Both `ifstream` and `ofstream` default to text mode. Use `binary` mode if you are reading or writing raw, nontext data. (See the next section in this chapter for a short explanation of binary mode.)

The | is the "binary OR" operator. The result of `in | out` is an `int` with the `in` bit set and the `out` bit set. You can OR any of the mode flags together.

If the file does not exist when you create the `ofstream` object, C++ will create an empty output file.

What is binary mode?

You can open a file for input or output in either binary or text mode. The primary difference between binary and text mode lies in the way that newlines are handled. The Unix operating system was written in the days when typewriters were still fashionable (when it was called "typing" instead of "keyboarding" or the soon to become fashionable "iPhoning"). Unix ends sentences with a carriage return followed by a line feed.

Subsequent operating systems saw no reason to continue using two characters to end a sentence, but they couldn't agree on which character to use. Some used the carriage return and others the line feed, now renamed newline. The C++ standard is the single newline.

When a file is opened in text mode, the C++ library converts the single newline character into what is appropriate for your operating system on output, whether it's a carriage return plus line feed, a single carriage return, or a line feed (or something else entirely). C++ performs the opposite conversion when reading a file. The C++ library does no such conversions for a file opened in binary mode.

Always use binary mode when manipulating a file that's not in human-readable format. If you don't, the C++ library will modify any byte in the data stream that happens to be the same as a carriage return or linefeed.

Hey, file, what state are you in?

A properly constructed ifstream or ofstream object becomes a stand-in for the file that it's associated with.

The programmer tends to think of operations on the fstream objects as being the same as operations on the file itself. However, this is only true so long as the object is properly constructed. If an fstream object fails to construct properly, it might not be associated with a file — for example, if an ifstream object is created for a file that doesn't exist. In this case, C++ rejects stream operations without taking any action at all.

Fortunately, C++ tells you when something is wrong — the member function bad() returns a true if something is wrong with the fstream object and if it cannot be used for input or output. This usually happens when the object cannot be constructed for input because the file doesn't exist or for output because the program doesn't have permission to write to the disk or directory. Other system errors can also cause the bad() state to become true.

The term "bad" is descriptive, if a bit excessive (I don't like to think of computer programs as being bad or good). A lesser state called fail() is set to true if the last read or write operation failed. For example, if you try to read an int and the stream operator can find only characters, then C++ will set the fail() flag. You can call the member function clear() to clear the fail flag and try again — the next call may or may not work. You cannot clear the bad() flag — just like wine, an object gone bad is not recoverable.

Attempts to perform input from or output to an object with either the bad() or fail() flag set are ignored.

I mean this literally — no input or output is possible as long as the internal state of the fstream object has an error. The program won't even try to perform I/O, which isn't so bad on output — it's pretty obvious when your program isn't performing output the way it's supposed to. This situation can lead to some tricky bugs in programs that perform input, however. It's very easy to mistake garbage left in the variable, perhaps from a previous read, for valid input from the file.

Consider the following ReadIntegers program, which contains an `unsafeFn()` that reads values from an input file:

```
//
//   ReadIntegers - this program reads integers from
//                  an input file MyFile.txt contained
//                  in the current directory.
//
#include <cstdio>
#include <cstdlib>
#include <fstream>
#include <iostream>
using namespace std;

void unsafeFn()
{
    ifstream myFile("MyFile.txt");
    int nInputValue;

    for(int n = 1; n <= 10; n++)
    {
        // read a value
        myFile >> nInputValue;

        // value successfully read - output it
        cout << n << " - " << nInputValue << endl;
    }
}

int main(int nNumberofArgs, char* pszArgs[])
{
    unsafeFn();

    // wait until user is ready before terminating program
    // to allow the user to see the program results
    system("PAUSE");
    return 0;
}
```

The preceding `unsafeFn()` function reads ten values from `MyFile.txt` and displays them on the console. That sounds okay, but what if there aren't ten values in `MyFile.txt` — what if there are only nine (or five or none!)? This version of the program generated the following output when provided a sample `MyFile.txt`:

```
1 - 1
2 - 2
3 - 3
4 - 4
5 - 5
6 - 6
7 - 7
8 - 7
```

```
9 - 7
10 - 7
Press any key to continue . . .
```

The question is, did the file really contain the value 7 four times, or did an error occur after the seventh read? There is no way for the user to tell because once the program gets to the End of File, all subsequent read requests fail. The value of nInputValue is not set to zero or some other "special value." It retains whatever value it had on the last successful read request, which in this case is 7.

The most flexible means to avoid this problem is to exit the loop as soon as an error occurs using the member function fail(), as demonstrated by the following safeFn() version of the same function (also part of the ReadIntegers program on the enclosed CD-ROM):

```
//
//   ReadIntegers - this program reads integers from
//                  an input file MyFile.txt contained
//                  in the current directory.
//
#include <cstdio>
#include <cstdlib>
#include <fstream>
#include <iostream>
using namespace std;

void safeFn()
{
    ifstream myFile("MyFile.txt");
    int nInputValue;

    for(int n = 0; n < 10; n++)
    {
        // read a value
        myFile >> nInputValue;

        // exit the loop on read error
        if (myFile.fail())
        {
            break;
        }

        // value successfully read - output it
        cout << n << " - " << nInputValue << endl;
    }
}

int main(int nNumberofArgs, char* pszArgs[])
```

```
{
    safeFn();

    // wait until user is ready before terminating program
    // to allow the user to see the program results
    system("PAUSE");
    return 0;
}
```

This version generated the following output when reading the same `MyFile.txt` file:

```
1 - 1
2 - 2
3 - 3
4 - 4
5 - 5
6 - 6
7 - 7
Press any key to continue . . .
```

Now it's obvious that there are only seven values in the file rather than the expected ten and that the number seven isn't repeated.

Always check the value of `fail()` after extracting data from an input file to make sure that you've actually read a new value.

Notice that the preceding ReadIntegers program adds the line `#include <fstream>` to the standard template I've used for all programs in earlier chapters. This extra include file is necessary to gain access to the `ifstream` and `ofstream` classes.

Don't overflow that buffer

If you look closely at some of the earlier programs in this book, you'll see C++ statements like the following:

```
char szStudentName[80];
cin >> szStudentName;
```

This snippet allocates 80 characters for the student's name (surely that's enough for anyone's name) and then extracts a string into that array. The problem is that the extractor doesn't know how large the array is — if the user types more than 80 characters before entering a return or whitespace, then the C++ library function will overflow the end of the array and overwrite memory. Hackers use this overflow capability in programs that interface directly to the Internet to overwrite the machine instructions in the program, thereby taking over control of your computer.

You can avoid this problem two ways. One way is to use the member function `getline()`. This function allows you to specify the length of the array as in the following:

```
char szStudentName[80];
cin.getline(szStudentName, 80);
```

This call reads input until the first newline or until 80 characters have been read, whichever comes first. Any characters not read are left in `cin` for the next read to pick up.

A second approach is to use the `string` class. This class acts like a char array except that it dynamically resizes to fit the amount of data. Thus, the following is safe:

```
string sStudentName;
cin >> sStudentName;
```

The string class will automatically allocate an array off the heap that's large enough to hold whatever data is input. Unfortunately, the `string` class is beyond the scope of a beginning book on programming.

Other Member Functions of the fstream Classes

The `fstream` classes provide a number of member functions, as shown in Table 31-3 (the list isn't a complete list of all the functions in these very large classes). The prototype declarations for these member functions reside in the `fstream` include file. They are described in the remainder of this section.

Table 31-3   Major Methods of the I/O Stream Classes

Method	Meaning
`bool bad()`	Returns true if a serious error has occurred.
`void clear(iostate flags = ios_base::goodbit)`	Clears (or sets) the I/O state flags.
`void close()`	Closes the file associated with a stream object.
`bool eof()`	Returns true if there are no more characters in the read pointer at the End of File.
`char fill()` `char fill(char newFill)`	Returns or sets the fill character.

(continued)

Table 31-3 *(continued)*

Method	Meaning
`fmtflags flags()` `fmtflags flags(fmtflags f)`	Returns or sets format flags. (See next section on format flags.)
`void flush()`	Flushes the output buffer to the disk.
`int gcount()`	Returns the number of bytes read during the last input.
`char get()`	Reads individual characters from file.

`char getline(`
  `char* buffer,`
  `int count,`
  `char delimiter = '\n')`
	Reads multiple characters up until either End of File, until delimiter encountered, or until `count - 1` characters read. Tacks a null onto the end of the line read. Does not store the delimiter read into the buffer. The delimiter defaults to newline, but you can provide a different one if you like.

`bool good()`	Returns true if no error conditions are set.

`void open(`
  `const char* filename,`
  `openmode mode)`
	Same arguments as the constructor. Performs the same file open on an existing object that the constructor performs when creating a new object.

`streamsize precision()`
`streamsize precision(`
  `streamsize s)`
	Reads or sets the number of digits displayed for floating point variables.

`ostream& put(char ch)`	Writes a single character to the stream.

`istream& read(`
  `char* buffer,`
  `streamsize num)`
	Reads a block of data. Reads either num bytes or until an End of File is encountered, whichever occurs first.

`fmtflags setf(fmtflags)`	Sets specific format flags. Returns old value.
`fmtflags unsetf(fmtflags)`	Clears specific format flags. Returns old value.
`int width()` `int width(int w)`	Reads or sets the number of characters to be displayed by the next formatted output statement.

`ostream& write(`
  `const char* buffer,`
  `streamsize num)`
	Writes a block of data to the output file.

Reading and writing streams directly

The inserter and extractor operators provide a convenient mechanism for reading formatted input. However, sometimes you just want to say, "Give it to me; I don't care what the format is." Several member functions are useful in this case.

The simplest function, get(), returns the next character in an input file. Its output equivalent is put(), which writes a single character to an output file. The function getline() returns a string of characters up to some terminator — the default terminator is a newline, but you can specify any other character you like as the third argument to the function. The getline() function strips off the terminator but makes no other attempt to reformat or otherwise interpret the input.

The member function read() is even more basic. This function reads the number of bytes that you specify, or less if the program encounters the End of File. The function gcount() always returns the actual number of bytes read. The output equivalent is write().

The following FileCopy program uses the read() and write() functions to create a backup of any file you give it by making a copy with the string ".backup" appended to the name:

```cpp
//
//   CopyFiles - make backup copies of whatever files
//               are passed to the program by creating
//               a file with the same name plus the name
//               ".backup" appended.
//
#include <cstdio>
#include <cstdlib>
#include <fstream>
#include <iostream>
#include <cstring>
using namespace std;

void copyFile(const char* pszSrcFileName)
{
    // create a copy of the specified filename with
    // ".backup" added to the end
    int nTargetNameLength = strlen(pszSrcFileName) + 10;
    char *pszTargetFileName = new char[nTargetNameLength];
    strcpy(pszTargetFileName, pszSrcFileName);
    strcat(pszTargetFileName, ".backup");

    // now open the source file for input and
```

```
    // the target file for output
    ifstream input(pszSrcFileName,
                   ios_base::in | ios_base::binary);
    if (input.good())
    {
        ofstream output(pszTargetFileName,
      ios_base::out | ios_base::binary | ios_base::trunc);
        if (output.good())
        {

            while (!input.eof() && input.good())
            {
                char buffer[4096];
                input.read(buffer, 4096);
                output.write(buffer, input.gcount());
            }
        }
    }

    // restore memory to the heap
    delete pszTargetFileName;
}

int main(int nNumberofArgs, char* pszArgs[])
{
    // pass every file name provided to main() to
    // the copyFile() function, one name at a time
    for (int i = 1; i < nNumberofArgs; i++)
    {
        cout << "Copying " << pszArgs[i] << endl;
        copyFile(pszArgs[i]);
    }

    // wait until user is ready before terminating program
    // to allow the user to see the program results
    system("PAUSE");
    return 0;
}
```

The program iterates through the arguments passed to it, remembering that
pszArgs[0] points to the name of the program itself. The program passes
each argument, one at a time, to the function copyFile().

The copyFile() function first creates a copy of the name passed it in the
array pszTargetFileName. It then concatenates the string ".backup" to
that name. Finally, you get to the good part: copyFile() opens the source
file whose name was passed as the argument to the copyFile() function for
binary input.

Note: The ios_base:: is necessary when using the in, out, binary, and trunc flags as these are const static members of the ios_base class.

Use binary mode if you are working with non-text files or you don't intend to display the contents. In this case, I did not limit the program to work only with text files.

The function only continues executing if input.good() is true, indicating that the input object was created successfully, since it will be impossible to read from the file if the open did not work properly.

In a real-world program, I would have displayed some useful error message before returning to the caller.

If the input object is created okay, copyFile() creates an output object using the pszTargetFileName created earlier. This file is opened for binary output. The mode flag is also set to truncate to delete the contents of the target file if it already exists. If output.good() is true, the function executes the next section of the function; otherwise, control jumps to the end.

The function is now ready to copy the contents of one file to the other: it enters a loop in which it reads 4K blocks from the input file and writes them to the output file.

Notice in the call to write(), copyFile() uses the value returned from input.gcount() rather than a hardcoded 4096. This is because unless the source file just happens to be an integer multiple of 4096 bytes in length (not very likely), the last call to read() will fetch less than the requested number of bytes before encountering the End of File.

The loop terminates when either input reaches the End of File or the input object is no longer good.

The ! operator (pronounced "the NOT operator") inverts the sense of a Boolean expression. In other words, !true is false and !false is true. (You read that last phrase as "NOT true is false and NOT false is true.")

Immediately before exiting, the function returns the pszTargetFileName array to the heap. Exiting the function causes the destructor for both input and output to be called, which closes both the input and output files.

To execute the program within the Code::Blocks environment, I first selected Project⇨Set Programs' Arguments to open the Select target dialog box. In the Program arguments field, I entered main.cpp and clicked OK. I could just as well have selected and dropped several files onto the name of the CopyFiles executable file or entered the command name followed by the names of the files to "backup" at the command prompt.

Chapter 18 discusses the various ways to pass arguments to your program.

When I run the program, I get the following output:

```
Copying main.cpp
Press any key to continue . . .
```

Looking into the folder containing the main.cpp source file, I now see a second main.cpp.backup file that has the identical size and contents as the original.

Controlling format

The flags(), setf(), and unsetf() member functions are all used to set or retrieve a set of format flags used to control the format of input extracted from an ifstream or inserted into an ofstream object. The flags get set to some default value that makes sense most of the time when the object is created. However, you can change these flags to control the format of input and/or output. Table 31-4 describes the flags that can be used with the flags(), setf(), and unsetf() member functions.

Table 31-4	I/O Stream Format Flags Used with setf(), unsetf(), and flags()
Flag	*If Flag Is True Then . . .*
boolalpha	Displays variables of type bool as either true or false rather than 1 or 0
dec	Reads or writes integers in decimal format (default)
fixed	Displays floating point in fixed point as opposed to scientific (default)
hex	Reads or writes integers in hexadecimal
left	Displays output left-justified (that is, pads on the right)
oct	Reads or writes integers in octal
right	Displays output right-justified (that is, pads on the left)
scientific	Displays floating point in scientific format
showbase	Displays a leading 0 for octal output and leading 0x for hexadecimal output
showpoint	Displays a decimal point for floating point output even if the fractional portion is zero
skipws	Skips over whitespace when reading using the extractor
unitbuf	Flushes output after each output operation
uppercase	Replaces lowercase letters with their uppercase equivalents on output

For example, the following code segment displays integer values in hexadecimal (rather than the default, decimal):

```
// fetch the previous value so we can restore it
ios_base::fmtflags prevValue = cout.flags();

// clear the decimal flag
cout.unsetf(cout.dec);

// now set the hexadecimal flag
cout.setf(cout.hex);

// ...do stuff...

// restore output to previous state
cout.flags(prevValue);
```

This example first queries the cout object for the current value of the format flags using the flags() member function. The type of the value returned is ios_base::fmtflags.

I didn't discuss user-defined types defined within classes — that's an advanced topic — so just trust me that this type makes sense.

It's always a good idea to record the format flags of an input or output object before changing them so that you can restore them to their previous value once you're finished.

The program then clears the decimal flag using the unsetf() function (it does this because hexadecimal, octal, and decimal are mutually exclusive format modes) before setting the hex mode using setf(). The setf() sets the hexadecimal flag without changing the value of any other format flags that may be set. Every time an integer is inserted into the cout object for the remainder of the function, C++ will display the value in hexadecimal.

Once the function finishes displaying values in hexadecimal format, it restores the previous value by calling flags(fmtflags). This member function overwrites the current flags without whatever value you pass it.

Further format control is provided by the width(int) member function that sets the minimum width of the next output operation. In the event that the field doesn't take up the full width specified, the inserter adds the requisite number of fill characters. The default fill character is a space, but you change this by calling fill(char). Whether C++ adds the fill characters on the left or right is determined by whether the left or right format flag is set.

For example, the code snippet

```
int i = 123;
cout.setf(cout.right);
cout.unsetf(cout.left);
cout.fill('+');
cout << "i = [";
cout.width(10);
cout << i;
cout << "]" << endl;
```

generates the following output:

```
i = [+++++++123]
```

Notice that the call to width(int) appears immediately before cout << i. Unlike the other formatting flags, the width(int) call applies only to the very next value that you insert. It must be reset after every value that you output.

What's up with endl?

Most programs in this book terminate an output stream by inserting the object endl. However, some programs include \n within the text to output a newline. What's the deal?

The endl object inserts a newline into the output stream, but it takes one more step. Disks are slow devices (compared to computer processors). Writing to disk more often than necessary will slow your program considerably. To avoid this, the ofstream class collects output into an internal buffer. The class writes the contents to disk when the buffer is full.

A memory buffer used to speed up output to a slow device like a disk is known as a *cache* — pronounced "cash." Writing the contents of the buffer to disk is known as *flushing the cache*.

The endl object adds a newline to the buffer and then flushes the cache to disk. You can also flush the cache manually by calling the member function flush().

Note that C++ does not cache output to the standard error object, cerr.

Manipulating Manipulators

The span of some formatting member functions is fairly short. The best example of this is the width(n) member function — this function is good only for the next value output. After that it must be reset. You saw this implication in the preceding snippet — the call to cout.width(n) had to appear right in the middle of the inserters:

```
cout << "i = [";
cout.width(10);
cout << i;
cout << "]" << endl;
```

The call to cout.width(10) is good only for the very next output cout << i; it has no effect on the following output cout << "]".

Other functions have a short span, usually because you need to change their value often. For example, switching back and forth between decimal and hexadecimal mode while performing output requires multiple calls to setf(hex) and setf(dec) throughout the program.

Since this process can be a bit clumsy, C++ defines a more convenient means to invoke these common member functions. Table 31-5 defines a set of so-called *manipulators* that can be inserted directly in the output stream. These manipulators defined in the include file iomanip have the same effect as calling the corresponding member function.

Table 31-5	Common Manipulators and Their Equivalent Member Functions	
Manipulator	*Member Function*	*Description*
dec	setf(dec)	Set display radix to decimal
hex	setf(hex)	Set display radix to hexadecimal
oct	setf(oct)	Set display radix to octal
setfill(c)	fill(c)	Set the fill character to c
setprecision(n)	precision(n)	Set the display precision to n
setw(n)	width(n)	Set the minimum field width for the next output to n

For example, the earlier snippet can be written as follows:

```
cout << "i = [" << setw(10) << i << "]" << endl;
```

I/O manipulators are nothing more than a labor-saving device — they don't add any new capability.

You must include iomanip if you intend to use I/O manipulators.

Using the stringstream Classes

After some practice, you get pretty good at parsing input from a file using the extractors and generating attractive output using the format controls provided with the inserter. It's a shame that you can't use that skill to parse character strings that are already in memory.

Well, of course, C++ provides just such a capability (I wouldn't have mentioned it otherwise). C++ provides two pairs of classes that allow you to parse a string in memory using the same member functions that you're accustomed to using for file I/O. An object of class istrstream or istringstream "looks and feels" like an ifstream object. Similarly, an object of class ostrstream or ostringstream responds to the same commands as an ofstream object.

The difference between the two sets of classes is not how they operate but how they are constructed. The istrstream class must be constructed with an ASCIIZ array as its base. All input is performed from this array. The istringstream class takes an object of class string as its base.

I don't discuss the string class in this book since in practice it's a little beyond the scope of a beginning programmer. However, the string class acts like an ASCIIZ array whose size changes automatically to conform to the size of the string it's asked to hold.

Similarly, the class ostrstream writes into an ASCIIZ array that is provided in the constructor, whereas the ostringstream class creates a string object for output.

The istrstream and ostrstream classes are defined in the strstream include file. The istringstream and ostringstream classes are defined in the sstream include file.

The following StringStream program parses Student information from an input file by first reading in a line using getline() before parsing it with istrstream.

The strstream classes are being phased out of the language in favor of the stringstream classes; however, I used the strstream classes here since they are based on the ASCIIZ character arrays that you are already familiar with. You will want to convert over to using the stringstream classes once you become familiar with the string class. The Code::Blocks compiler generates a warning when building the StringStream program that the strstream classes are *deprecated*, meaning that they are subject to removal.

```
// StringStream - demonstrate the use of string stream
//                   classes for parsing input safely
#include <cstdio>
#include <cstdlib>
#include <iostream>
#include <strstream>
#include <cstring>
using namespace std;

struct Student
{
  protected:
    char szFirstName[128];
    char szLastName[128];
    int  nStudentID;

  public:
    Student(const char* pszFN, const char* pszLN,int nSID)
    {
        strncpy(szFirstName, pszFN, 128);
        strncpy(szLastName, pszLN, 128);
        nStudentID = nSID;
    }

    // display - write the student's data into the
    //           array provided; don't exceed the size
    //           of the array set by nLength
    void display(char* pszBuffer, int nLength)
    {
        ostrstream out(pszBuffer, nLength);

        out << szFirstName << " " << szLastName
            << " [" << nStudentID << "]" << ends;
    }
};

int main(int nNumberofArgs, char* pszArgs[])
{
    Student *pStudents[128];
    int nCount = 0;

    cout << "Input student <last name, first name ID>\n"
         << "(Input a blank line to stop input)" << endl;

    for(;;)
    {
        // get another line to parse
```

```
        char szLine[256];
        cin.getline(szLine, 256);

        // terminate if line is blank
        if (strlen(szLine) == 0)
        {
            break;
        }

        // associate an istrstream object with the
        // array that we just read
        istrstream input(szLine, 256);

        // now try to parse the buffer read
        char szLastName[256];
        char szFirstName[256];
        int nSSID;

        // read the last name up to a comma separator
        input.getline(szLastName, 256, ',');

        // read the first name until encountering white
        // space
        input >> szFirstName;

        // now read the student id
        input >> nSSID;

        // skip this line if anything didn't work
        if (input.fail())
        {
            cerr << "Bad input: " << szLine << endl;
            continue;
        }

        // create a Student object with the data
        // input and store it in the array of pointers
        pStudents[nCount++] = new Student(szFirstName,
                                   szLastName, nSSID);
    }

    // display the students input - use the Student's
    // output function to format the student data
    for(int n = 0; n < nCount; n++)
    {
        char szBuffer[256];
        pStudents[n]->display(szBuffer, 256);
        cout << szBuffer << endl;
    }
```

```
    // wait until user is ready before terminating program
    // to allow the user to see the program results
    system("PAUSE");
    return 0;
}
```

The program starts by creating an array of pointers that it will use to store the Student objects that it creates. It then prompts the user for the format that it expects for the student data to be read.

The program then enters a loop in which it first reads an entire line of input up to and including the terminating newline. If the length of the line read is zero, meaning that nothing was entered but a newline, the program breaks out of the input loop.

If something was input, the program associates an istrstream object input with the buffer. Subsequent read requests will be from this szLine buffer. The istrstream buffer must also tell the constructor how long the buffer is so that it doesn't read beyond the end.

The next section reads the last name, first name, and Social Security number.

These reads are safe — they cannot overflow the szLastName and szFirstName buffers because the extractor cannot possibly return more than 256 characters in any single read — that's how long the szLine array is.

Notice how the program calls getline() passing a ',' as the terminator. This reads characters up to and including the comma that separates the last name and first name.

Once the program has read the three student fields, it checks the input object to see if everything worked by calling input.fail(). If fail() is true, the program throws away whatever it read and spits back out the line to the user with an error message.

The Student constructor is typical of those you've seen elsewhere in the book. The program uses the Student::display() function to display the contents of a Student object. It does this in a fairly elegant fashion by simply associating an ostrstream object with the array provided and then inserting to the object. All main() has to do is output the result.

This is much more flexible than the alternative of inserting output directly to cout — the program can do anything it wants with the szBuffer array containing the Student data. It can write it to a file, send it to cout, or put it in a table, to name just three possibilities.

Notice that the last object `display()` inserts is the object `ends`. This is sort of the `strstream` version of `endl`; however, `ends` does not insert a newline. Instead, it inserts a null to terminate the ASCIIZ string within the buffer.

Always insert an `ends` last to terminate the ASCIIZ string that you build.

The output from the program appears as follows:

```
Input student <last name, first name ID>
(Input a blank line to stop input)
Davis, Stephen 12345678
Ashley 23456789
Bad input: Ashley 23456789
Webb, Jessalyn 34567890

Stephen Davis [12345678]
Jessalyn Webb [34567890]
Press any key to continue . . .
```

Notice how the second line is rejected since it doesn't follow the specified input format, but the program recovers gracefully to accept input again on the third line. This graceful recovery is very difficult to do any other way.

Chapter 32

I Take Exception!

I know it's hard to accept, but occasionally programs don't work properly — not even mine. The traditional means of reporting a failure within a function is to return some indication to the caller, usually as a return value. Historically, C and C++ programmers have used 0 as the "all clear" indicator and anything else as meaning an error occurred — the exact value returned indicates the nature of the error.

The problem with this approach is that people generally don't check all of the possible error returns. It's too much trouble. And if you were to check all of the possible error returns, pretty soon you wouldn't see the "real code" because of all the error paths that are almost never executed.

Finally, you can embed just so much information in a single return value. For example, the `factorial()` function could return a -1 for "negative argument" (the factorial of a negative number is not defined) and a -2 for "argument too large" (factorials get large very quickly — factorial(100) is well beyond the range of an `int`). But if the program were to return a -2, wouldn't you like to know the value of that "too large argument"? There's no easy way to embed that information in the return.

The fathers (and mothers) of C++ decided that the language needed a better way of handling errors, so they invented the exception mechanism that has since been duplicated in many similar languages. Exceptions are the subject of this chapter.

The Exception Mechanism

The exception mechanism is a way for functions to report errors so that the error is handled even if the calling function does nothing. It's based on three new keywords: `try`, `catch`, and `throw` (that's right, more variable names that you can't use). The exception mechanism works like this: A function *trys* to make it through a block of code without error. If the program does detect a problem, it *throws* an error indicator that a calling function can *catch* for processing.

The following FactorialException demonstrates how this works in ones and zeros:

```cpp
// FactorialException - demonstrate the Exception error
//                      handling mechanism with a
//                      factorial function.
#include <cstdio>
#include <cstdlib>
#include <iostream>
using namespace std;

// factorial - compute factorial
int factorial(int n)
{
    // argument must be positive; throw exception if
    // n is negative
    if (n < 0)
    {
        throw "Argument for factorial is negative";
    }

    // anything over 100 will overflow
    if (n > 100)
    {
        throw "Argument too large";
    }

    // go ahead and calculate factorial
    int nAccum = 1;
    while(n > 1)
    {
        nAccum *= n--;
    }
    return nAccum;
}

int main(int nNumberofArgs, char* pszArgs[])
{
    try
    {
        cout << "Factorial of 3 is "
             << factorial(3)
             << endl;

        cout << "Factorial of -1 is "
```

```
             << factorial(-1)
             << endl;

        cout << "Factorial of 5 is "
             << factorial(5)
             << endl;
    }
    catch(const char* pMsg)
    {
        cerr << "Error occurred: " << pMsg << endl;
    }
    catch(...)
    {
        cerr << "Unexpected error thrown" << endl;
    }

    // wait until user is ready before terminating program
    // to allow the user to see the program results
    system("PAUSE");
    return 0;
}
```

The `main()` function starts with the keyword `try` followed by an open brace and, eventually, a closed brace. Everything within the braces is said to be within a *try block*. The function then proceeds to display the factorial of three values: 3, –1, and 5. The only problem is that the factorial of a negative number is not defined.

You can see this within the `factorial()` function. This version of the function now contains a check for a negative argument and for an argument that is so large that it will overflow the `int`. In the event that either condition is true, control passes to a statement consisting of the keyword `throw` followed by an ASCIIZ string containing a description of the error.

Back in `main()`, at the end of the try block are two *catch phrases*. Each consists of the keyword `catch` followed by an argument. These catch phrases are designed to catch any exceptions thrown from within the try block. The first catch phrase will catch a pointer to an ASCIIZ string. This catch phrase displays the string. The second catch phrase, the one with the ellipses for an argument, is designed to catch anything. This wild-card catch phrase also displays a message, but since the catch phrase is so generic, it has no idea from where the exception was thrown or how to interpret the exception, so it just outputs a generic error message.

In practice, the program works like this: The first call to `factorial(3)` skips over both error conditions and returns the value 6. No problem so far.

The second call, `factorial(-1)` causes control to pass to the statement `throw "Argument for factorial is negative"`. This command passes control immediately out of `factorial()` and to the end of the try block where C++ starts comparing the type of "`Argument for factorial is negative`" (which is `const char*` by the way — but you knew that) to each of the catch arguments.

Fortunately, the type of object thrown matches the type of the first catch phrase. This displays the string `"Error occurred: "` followed by the string thrown from within `factorial()`. Control then passes to the first statement after the last catch phrase, which is the usual call to `system("PAUSE")`.

In execution, the output from the program appears as follows:

```
Factorial of 3 is 6
Error occurred: Argument for factorial is negative
Press any key to continue . . .
```

Notice that the call to `factorial(5)` never gets executed. There is no way to return from a catch.

Examining the exception mechanism in detail

Now, take a closer look at how C++ processes an exception.

When C++ encounters a throw, it first copies the object thrown to some neutral place other than the local memory of the function. It then starts looking in the current function for the end of the current try block. If it does not encounter one, it then executes a return from the function and continues the search. C++ continues to return and search, return and search until it finds the end of the current try block. This is known as *unwinding the stack*.

An important feature of stack unwinding is that as each stack is unwound, objects that go out of scope are destructed just as though the function had executed a `return` statement. This keeps the program from losing assets or leaving objects dangling.

When an enclosing try block is found, the code searches the first catch phrase to see if the argument type matches the object thrown. If not, it checks the next catch phrase and so on until a match is found.

If no matching catch phrase is found, then C++ resumes looking for the next higher try block in an ever outward spiral until an appropriate catch can be found. If no matching catch phrase is found, the program terminates.

Once a catch phrase is found, the exception is said to be handled and control passes to the statement following the last catch phrase.

The phrase `catch(...)` catches all exceptions.

Special considerations for throwing

I need to mention a few special considerations in regard to throwing exceptions. You need to be careful not to throw a pointer to an object in local memory. As the stack is unwound, all local variables are destroyed. C++ will copy the object into a safe memory location to keep it from being destroyed, but there's no way that C++ can tell what a pointer might be pointing to.

Note that I avoided this problem in the earlier example by throwing a pointer to a `const` string — these are kept in a different memory area and not on the stack. You'll see a better way to avoid this problem in the next section.

Don't catch an exception if you don't know what to do with the error. That may sound obvious, but it isn't really. The exception mechanism allows programmers to handle errors at a level at which they can truly do something about them. For example, if you are writing a data storage function and you get an exception from a write to the disk, there's not much point in catching it. The destructor for the output object should close the file, and C++ calls that automagically. Better to let the error propagate up to a level where the program knows what it's trying to do.

A catch phrase can rethrow an exception by executing the keyword `throw;` alone (without an argument). This allows the programmer to partially process an error. For example, a database function might catch an exception, close any open tables or databases, and rethrow the exception to the application software to be handled there for good. (Assuming that the destructors haven't done that stuff already.)

Finally, a function can declare the types of objects that it will throw as part of the declaration. In other words, I could have declared `factorial()` as follows:

```
int factorial(int n) throw(const char*);
```

I say "could" because, though some people consider exception declarations good form, they aren't mandatory. It isn't even clear, if exception declarations are a good idea. (Personally, I don't think so.)

If you declare the types of object that a function throws, then each of the throws is compared to that list, and an error is generated if the function tries to throw something else. If you do not include a throw in the declaration, then the function can throw anything it likes.

Creating a Custom Exception Class

The thing following a throw is actually an expression that creates an object of some kind. In the earlier example, the object was a pointer, but it could have been any object that you like (with one exception that I'll mention a little later in this section).

For example, I could have created my own class specifically for the purpose of holding information about errors. For the factorial() example, I could have created a class ArgOutOfRange that included everything you need to know about out-of-range arguments. In this way, I could store as much information as needed to debug the error (if it is an error), process the exception, and report the problem accurately to the user.

The following CustomExceptionClass program creates an ArgOutOfRange class and uses it to provide an accurate description of the error encountered in factorial():

```
// CustomExceptionClass - demonstrate the flexibility of
//                        the exception mechanism by creating
//                        a custom exception class.
#include <cstdio>
#include <cstdlib>
#include <iostream>
#include <cstring>
#include <exception>
#include <strstream>
using namespace std;

class ArgOutOfRange : public exception
{
  protected:
    char szMsg[256];
    int nValue;
    int nMaxLegal;
    int nMinLegal;

  public:
    ArgOutOfRange(const char* pszFName, int nVal,
                  int nMin = 0, int nMax = 0)
    {
```

```
        nValue = nVal;
        nMinLegal = nMin;
        nMaxLegal = nMax;

        ostrstream out(szMsg, 256);
        out << "Argument out of range in " << pszFName
            << ", arg is " << nValue;
        if (nMin != nMax)
        {
            out << ", legal range is "
                << nMin << " to " << nMax;
        }
        out << ends;
    }

    virtual const char* what()
    {
        return szMsg;
    }
};


// factorial - compute factorial
int factorial(int n)
{
    // argument must be positive; throw exception if
    // n is negative
    if (n < 0)
    {
        throw ArgOutOfRange("factorial()", n, 0, 100);
    }

    // anything over 100 will overflow
    if (n > 100)
    {
        throw ArgOutOfRange("factorial()", n, 0, 100);
    }

    // go ahead and calculate factorial
    int nAccum = 1;
    while(n > 1)
    {
        nAccum *= n--;
    }
    return nAccum;
}

int main(int nNumberofArgs, char* pszArgs[])
{
    try
```

```
    {
        cout << "Factorial of 3 is "
             << factorial(3)
             << endl;

        cout << "Factorial of -1 is "
             << factorial(-1)
             << endl;

        cout << "Factorial of 5 is "
             << factorial(5)
             << endl;
    }
    catch(ArgOutOfRange e)
    {
        cerr << "Error occurred:\n" << e.what() << endl;
    }
    catch(...)
    {
        cerr << "Unexpected error thrown" << endl;
    }

    // wait until user is ready before terminating program
    // to allow the user to see the program results
    system("PAUSE");
    return 0;
}
```

The main() program starts just like the previous example. The factorial() function contains the same tests. Rather than throw a simple character string, however, this version of factorial() throws an object of class ArgOutRange. The constructor for ArgOutOfRange provides room for the name of the function, the value of the offending argument, and the range of legal values for the argument.

All the real work is done in the ArgOutOfRange class. First, this class extends the class exception, which is defined in the exception include file. The exception class defines the virtual member function what() that you must override with a version that outputs your message. Everything else is optional.

User-defined exception classes should extend exception so that C++ will know what to do with your exception should you fail to catch it.

The constructor to ArgOutOfRange accepts the name of the function, the value of the argument, and the minimum and maximum legal argument values. Providing a default value for these arguments makes them optional.

The constructor uses the `ostrstream` class (discussed in Chapter 31) to create a complex description of the problem in the internal array `szMsg`. It also saves off the arguments themselves.

A complete version of `ArgOutOfRange` would provide access functions to allow each of these values to be queried from the application code, if desired. I have to leave these details out in order to keep the programs as short as possible.

Back in `factorial()`, the two throws now throw `ArgOutOfRange` objects with the appropriate information. The catch back in `main()` is for an `ArgOutOfRange` object. This block does nothing more than display an error message along with the description returned by `ArgOutRange::what()`.

Since all the real work was done in the constructor, the `what()` function doesn't have to do anything except return a pointer to the message stored within the object.

The output from the program is now very descriptive:

```
Factorial of 3 is 6
Error occurred:
Argument out of range in factorial(), arg is -1, legal
          range is 0 to 100
Press any key to continue . . .
```

Restrictions on exception classes

I mentioned that the exception mechanism can throw almost any type of object. The only real restriction is that the class must be copyable. That means either the default copy constructor provided by C++ is sufficient (that was the case for `ArgOutOfRange`) or the class provides its own copy constructor.

This restriction is because C++ has to copy the exception object out of local storage and to some "safe place" before unwinding the stack. C++ uses the copy constructor again to copy the object to the catch's storage area.

Part VII
The Part of Tens

In this part . . .

No *For Dummies* book would be complete without its Part of Tens. In this part, you'll see ten ways to avoid the most common coding mistakes and ten advanced language features you may want to tackle when you're a little more experienced with the C++ language.

Chapter 33

Ten Ways to Avoid Bugs

. . . .

In This Chapter

▶ Enable all compiler warning messages

▶ Adopt a clear and consistent coding style

▶ Comment your code while you write it

▶ Single-step every path in the debugger at least once

▶ Limit the visibility of members

▶ Keep track of heap memory

▶ Zero out pointers after deleting what they point to

▶ Use exceptions to handle errors

▶ Declare destructors virtual

▶ Provide a copy constructor and overloaded assignment operator

. . . .

*I*t's an unfortunate fact that you will spend more time searching for and removing bugs than you will spend actually writing your programs in the first place. The suggestions in this section may help you minimize the number of errors you introduce into your programs to make programming a more enjoyable experience.

Enable All Warnings and Error Messages

The syntax of C++ allows for a lot of error checking. When the compiler encounters a construct that it just can't decipher, it has no choice but to output a message. It tries to sync back up with the source code (sometimes less than successfully), but it will not generate an executable. This forces the programmer to fix all error messages — she has no choice.

However, when C++ comes across a structure that it can figure out but the structure smells fishy anyway, C++ generates a warning message. Because C++ is pretty sure that it understands what you want, it goes ahead and creates an executable file so you can ignore warnings if you like. In fact, if you really don't want to be bothered, you can disable warnings.

Disabling or otherwise ignoring warnings is an extraordinarily bad idea. It's a bit like unplugging the check engine light on your car's dashboard because it bothers you. Ignoring the problem doesn't make it go away. It doesn't mean that you can always fix the problem — for example, I chose to overlook the warnings in Chapter 31 about `strstream` being deprecated — but you need to at least understand the warning. What you don't know will hurt you.

If your compiler has a Syntax Check from Hell mode, enable it.

Adopt a Clear and Consistent Coding Style

Writing your C++ code in a clear and consistent style not only enhances the readability of your program, but also it results in fewer coding mistakes. This somewhat surprising state of affairs results from the fact that our brains have only a limited amount of computing power. When you read code that is clean and neat and that follows a style you're familiar with, you spend very little brain power parsing the syntax of the C++ statements. This leaves more brain CPU power to decode what the program is trying to do and not how it's doing it.

A good coding style lets you do the following with ease:

✔ Differentiate between class names, object names, and function names

✔ Understand what the class, function, or object is used for based on its name

✔ Differentiate preprocessor symbols from C++ symbols (that is, `#define` objects should stand out)

✔ Identify blocks of C++ code at the same level (this is the result of consistent indentation)

In addition, you need to establish a standard module header format that provides information about the functions or classes in the module, the author (presumably, that's you), the date, the version, and something about the modification history.

All programmers involved in a single project should use the same coding style. A program written in a patchwork of different coding styles is confusing and looks unprofessional.

Comment the Code While You Write It

You can avoid errors if you comment your code while you write it rather than wait until everything works and then go back and add comments. I can understand not taking the time to write voluminous headers and function descriptions until later, but I have never understood not writing short comments as you are coding.

Have you ever had the experience of asking someone a question, and even as you got to the end of the question you knew the answer? Somehow formulating the question forced you to organize your thoughts sufficiently so that the answer became clear.

Writing comments is like that. Formulating comments forces you to take stock of what it is you're trying to do. Short comments are enlightening, both when you read them later and as you're writing them.

Write comments like you're talking to another, knowledgeable programmer. You can assume that the reader understands the basics of the program, so please don't explain how C++ works. There's no point in writing comments that explain how a `switch` statement works unless you're relying on some obscure point of the language (like the fall-through capability of the `switch` statement).

Single-Step Every Path in the Debugger at Least Once

It may seem like an obvious statement, but I'll say it anyway: As a programmer, it's important that you understand what your program is doing. It isn't sufficient that the program outputs the expected value. You need to understand everything your program is doing. Nothing gives you a better feel for what's going on under the hood than single-stepping the program with a good debugger (like the one that comes with Code::Blocks).

Beyond that, as you debug a program, you sometimes need raw material to figure out some bizarre behavior. Nothing gives you that material better than single-stepping through each function as it comes into service.

Finally, when a function is finished and ready to be added to the program, every logical path needs to be traveled at least once. Bugs are much easier to find when the function is examined by itself rather than after it has been thrown into the pot with the rest of the functions — and your attention has gone on to new programming challenges.

Limit the Visibility

Limiting the visibility of class internals to the outside world is a cornerstone of object-oriented programming. The class should be responsible for its internal state — if something gets screwed up in the class, then it's the class programmer's fault. The application programmer should worry about solving the problem at hand.

Specifically, limited visibility means that data members should not be accessible outside of the class — that is, they should be marked as protected. In addition, member functions that the application software does not need to know about should also be marked protected. Don't expose any more of the class internals than necessary to get the job done.

A related rule is that public member functions should trust application code as little as possible, even if the class programmer and the application programmer are the same person. The class programmer should act like it's a fact that the application programmer is a felonious hacker; if your programmer is accessible over the Internet, all too often this assumption is true.

Keep Track of Heap Memory

Losing track of heap memory is the most common source of fatal errors in programs that have been released into the field and, at the same time, the hardest problem to track down and remove (because this class of error is so hard to find and remove, it's prevalent in programs that you buy). You may have to run a program for hours before problems start to arise (depending upon how big the memory leak is).

As a general rule, programmers should always allocate and release heap memory at the same "level." If a member function `MyClass::create()` allocates a block of heap memory and returns it to the caller, then there should be a member `MyClass::release()` that returns it to the heap. Specifically, `MyClass::create()` should not require the parent function to release the memory.

If at all possible, `MyClass` should keep track of such memory pointers on its own and delete them in the destructor.

Certainly, this doesn't avoid all memory problems, but it does reduce their prevalence somewhat.

Zero Out Pointers after Deleting What They Point To

Sort of a corollary to the warning in the preceding section is to make sure that you zero out pointers after they are no longer valid. The reasons for this become clear with experience: you can often continue to use a memory block that has been returned to the heap and not even know it. A program might run fine 99 percent of the time, making it very difficult to find the 1 percent of cases where the block gets reallocated and the program doesn't work.

If you zero out pointers that are no longer valid and you attempt to use them to store a value (you can't store anything at or near location 0), your program will crash immediately. Crashing sounds bad, but it's not. The problem is there; it's merely a question of whether you find it or not before putting it into production.

It's like finding a tumor at an early stage in an x-ray. Finding a tumor early when it's easy to treat is a good thing. Given that the tumor is there either way, not finding it is much worse.

Use Exceptions to Handle Errors

The exception mechanism in C++ is designed to handle errors conveniently and efficiently. In general, you should throw an error indicator rather than return an error flag. The resulting code is easier to write, read, and maintain. Besides, other programmers have come to expect it, and you wouldn't want to disappoint them, would you?

Having said that, limit your use of exceptions to true errors. It is not necessary to throw an exception from a function that returns a "didn't work" indicator if this is a part of everyday life for that function. Consider a function lcd() that returns the least common denominator of its two arguments. That function will not return any values when presented with two mutually prime numbers. This is not an error and should not result in an exception.

Declare Destructors Virtual

Don't forget to create a destructor for your class if the constructor allocates resources such as heap memory that need to be returned when the object reaches its ultimate demise. This rule is pretty easy to teach. What's a little harder for students to remember is this: Having created a destructor, don't forget to declare it virtual.

"But," you say, "My class doesn't inherit from anything, and it's not subclassed by another class." Yes, but it *could* become a base class in the future. Unless you have some good reason for not declaring the destructor virtual, then do so when you first create the class. (See Chapter 29 for a detailed discussion of virtual destructors.)

Provide a Copy Constructor and Overloaded Assignment Operator

Here's another rule to live by: If your class needs a destructor, it almost surely needs a copy constructor and an overloaded assignment operator. If your constructor allocates resources such as heap memory, the default copy constructor and assignment operator will do nothing but create havoc by generating multiple pointers to the same resources. When the destructor for one of these objects is invoked, it will restore the assets. When the destructor for the other copy comes along, it will screw things up.

If you are too lazy or too confused or you just don't need a copy constructor and assignment operator, then declare "do nothing" versions, but make them protected so that application software doesn't try to invoke them by accident. See Chapter 30 for more details. (The 2009 C++ standard allows you to delete both the default copy constructor and assignment operator, but declaring them protected works almost as well.)

Chapter 34

Ten Features Not Covered in This Book

*T*he C++ language contains so many features that covering every one in a single book — especially a book intended for beginning programmers — is impossible. Fortunately, you don't need to master all of the features of the language in order to write big, real-world programs.

Nevertheless, you may want to look ahead at some of the features that didn't make the cut for this beginner's book, just in case you see them in other people's programs.

The goto Command

This command goes all the way back to C, the progenitor of C++. In principle, using this command is easy. You can place `goto label;` anywhere you want. When C++ comes across this command, control passes immediately to the label, as demonstrated in this code snippet:

```
for(;;)
{
    if (conditional expression)
    {
        goto outahere;
    }
    // ...whatever you want...
}
outahere:
    // ...program continues here...
```

In practice, however, `goto` introduces a lot of ways to screw up — many more than I can go into here. In any case, it didn't take long before programmers noticed that the two most common uses of the `goto` were to exit loops and to go to the next case within a loop. The C Standards Committee introduced `break` and `continue` and almost completely removed the need for the `goto` command. I can say that I've been programming in C and C++ for almost 20 years, and I've never had an application for a `goto` that I couldn't handle in some other way more clearly.

The Ternary Operator

The ternary operator is an operator unique to C and C++. It works as follows:

```
int n = (conditional) ? expression1 : expression2;
```

The `?` operator first evaluates the `conditional`. If the condition is true, then the value of the expression is equal to the value of `expression1`; otherwise, it's equal to the value of `expression2`.

For example, you could implement a `maximum()` function as follows:

```
int max(int n1, int n2)
{
    return (n1 > n2) ? n1 : n2;
}
```

The ternary operator can be applied to any type of numeric but cannot be overloaded. The ternary operator is truly an expression and not a control statement like an `if`.

Binary Logic

I chose to skip entirely the topic of binary arithmetic. Some readers will consider this scandalous. After all, how can you talk about programming without getting down to ones and zeros? It's not that I don't consider the topic worthwhile — it's just that I find explaining the topic properly takes many pages of text and leaves readers somewhat confused, when in practice it's rarely used. Google the topic once you feel comfortable with the basics of C++ programming.

Enumerated Types

This is a topic that barely missed the cut for inclusion in the book. The simple idea is that you can define constants and let C++ assign them values, as shown here:

```
enum Colors {BLACK, BLUE, GREEN, YELLOW, RED};
Colors myColor = BLACK;
```

The problem with enumerated types lies in the implementation: Rather than create a true type, C++ uses integers. In this case, BLACK is assigned the value 0, BLUE is assigned 1, GREEN 2, and so on. This leads to special cases that make the topic not worth the trouble.

The 2009 Standard Library for C++ "fixed" this problem by creating true enumerated types, but it didn't do away with the integer version in order to retain compatibility with existing programs. The result is even more confusing than before.

Namespaces

It's possible to give different entities in two different libraries the same name. For example, the grade() function within the Student library probably assigns a grade, whereas the grade() function within the Civil Engineering library might set the slope on the side of a hill. To avoid this problem, C++ allows the programmer to place her code in a separate namespace. Thus, the grade within the Student namespace is different from the grade within CivilEngineering.

The namespace is above and beyond the class name. The `grade()` member function of the class `BullDozer` in the `CivilEngineering` namespace has the extended name `CivilEngineering::BullDozer::grade()`.

All library objects and functions are in the namespace `std`. The statement at the beginning of the program template `using namespace std;` says if you don't see the specified object in the default namespace, then go look in `std`. Without this I would have to include the namespace explicitly, as in the following snippet:

```
std::cout << "Hello, world!" << std::endl;
```

Pure Virtual Functions

You saw how to declare functions virtual in Chapter 29. What I didn't mention there is that you don't have to define a function declared virtual. Such an undefined function is known as a *pure virtual member function*. However, things get complicated. For example, a class with one or more pure virtual functions is said to be abstract and cannot be used to create an object (see what I mean?). Tackle this subject after you feel comfortable with virtual functions and late binding.

The string Class

This is another topic that barely missed the cut. Most languages include a `string` class as an intrinsic type for handling strings of characters easily. In theory, the string class should do the same for C++. In practice, however, it's not that simple. Because `string` is not an intrinsic type, the error messages that the compiler generates when something goes wrong are more like those associated with user-defined classes. For a beginner, these messages can be very difficult to interpret.

It's actually worse than I'm describing here — `string` isn't even a class. It's an instance of a template class. The error messages can be breathtaking.

Multiple Inheritance

I describe how to base one class on another using inheritance in Chapter 28. What I didn't mention there is that one class can actually extend more than one base class. This sounds simple but can get quite complicated when the two base classes contain member functions with the same name. Or worse, when both base classes are themselves subclasses of some common class. In fact, there are so many problems that arise that C++ is the only C-like language that supports multiple inheritance. Java and C#, both languages derived from C++, decided to drop support for multiple inheritance. I recommend that beginning programmers avoid the subject.

Templates and the Standard Template Library

The makers of C++ noticed how similar functions like the following are:

```cpp
int max(int n1, int n2)
{
    if (n1 > n2)
    {
        return n1;
    }
    return n2;
}
double max(double n1, double n2)
{
    if (n1 > n2)
    {
        return n1;
    }
    return n2;
}
char max(char n1, char n2)
{
    if (n1 > n2)
    {
        return n1;
    }
    return n2;
}
```

I can almost imagine the scene: "Wouldn't it be cool," one said to another, "if we could replace the type with a pseudo-type T that we could define at compile time?" Before you knew it, templates were a part of C++:

```
template <class T> T max(T t1, T t2)
{
    if (t1 > t2)
    {
        return t1;
    }
    return t2;
}
```

Now the programmer can create a max(int, int) by replacing T with int and compiling the result, create a max(double, double) by replacing T with double, and so forth. The Standards Committee even released an entire library of classes, known as the Standard Template Library (STL for short), based upon template classes.

For a beginner, however, the subject of template classes starts to get syntactically very complicated. In addition, the errors that the compiler generates when you get a template instantiation wrong are bewildering to an expert, never mind a beginner. This is definitely a topic that needs to wait until you feel comfortable with the basic language.

The 2009 C++ Standard

The C++ Standard was released and agreed to in the late 1990s. Things changed relatively little in the ensuing years, but the demand for additions to the language grew until finally the 2009 Standard was released for comment in late 2008. The problem with this standard is that it introduces a lot of new features for which there seems to be very little demand. The standard is more than 1,400 pages. (Admittedly, it includes a lot of very dry, very repetitive library definitions, but even so, that C++ is not a small language any more.) As of this writing (early 2010), no compilers implement the full 2009 standard.

Appendix

About the CD

In This Appendix
▶ System requirements

▶ Using the CD with Windows, Linux, and Mac

▶ What you'll find on the CD

▶ Troubleshooting

*T*his section describes the CD-ROM enclosed in the back of *Beginning Programs with C++ for Dummies*. All readers will appreciate the source code to the programs that appear in the book — using this code can save you a lot of typing. In addition, 32-bit Windows users will welcome the Code::Blocks C++ development environment coupled with the GNU C++ compiler ready to be installed on Windows 2000, Windows XP, Windows Vista, or Windows 7. (Macintosh, Linux, and 64-bit Windows users can download Code::Blocks from www.codeblocks.org.)

System Requirements

Make sure that your computer meets the minimum system requirements shown in the following list. If your computer doesn't match up to most of these requirements, you may have problems using the software and files on the CD. For the latest and greatest information, please refer to the ReadMe file located at the root of the CD-ROM.

- ✔ A PC running Microsoft Windows or Linux with kernel 2.4 or later

- ✔ A Macintosh running Apple OS X or later

- ✔ An Internet connection (only required for downloading versions of Code::Blocks for Macintosh or Linux)

- ✔ A CD-ROM drive

If you need more information on the basics, check out these books published by Wiley Publishing, Inc.: *PCs For Dummies* by Dan Gookin; *Macs For Dummies* by Edward C. Baig; *iMacs For Dummies* by Mark L. Chambers; and *Windows XP*

For Dummies, Windows Vista For Dummies, and *Windows 7 For Dummies,* all by Andy Rathbone.

Using the CD

These steps will help you install the items from the CD to your hard drive:

1. **Insert the CD into your computer's CD-ROM drive.**

   The license agreement appears.

   Note to Windows users: The interface won't launch if you have autorun disabled. In that case, choose Start⇨Run. (For Windows Vista, choose Start⇨All Programs⇨Accessories⇨Run.) In the dialog box that appears, type **D:\Start.exe**. (Replace *D* with the proper letter if your CD drive uses a different letter. If you don't know the letter, see how your CD drive is listed under My Computer.) Click OK.

   Note for Mac Users: When the CD icon appears on your desktop, double-click the icon to open the CD and double-click the Start icon.

   Note for Linux Users: The specifics of mounting and using CDs vary greatly between different versions of Linux. Please see the manual or help information for your specific system if you experience trouble using this CD.

2. **Read through the license agreement and then click the Accept button if you want to use the CD.**

   The CD interface appears. The interface allows you to browse the contents and install the programs with just a click of a button (or two).

3. **Copy the C++ source code onto your hard disk.**

   You can view the source code on the CD-ROM but you cannot build or execute programs there.

4. **Windows users will want to install the Code::Blocks environment.**

   Chapter 2 takes you through step-by-step instructions on how to install Code::Blocks and how to create your first program.

What You'll Find on the CD

The following sections are arranged by category and provide a summary of the software and other goodies you'll find on the CD. If you need help with installing the items provided on the CD, refer to the installation instructions in the preceding section.

For each program listed, I provide the program platform (Windows or Mac) plus the type of software. The programs fall into one of the following categories:

- ✔ *Shareware programs* are fully functional, free, trial versions of copyrighted programs. If you like particular programs, register with their authors for a nominal fee and receive licenses, enhanced versions, and technical support.

- ✔ *Freeware programs* are free, copyrighted games, applications, and utilities. You can copy them to as many computers as you like — for free — but they offer no technical support.

- ✔ *GNU software* is governed by its own license, which is included inside the folder of the GNU software. There are no restrictions on distribution of GNU software. See the GNU license at the root of the CD for more details.

- ✔ *Trial, demo,* or *evaluation* versions of software are usually limited either by time or functionality (such as not letting you save a project after you create it).

CPP programs

For all environments. All the examples provided in this book are located in the Beginning_Programming-CPP directory on the CD and work with Macintosh, Linux, Unix, and Windows and later computers. These files contain the sample code from the book. Each example program is in its own folder. For example, the Conversion program is in:

```
Beginning_Programming-CPP\Conversion
```

For Windows. I have built a set of workspace and set of project files for Code::Blocks that allows you to recompile all the programs in the book with a single mouse click. The AllPrograms.workspace file is located in the Beginning_Programming-CPP folder. (See Chapter 2 for an explanation of Code::Blocks Project files.) You **must** copy the source code from the CD-ROM onto your hard disk before you use it.

Code::Blocks development environment

For Windows. Code::Blocks is an "open source, cross platform" freeware environment designed to work with a number of different compilers. The version included on the CD-ROM is bundled with the GNU gcc C++ compiler (version 4.4) for 32-bit versions of Windows (if you don't know whether your Windows is 32-bit or not, it almost certainly is). Code::Blocks is supported by "The Code::Blocks Team/" You can find more information at www.codeblocks.org.

For non-Windows. You can download a version of Code::Blocks that works for your operating system at www.codeblocks.org. They've got versions of Code::Blocks for just about every environment short of the iPhone.

Troubleshooting

I tried my best to compile programs that work on most computers with the minimum system requirements. Alas, your computer may differ, and some programs may not work properly for some reason.

I include Code::Blocks workspace and project files for the included C++ source. This allows you to recompile all the programs with literally a single click. However, these project files assume that the programs are installed in the directory `C:\\Beginning_Programming-CPP`. You'll have to set up your own project files if you decide to install the source code in a different directory.

Other common problems are that you don't have enough memory (RAM) for the programs you want to use, or you have other programs running that are affecting installation or running of a program. If you get an error message such as `Not enough memory` or `Setup cannot continue`, try one or more of the following suggestions and then try using the software again:

- **Turn off any antivirus software running on your computer.** Installation programs sometimes mimic virus activity and may make your computer incorrectly believe that it's being infected by a virus.

- **Close all running programs.** The more programs you have running, the less memory is available to other programs. Installation programs typically update files and programs; so if you keep other programs running, installation may not work properly.

- **Have your local computer store add more RAM to your computer.** This is, admittedly, a drastic and somewhat expensive step. However, adding more memory can really help the speed of your computer and allow more programs to run at the same time.

Customer Care

If you have trouble with the CD-ROM, please call Wiley Product Technical Support at 800-762-2974. Outside the United States, call 317-572-3993. You can also contact Wiley Product Technical Support at `http://support.wiley.com`. John Wiley & Sons, Inc. will provide technical support only for installation and other general quality control items. For technical support on the applications themselves, consult the program's vendor or the author at `www.stephendavis.com`.

To place additional orders or to request information about other Wiley products, please call 877-762-2974.

Index

• E •

● **R** ●

● **S** ●

John Wiley & Sons, Inc.
End-User License Agreement

READ THIS. You should carefully read these terms and conditions before opening the software packet(s) included with this book "Book". This is a license agreement "Agreement" between you and John Wiley & Sons, Inc. "WILEY". By opening the accompanying software packet(s), you acknowledge that you have read and accept the following terms and conditions. If you do not agree and do not want to be bound by such terms and conditions, promptly return the Book and the unopened software packet(s) to the place you obtained them for a full refund.

1. **License Grant.** WILEY grants to you (either an individual or entity) a nonexclusive license to use one copy of the enclosed software program(s) (collectively, the "Software") solely for your own personal or business purposes on a single computer (whether a standard computer or a workstation component of a multi-user network). The Software is in use on a computer when it is loaded into temporary memory (RAM) or installed into permanent memory (hard disk, CD-ROM, or other storage device). WILEY reserves all rights not expressly granted herein.

2. **Ownership.** WILEY is the owner of all right, title, and interest, including copyright, in and to the compilation of the Software recorded on the physical packet included with this Book "Software Media". Copyright to the individual programs recorded on the Software Media is owned by the author or other authorized copyright owner of each program. Ownership of the Software and all proprietary rights relating thereto remain with WILEY and its licensers.

3. **Restrictions on Use and Transfer.**

   (a) You may only (i) make one copy of the Software for backup or archival purposes, or (ii) transfer the Software to a single hard disk, provided that you keep the original for backup or archival purposes. You may not (i) rent or lease the Software, (ii) copy or reproduce the Software through a LAN or other network system or through any computer subscriber system or bulletin-board system, or (iii) modify, adapt, or create derivative works based on the Software.

   (b) You may not reverse engineer, decompile, or disassemble the Software. You may transfer the Software and user documentation on a permanent basis, provided that the transferee agrees to accept the terms and conditions of this Agreement and you retain no copies. If the Software is an update or has been updated, any transfer must include the most recent update and all prior versions.

4. **Restrictions on Use of Individual Programs.** You must follow the individual requirements and restrictions detailed for each individual program in the "About the CD" appendix of this Book or on the Software Media. These limitations are also contained in the individual license agreements recorded on the Software Media. These limitations may include a requirement that after using the program for a specified period of time, the user must pay a registration fee or discontinue use. By opening the Software packet(s), you agree to abide by the licenses and restrictions for these individual programs that are detailed in the "About the CD" appendix and/or on the Software Media. None of the material on this Software Media or listed in this Book may ever be redistributed, in original or modified form, for commercial purposes.

5. **Limited Warranty.**

   (a) WILEY warrants that the Software and Software Media are free from defects in materials and workmanship under normal use for a period of sixty (60) days from the date of purchase of this Book. If WILEY receives notification within the warranty period of defects in materials or workmanship, WILEY will replace the defective Software Media.

(b) WILEY AND THE AUTHOR(S) OF THE BOOK DISCLAIM ALL OTHER WARRANTIES, EXPRESS OR IMPLIED, INCLUDING WITHOUT LIMITATION IMPLIED WARRANTIES OF MERCHANTABILITY AND FITNESS FOR A PARTICULAR PURPOSE, WITH RESPECT TO THE SOFTWARE, THE PROGRAMS, THE SOURCE CODE CONTAINED THEREIN, AND/OR THE TECHNIQUES DESCRIBED IN THIS BOOK. WILEY DOES NOT WARRANT THAT THE FUNCTIONS CONTAINED IN THE SOFTWARE WILL MEET YOUR REQUIREMENTS OR THAT THE OPERATION OF THE SOFTWARE WILL BE ERROR FREE.

(c) This limited warranty gives you specific legal rights, and you may have other rights that vary from jurisdiction to jurisdiction.

6. Remedies.

(a) WILEY's entire liability and your exclusive remedy for defects in materials and workmanship shall be limited to replacement of the Software Media, which may be returned to WILEY with a copy of your receipt at the following address: Software Media Fulfillment Department, Attn.: *Beginning Programming with C++ For Dummies*, John Wiley & Sons, Inc., 10475 Crosspoint Blvd., Indianapolis, IN 46256, or call 1-800-762-2974. Please allow four to six weeks for delivery. This Limited Warranty is void if failure of the Software Media has resulted from accident, abuse, or misapplication. Any replacement Software Media will be warranted for the remainder of the original warranty period or thirty (30) days, whichever is longer.

(b) In no event shall WILEY or the author be liable for any damages whatsoever (including without limitation damages for loss of business profits, business interruption, loss of business information, or any other pecuniary loss) arising from the use of or inability to use the Book or the Software, even if WILEY has been advised of the possibility of such damages.

(c) Because some jurisdictions do not allow the exclusion or limitation of liability for consequential or incidental damages, the above limitation or exclusion may not apply to you.

7. U.S. Government Restricted Rights. Use, duplication, or disclosure of the Software for or on behalf of the United States of America, its agencies and/or instrumentalities "U.S. Government" is subject to restrictions as stated in paragraph (c)(1)(ii) of the Rights in Technical Data and Computer Software clause of DFARS 252.227-7013, or subparagraphs (c) (1) and (2) of the Commercial Computer Software - Restricted Rights clause at FAR 52.227-19, and in similar clauses in the NASA FAR supplement, as applicable.

8. General. This Agreement constitutes the entire understanding of the parties and revokes and supersedes all prior agreements, oral or written, between them and may not be modified or amended except in a writing signed by both parties hereto that specifically refers to this Agreement. This Agreement shall take precedence over any other documents that may be in conflict herewith. If any one or more provisions contained in this Agreement are held by any court or tribunal to be invalid, illegal, or otherwise unenforceable, each and every other provision shall remain in full force and effect.

GNU GENERAL PUBLIC LICENSE

Version 3, 29 June 2007
Copyright © 2007 Free Software Foundation, Inc.
<http://fsf.org/>

Everyone is permitted to copy and distribute verbatim copies of this license document, but changing it is not allowed.

Preamble

The GNU General Public License is a free, copyleft license for software and other kinds of works.

The licenses for most software and other practical works are designed to take away your freedom to share and change the works. By contrast, the GNU General Public License is intended to guarantee your freedom to share and change all versions of a program–to make sure it remains free software for all its users. We, the Free Software Foundation, use the GNU General Public License for most of our software; it applies also to any other work released this way by its authors. You can apply it to your programs, too.

When we speak of free software, we are referring to freedom, not price. Our General Public Licenses are designed to make sure that you have the freedom to distribute copies of free software (and charge for them if you wish), that you receive source code or can get it if you want it, that you can change the software or use pieces of it in new free programs, and that you know you can do these things.

To protect your rights, we need to prevent others from denying you these rights or asking you to surrender the rights. Therefore, you have certain responsibilities if you distribute copies of the software, or if you modify it: responsibilities to respect the freedom of others.

For example, if you distribute copies of such a program, whether gratis or for a fee, you must pass on to the recipients the same freedoms that you received. You must make sure that they, too, receive or can get the source code. And you must show them these terms so they know their rights.

Developers that use the GNU GPL protect your rights with two steps: (1) assert copyright on the software, and (2) offer you this License giving you legal permission to copy, distribute and/or modify it.

For the developers' and authors' protection, the GPL clearly explains that there is no warranty for this free software. For both users' and authors' sake, the GPL requires that modified versions be marked as changed, so that their problems will not be attributed erroneously to authors of previous versions.

Some devices are designed to deny users access to install or run modified versions of the software inside them, although the manufacturer can do so. This is fundamentally incompatible with the aim of protecting users' freedom to change the software. The systematic pattern of such abuse occurs in the area of products for individuals to use, which is precisely where it is most unacceptable. Therefore, we have designed this version of the GPL to prohibit the practice for those products. If such problems arise substantially in other domains, we stand ready to extend this provision to those domains in future versions of the GPL, as needed to protect the freedom of users.

Finally, every program is threatened constantly by software patents. States should not allow patents to restrict development and use of software on general-purpose computers, but in those that do, we wish to avoid the special danger that patents applied to a free program could make it effectively proprietary. To prevent this, the GPL assures that patents cannot be used to render the program non-free.

The precise terms and conditions for copying, distribution and modification follow.

TERMS AND CONDITIONS

0. Definitions. "This License" refers to version 3 of the GNU General Public License. "Copyright" also means copyright-like laws that apply to other kinds of works, such as semiconductor masks. "The Program" refers to any copyrightable work licensed under this License. Each licensee is addressed as "you". "Licensees" and "recipients" may be individuals or organizations. To "modify" a work means to copy from or adapt all or part of the work in a fashion requiring copyright permission, other than the making of an exact copy. The resulting work is called a "modified version" of the earlier work or a work "based on" the earlier work. A "covered work" means either the unmodified Program or a work based on the Program.

   To "propagate" a work means to do anything with it that, without permission, would make you directly or secondarily liable for infringement under applicable copyright law, except executing it on a computer or modifying a private copy. Propagation includes copying, distribution (with or without modification), making available to the public, and in some countries other activities as well.

   To "convey" a work means any kind of propagation that enables other parties to make or receive copies. Mere interaction with a user through a computer network, with no transfer of a copy, is not conveying.

   An interactive user interface displays "Appropriate Legal Notices" to the extent that it includes a convenient and prominently visible feature that (1) displays an appropriate copyright notice, and (2) tells the user that there is no warranty for the work (except to the extent that warranties are provided), that licensees may convey the work under this License, and how to view a copy of this License. If the interface presents a list of user commands or options, such as a menu, a prominent item in the list meets this criterion.

1. Source Code. The "source code" for a work means the preferred form of the work for making modifications to it. "Object code" means any non-source form of a work. A "Standard Interface" means an interface that either is an official standard defined by a recognized standards body, or, in the case of interfaces specified for a particular programming language, one that is widely used among developers working in that language.

   The "System Libraries" of an executable work include anything, other than the work as a whole, that (a) is included in the normal form of packaging a Major Component, but which is not part of that Major Component, and (b) serves only to enable use of the work with that Major Component, or to implement a Standard Interface for which an implementation is available to the public in source code form. A "Major Component", in this context, means a major essential component (kernel, window system, and so on) of the specific operating system (if any) on which the executable work runs, or a compiler used to produce the work, or an object code interpreter used to run it.

   The "Corresponding Source" for a work in object code form means all the source code needed to generate, install, and (for an executable work) run the object code and to modify the work, including scripts to control those activities. However, it does not include the work's System Libraries, or general-purpose tools or generally available free programs which are used unmodified in performing those activities but which are not part of the work. For example, Corresponding Source includes interface definition files associated with source files for the work, and the source code for shared libraries and dynamically linked subprograms that the work is specifically designed to require, such as by intimate data communication or control flow between those subprograms and other parts of the work.

The Corresponding Source need not include anything that users can regenerate automatically from other parts of the Corresponding Source.

The Corresponding Source for a work in source code form is that same work.

2. Basic Permissions. All rights granted under this License are granted for the term of copyright on the Program, and are irrevocable provided the stated conditions are met. This License explicitly affirms your unlimited permission to run the unmodified Program. The output from running a covered work is covered by this License only if the output, given its content, constitutes a covered work. This License acknowledges your rights of fair use or other equivalent, as provided by copyright law.

You may make, run and propagate covered works that you do not convey, without conditions so long as your license otherwise remains in force. You may convey covered works to others for the sole purpose of having them make modifications exclusively for you, or provide you with facilities for running those works, provided that you comply with the terms of this License in conveying all material for which you do not control copyright. Those thus making or running the covered works for you must do so exclusively on your behalf, under your direction and control, on terms that prohibit them from making any copies of your copyrighted material outside their relationship with you.

Conveying under any other circumstances is permitted solely under the conditions stated below. Sublicensing is not allowed; section 10 makes it unnecessary.

3. Protecting Users' Legal Rights From Anti-Circumvention Law. No covered work shall be deemed part of an effective technological measure under any applicable law fulfilling obligations under article 11 of the WIPO copyright treaty adopted on 20 December 1996, or similar laws prohibiting or restricting circumvention of such measures.

When you convey a covered work, you waive any legal power to forbid circumvention of technological measures to the extent such circumvention is effected by exercising rights under this License with respect to the covered work, and you disclaim any intention to limit operation or modification of the work as a means of enforcing, against the work's users, your or third parties' legal rights to forbid circumvention of technological measures.

4. Conveying Verbatim Copies. You may convey verbatim copies of the Program's source code as you receive it, in any medium, provided that you conspicuously and appropriately publish on each copy an appropriate copyright notice; keep intact all notices stating that this License and any non-permissive terms added in accord with section 7 apply to the code; keep intact all notices of the absence of any warranty; and give all recipients a copy of this License along with the Program.

You may charge any price or no price for each copy that you convey, and you may offer support or warranty protection for a fee.

5. You may convey a work based on the Program, or the modifications to produce it from the Program, in the form of source code under the terms of section 4, provided that you also meet all of these conditions:

a) The work must carry prominent notices stating that you modified it, and giving a relevant date.

b) The work must carry prominent notices stating that it is released under this License and any conditions added under section 7. This requirement modifies the requirement in section 4 to "keep intact all notices".

c) You must license the entire work, as a whole, under this License to anyone who comes into possession of a copy. This License will therefore apply, along with any applicable section 7 additional terms, to the whole of the work, and all its parts, regardless of how they are packaged. This License gives no permission to license the work in any other way, but it does not invalidate such permission if you have separately received it.

d) If the work has interactive user interfaces, each must display Appropriate Legal Notices; however, if the Program has interactive interfaces that do not display Appropriate Legal Notices, your work need not make them do so.

A compilation of a covered work with other separate and independent works, which are not by their nature extensions of the covered work, and which are not combined with it such as to form a larger program, in or on a volume of a storage or distribution medium, is called an "aggregate" if the compilation and its resulting copyright are not used to limit the access or legal rights of the compilation's users beyond what the individual works permit. Inclusion of a covered work in an aggregate does not cause this License to apply to the other parts of the aggregate.

6. Conveying Non-Source Forms. You may convey a covered work in object code form under the terms of sections 4 and 5, provided that you also convey the machine-readable Corresponding Source under the terms of this License, in one of these ways:

a) Convey the object code in, or embodied in, a physical product (including a physical distribution medium), accompanied by the Corresponding Source fixed on a durable physical medium customarily used for software interchange.

b) Convey the object code in, or embodied in, a physical product (including a physical distribution medium), accompanied by a written offer, valid for at least three years and valid for as long as you offer spare parts or customer support for that product model, to give anyone who possesses the object code either (1) a copy of the Corresponding Source for all the software in the product that is covered by this License, on a durable physical medium customarily used for software interchange, for a price no more than your reasonable cost of physically performing this conveying of source, or (2) access to copy the Corresponding Source from a network server at no charge.

c) Convey individual copies of the object code with a copy of the written offer to provide the Corresponding Source. This alternative is allowed only occasionally and noncommercially, and only if you received the object code with such an offer, in accord with subsection 6b.

d) Convey the object code by offering access from a designated place (gratis or for a charge), and offer equivalent access to the Corresponding Source in the same way through the same place at no further charge. You need not require recipients to copy the Corresponding Source along with the object code. If the place to copy the object code is a network server, the Corresponding Source may be on a different server (operated by you or a third party) that supports equivalent copying facilities, provided you maintain clear directions next to the object code saying where to find the Corresponding Source. Regardless of what server hosts the Corresponding Source, you remain obligated to ensure that it is available for as long as needed to satisfy these requirements.

e) Convey the object code using peer-to-peer transmission, provided you inform other peers where the object code and Corresponding Source of the work are being offered to the general public at no charge under subsection 6d.

A separable portion of the object code, whose source code is excluded from the Corresponding Source as a System Library, need not be included in conveying the object code work.

A "User Product" is either (1) a "consumer product", which means any tangible personal property which is normally used for personal, family, or household purposes, or (2) anything designed or sold for incorporation into a dwelling. In determining whether a product is a consumer product, doubtful cases shall be resolved in favor of coverage. For a particular product received by a particular user, "normally used" refers to a typical or common use of that class of product, regardless of the status of the particular user or of the way in which the particular user actually uses, or expects or is expected to use, the product. A product is a consumer product regardless of whether the product has substantial commercial, industrial or non-consumer uses, unless such uses represent the only significant mode of use of the product.

"Installation Information" for a User Product means any methods, procedures, authorization keys, or other information required to install and execute modified versions of a covered work in that User Product from a modified version of its Corresponding Source. The information must suffice to ensure that the continued functioning of the modified object code is in no case prevented or interfered with solely because modification has been made.

If you convey an object code work under this section in, or with, or specifically for use in, a User Product, and the conveying occurs as part of a transaction in which the right of possession and use of the User Product is transferred to the recipient in perpetuity or for a fixed term (regardless of how the transaction is characterized), the Corresponding Source conveyed under this section must be accompanied by the Installation Information. But this requirement does not apply if neither you nor any third party retains the ability to install modified object code on the User Product (for example, the work has been installed in ROM).

The requirement to provide Installation Information does not include a requirement to continue to provide support service, warranty, or updates for a work that has been modified or installed by the recipient, or for the User Product in which it has been modified or installed. Access to a network may be denied when the modification itself materially and adversely affects the operation of the network or violates the rules and protocols for communication across the network.

Corresponding Source conveyed, and Installation Information provided, in accord with this section must be in a format that is publicly documented (and with an implementation available to the public in source code form), and must require no special password or key for unpacking, reading or copying.

7. Additional Terms. "Additional permissions" are terms that supplement the terms of this License by making exceptions from one or more of its conditions. Additional permissions that are applicable to the entire Program shall be treated as though they were included in this License, to the extent that they are valid under applicable law. If additional permissions apply only to part of the Program, that part may be used separately under those permissions, but the entire Program remains governed by this License without regard to the additional permissions.

When you convey a copy of a covered work, you may at your option remove any additional permissions from that copy, or from any part of it. (Additional permissions may be written to require their own removal in certain cases when you modify the work.) You may place additional permissions on material, added by you to a covered work, for which you have or can give appropriate copyright permission.

Notwithstanding any other provision of this License, for material you add to a covered work, you may (if authorized by the copyright holders of that material) supplement the terms of this License with terms:

a) Disclaiming warranty or limiting liability differently from the terms of sections 15 and 16 of this License; or

b) Requiring preservation of specified reasonable legal notices or author attributions in that material or in the Appropriate Legal Notices displayed by works containing it; or

c) Prohibiting misrepresentation of the origin of that material, or requiring that modified versions of such material be marked in reasonable ways as different from the original version; or

d) Limiting the use for publicity purposes of names of licensors or authors of the material; or

e) Declining to grant rights under trademark law for use of some trade names, trademarks, or service marks; or

f) Requiring indemnification of licensors and authors of that material by anyone who conveys the material (or modified versions of it) with contractual assumptions of liability to the recipient, for any liability that these contractual assumptions directly impose on those licensors and authors.

All other non-permissive additional terms are considered "further restrictions" within the meaning of section 10. If the Program as you received it, or any part of it, contains a notice stating that it is governed by this License along with a term that is a further restriction, you may remove that term. If a license document contains a further restriction but permits relicensing or conveying under this License, you may add to a covered work material governed by the terms of that license document, provided that the further restriction does not survive such relicensing or conveying.

If you add terms to a covered work in accord with this section, you must place, in the relevant source files, a statement of the additional terms that apply to those files, or a notice indicating where to find the applicable terms.

Additional terms, permissive or non-permissive, may be stated in the form of a separately written license, or stated as exceptions; the above requirements apply either way.

8. Termination. You may not propagate or modify a covered work except as expressly provided under this License. Any attempt otherwise to propagate or modify it is void, and will automatically terminate your rights under this License (including any patent licenses granted under the third paragraph of section 11).

   However, if you cease all violation of this License, then your license from a particular copyright holder is reinstated (a) provisionally, unless and until the copyright holder explicitly and finally terminates your license, and (b) permanently, if the copyright holder fails to notify you of the violation by some reasonable means prior to 60 days after the cessation.

   Moreover, your license from a particular copyright holder is reinstated permanently if the copyright holder notifies you of the violation by some reasonable means, this is the first time you have received notice of violation of this License (for any work) from that copyright holder, and you cure the violation prior to 30 days after your receipt of the notice.

   Termination of your rights under this section does not terminate the licenses of parties who have received copies or rights from you under this License. If your rights have been terminated and not permanently reinstated, you do not qualify to receive new licenses for the same material under section 10.

9. Acceptance Not Required for Having Copies. You are not required to accept this License in order to receive or run a copy of the Program. Ancillary propagation of a covered work occurring solely as a consequence of using peer-to-peer transmission to receive a copy likewise does not require acceptance. However, nothing other than this License grants you permission to propagate or modify any covered work. These actions infringe copyright if you do not accept this License. Therefore, by modifying or propagating a covered work, you indicate your acceptance of this License to do so.

10. Automatic Licensing of Downstream Recipients. Each time you convey a covered work, the recipient automatically receives a license from the original licensors, to run, modify and propagate that work, subject to this License. You are not responsible for enforcing compliance by third parties with this License.

    An "entity transaction" is a transaction transferring control of an organization, or substantially all assets of one, or subdividing an organization, or merging organizations. If propagation of a covered work results from an entity transaction, each party to that transaction who receives a copy of the work also receives whatever licenses to the work the party's predecessor in interest had or could give under the previous paragraph, plus a right to possession of the Corresponding Source of the work from the predecessor in interest, if the predecessor has it or can get it with reasonable efforts.

    You may not impose any further restrictions on the exercise of the rights granted or affirmed under this License. For example, you may not impose a license fee, royalty, or other charge for exercise of rights granted under this License, and you may not initiate litigation (including a cross-claim or counterclaim in a lawsuit) alleging that any patent claim is infringed by making, using, selling, offering for sale, or importing the Program or any portion of it.

11. Patents. A "contributor" is a copyright holder who authorizes use under this License of the Program or a work on which the Program is based. The work thus licensed is called the contributor's "contributor version".

A contributor's "essential patent claims" are all patent claims owned or controlled by the contributor, whether already acquired or hereafter acquired, that would be infringed by some manner, permitted by this License, of making, using, or selling its contributor version, but do not include claims that would be infringed only as a consequence of further modification of the contributor version. For purposes of this definition, "control" includes the right to grant patent sublicenses in a manner consistent with the requirements of this License.

Each contributor grants you a non-exclusive, worldwide, royalty-free patent license under the contributor's essential patent claims, to make, use, sell, offer for sale, import and otherwise run, modify and propagate the contents of its contributor version.

In the following three paragraphs, a "patent license" is any express agreement or commitment, however denominated, not to enforce a patent (such as an express permission to practice a patent or covenant not to sue for patent infringement). To "grant" such a patent license to a party means to make such an agreement or commitment not to enforce a patent against the party.

If you convey a covered work, knowingly relying on a patent license, and the Corresponding Source of the work is not available for anyone to copy, free of charge and under the terms of this License, through a publicly available network server or other readily accessible means, then you must either (1) cause the Corresponding Source to be so available, or (2) arrange to deprive yourself of the benefit of the patent license for this particular work, or (3) arrange, in a manner consistent with the requirements of this License, to extend the patent license to downstream recipients. "Knowingly relying" means you have actual knowledge that, but for the patent license, your conveying the covered work in a country, or your recipient's use of the covered work in a country, would infringe one or more identifiable patents in that country that you have reason to believe are valid.

If, pursuant to or in connection with a single transaction or arrangement, you convey, or propagate by procuring conveyance of, a covered work, and grant a patent license to some of the parties receiving the covered work authorizing them to use, propagate, modify or convey a specific copy of the covered work, then the patent license you grant is automatically extended to all recipients of the covered work and works based on it.

A patent license is "discriminatory" if it does not include within the scope of its coverage, prohibits the exercise of, or is conditioned on the non-exercise of one or more of the rights that are specifically granted under this License. You may not convey a covered work if you are a party to an arrangement with a third party that is in the business of distributing software, under which you make payment to the third party based on the extent of your activity of conveying the work, and under which the third party grants, to any of the parties who would receive the covered work from you, a discriminatory patent license (a) in connection with copies of the covered work conveyed by you (or copies made from those copies), or (b) primarily for and in connection with specific products or compilations that contain the covered work, unless you entered into that arrangement, or that patent license was granted, prior to 28 March 2007.

Nothing in this License shall be construed as excluding or limiting any implied license or other defenses to infringement that may otherwise be available to you under applicable patent law.

12. No Surrender of Others' Freedom. If conditions are imposed on you (whether by court order, agreement or otherwise) that contradict the conditions of this License, they do not excuse you from the conditions of this License. If you cannot convey a covered work so as to satisfy simultaneously your obligations under this License and any other pertinent obligations, then as a consequence you may not convey it at all. For example, if you agree to terms that obligate you to collect a royalty for further conveying from those to whom you convey the Program, the only way you could satisfy both those terms and this License would be to refrain entirely from conveying the Program.

13. Use with the GNU Affero General Public License. Notwithstanding any other provision of this License, you have permission to link or combine any covered work with a work licensed under version 3 of the GNU Affero General Public License into a single combined work, and to convey the resulting work. The terms of this License will continue to apply to the part which is the covered work, but the special requirements of the GNU Affero General Public License, section 13, concerning interaction through a network will apply to the combination as such.

14. Revised Versions of this License. The Free Software Foundation may publish revised and/or new versions of the GNU General Public License from time to time. Such new versions will be similar in spirit to the present version, but may differ in detail to address new problems or concerns.

    Each version is given a distinguishing version number. If the Program specifies that a certain numbered version of the GNU General Public License "or any later version" applies to it, you have the option of following the terms and conditions either of that numbered version or of any later version published by the Free Software Foundation. If the Program does not specify a version number of the GNU General Public License, you may choose any version ever published by the Free Software Foundation.

    If the Program specifies that a proxy can decide which future versions of the GNU General Public License can be used, that proxy's public statement of acceptance of a version permanently authorizes you to choose that version for the Program.

    Later license versions may give you additional or different permissions. However, no additional obligations are imposed on any author or copyright holder as a result of your choosing to follow a later version.

15. Disclaimer of Warranty. THERE IS NO WARRANTY FOR THE PROGRAM, TO THE EXTENT PERMITTED BY APPLICABLE LAW. EXCEPT WHEN OTHERWISE STATED IN WRITING THE COPYRIGHT HOLDERS AND/OR OTHER PARTIES PROVIDE THE PROGRAM "AS IS" WITHOUT WARRANTY OF ANY KIND, EITHER EXPRESSED OR IMPLIED, INCLUDING, BUT NOT LIMITED TO, THE IMPLIED WARRANTIES OF MERCHANTABILITY AND FITNESS FOR A PARTICULAR PURPOSE. THE ENTIRE RISK AS TO THE QUALITY AND PERFORMANCE OF THE PROGRAM IS WITH YOU. SHOULD THE PROGRAM PROVE DEFECTIVE, YOU ASSUME THE COST OF ALL NECESSARY SERVICING, REPAIR OR CORRECTION.

16. Limitation of Liability. IN NO EVENT UNLESS REQUIRED BY APPLICABLE LAW OR AGREED TO IN WRITING WILL ANY COPYRIGHT HOLDER, OR ANY OTHER PARTY WHO MODIFIES AND/OR CONVEYS THE PROGRAM AS PERMITTED ABOVE, BE LIABLE TO YOU FOR DAMAGES, INCLUDING ANY GENERAL, SPECIAL, INCIDENTAL OR CONSEQUENTIAL DAMAGES ARISING OUT OF THE USE OR INABILITY TO USE THE PROGRAM (INCLUDING BUT NOT LIMITED TO LOSS OF DATA OR DATA BEING RENDERED INACCURATE OR LOSSES SUSTAINED BY YOU OR THIRD PARTIES OR A FAILURE OF THE PROGRAM TO OPERATE WITH ANY OTHER PROGRAMS), EVEN IF SUCH HOLDER OR OTHER PARTY HAS BEEN ADVISED OF THE POSSIBILITY OF SUCH DAMAGES.

17. Interpretation of Sections 15 and 16. If the disclaimer of warranty and limitation of liability provided above cannot be given local legal effect according to their terms, reviewing courts shall apply local law that most closely approximates an absolute waiver of all civil liability in connection with the Program, unless a warranty or assumption of liability accompanies a copy of the Program in return for a fee.

END OF TERMS AND CONDITIONS